Damaged Rudders

DAMAGED RUDDERS:

Healing Trauma through Yoga, Creativity, and the Connections to Our Divinity

Laura Weber Garrison, PhD

All Rights Reserved. Any unauthorized reprinting or use of this material is strictly prohibited. No part of this book may be reproduced or transmitted in any form or by any means, electronic or mechanical, including photocopying, recording, or by any information storage and retrieval system without express written permission from the author.

All reasonable attempts have been made to verify the accuracy of the information provided in this publication. Nevertheless, the author assumes no responsibility for any errors and/or omissions.

The content of this book is intended for educational and inspirational purposes only and is not meant as a substitute for professional medical advice, diagnosis, or treatment. My goal is to provide insights and guidance that may support your personal growth and well-being. However, this book should not be used as a replacement for the care provided by your physician or other qualified healthcare professionals. Always seek the advice of a medical professional with any questions you may have regarding a health condition. Do not disregard professional medical advice or delay in seeking it because of something you have read in this book. The opinions and information presented here are based on my experience and knowledge but may not apply to all individuals or situations.

Better Wellness Naturally, LLC

Sarasota, FL

www.BetterWellnessNaturally.com

Cover photo by the author

Copyright © 2024

Laura Weber Garrison, PhD

ISBN: 979898841903

For Lollie McGee

TABLE OF CONTENTS

CHAPTER 1 THE WHOLE OF OUR LIVES..1

CHAPTER 2 OBSCURE LESSONS..9

CHAPTER 3 YOGA ARRIVED...13

CHAPTER 4 INTO THE TRANCE...49

CHAPTER 5 OUTDATED ATTACHMENTS..55

CHAPTER 6 PATHWAYS OF FIRE...65

CHAPTER 7 WHEN OTHER LANDS CALL..87

CHAPTER 8 INTO THE HEART..99

CHAPTER 9 INSIDE INFORMATION..123

CHAPTER 10 ATTACHMENTS AND PINNACLES..139

CHAPTER 11 COMPULSORY LESSONS..147

CHAPTER 12 WALKING HOME...167

CHAPTER 13 FINDING HOME...187

CHAPTER 14 PARALLEL PROCESSING...195

CHAPTER 15 THE OPPORTUNITY OF ABILITIES...221

CHAPTER 16 THE ENERGY OF AFFLICTIONS..227

CHAPTER 17 AT ONE...233

CHAPTER 18 PARADIGMS..253

CHAPTER 19 THE COURAGE OF CREATIVITY...263

CHAPTER 20 JOY AS A DAILY EPITOME..291

ACKNOWLEDGEMENTS

As with most acknowledgments, there are far more people to thank than space might allow. Bringing my personal stories forward within the context of this book and in conjunction with my practice presented a unique set of challenges and circumstances. Do I create even more ripples than I normally do by sharing ... or do I attempt to stay quietly in my lane?

Ripples it is.

I have been told by my clients that I am a "Unicorn in a Field of Jackasses"—a title I do not take lightly—as I do often find that I'm standing toe to toe with practitioners who insist a prescription will rapidly fix "it," whatever the "it" may present as. I, contrarily, advocate for a more holistic, sustainable, Rx-free approach.

To obtain genuine healing, I believe we have to go beyond the temporary relief that prescription medications may provide and seek understanding from a place we haven't gone to before. We must comprehend certain issues from a more qualified perspective. We must venture into the vast unknown, the yet unfamiliar to us, in order to heal the concerns that prevented us from evolving at some earlier juncture.

Does going to this new, unknown place mean incurring loss? Yes. We may have to let go of a life or of people or jobs or a version of who we thought we were.

We do, however, get to take what is fundamentally good and supportive with us as we scaffold into the updated version of who we are becoming.

Does going through this work mean lancing a festering boil of toxic memories sometimes? Yes. Does this mean reconnecting with the body even when it is terrifying and, on occasion, exquisitely painful to do so? Yes. There are intimate, complex connections between the intellect, the body, the emotions, and the Spirit that must be compassionately explored if someone is to truly heal.

Practitioners like David Hartman and Diane Zimberoff, who remain my teachers and mentors, embody this philosophy. They also know personally what it means to be completely broken open. Miki, Joy, and Neely have likewise remained steadfastly present over the years, and these three amazing women know what it means as well. People like my lovely friend Cindy, the Dancing Queen, who walked the Camino de Santiago solo at age sixty-nine, get it too. Not only did Cindy start taking dance lessons just after her Camino, but she has also since gone on to become one of the top amateur ballroom dancers in the nation. She also recently opened the Vision of Dance ballroom dance studio.

What a gift some people are. These are people I would have never met if I had not lost the "Me," or the life I'd had before.

And I took what was intrinsically good and supportive forward into my own scaffolding. A special heartfelt thank you belongs to my husband, Dan, for continuing to weather the seasons of our life in partnership and for loving me tenaciously through the stupefying storms of our life together. I am immensely grateful that we are still growing, evolving, Be-ing, and holding hands.

I am also deeply indebted to those who have bravely shared their stories, lives, and healing journeys with me. I love—and invest myself in and with—the people who grace my practice. The work of healing can be so damn hard; it's not pretty or comfortable or fun, yet heal we must—for ourselves, for our tribes, and for the world.

Showing up for oneself requires courage, tenacity, transparency, brutal honesty, guts, and often, defiance. I genuinely love my people. People like Emily, a brilliant, amazingly detail-oriented mom of six who has gone from visiting the temporary-might-become-permanent precipice that so many of us who have been traumatized are familiar with to creating enormous waves of precessional positive changes. She "moms" incredibly, like no other mother I have ever met, and has a beautifully inimitable way of compassionately lighting up the world just by being her truest Self. People like Jade, a truly magical being and talented songwriter who found the courage to save herself and her baby and extricate herself from a highly toxic and horribly abusive marriage. People whose bodies and lives have been altered by tactical Western medicine, such as Jody, who has gone from bed-bound (for a decade) and taking a laundry list of prescription meds to a hyper-mobile, unstoppable, fantasy-fiction writer, and Jess, who survived and defied the defeatists and "realists" and is now pregnant with her second baby. People like Christine, who has moved beyond the confines of generational "truths" and now defies imagination by simply sharing a small fraction of her patent-questing genius and being the delightful, captivating, "164+ simmering crockpots" person she is. People like Fred, Jeff, Rebekka, and Kelly, all wondrously introduced to me by the Universe in the most confounding series of parallels, who are in the midst of complicated personal transformations and are nonetheless steadfastly positioning themselves to bring their own unique, joy-filled magic to the world in a much, much larger way. People like Rebecca, Dee, Naydaliz, and Denise—all fabulous, beautiful, brainy, incredible women who have gone from being perpetually angry, anxious, and stuck in chronic, toxic patterns to embodying radiance, autonomy, self-sufficiency, and positive personal growth. People like Alie, who showed up precipitously shattered and severely depleted and is now a true Boss Babe with a thriving, kick-ass, woman-owned business—replete with a ginormous truck (the first of many, no doubt) named after her granddad.

There are so many, many more. I've held hands and the flashlight, bearing witness to the most extraordinary miracles. I am both honored and deeply grateful to be a part of the journey home with each of you.

FOREWORD

Please be gentle with yourself as you navigate these next stages of your precious life. You're growing, and sometimes that can be wrought with unexpected judgments, challenges, passings, and grievances.

Please be gentle with yourself as you grow. Those around you may not understand, and instead—and quite likely—may be fearful of change. They may do everything they can to undermine your confidence and uproot you. It is from the depths of their fears that they may find disagreement with the You that you are becoming. Please remember that baggage belongs to them and is part of their own unique set of life lessons.

You are responsible for *You;* you are not responsible for them, their responses, or their reactions. Please also remember that everyone is at their own stages of learning and that their "hatred" of you, of what you are becoming, or of the boundaries you are holding reflects their fears. They may observe, and they will have their opinions; please do not allow their judgments to result in shame for you.

Please be gentle with the You that you are about to meet. With awareness, changes are not only plausible, they also become probable. As we become more awake, the trappings of our outdated ways of being may no longer fit the Life we endeavor to have and may feel like the equivalent of a scratchy wool sweater during a more humid-than-average Florida summer. Things and people that once felt good may begin to feel like unwanted anchors; you may realize your current employment is no longer in alignment with your Higher calling. You may feel the undeniable pull of the lessons meant for you from across the globe. Some may even accuse you of running away when you know in your heart that you are running into instead of away from that which is intended for you.

Laura Weber Garrison, PhD

We may step in the river, but it is never the same way twice, to paraphrase Heraclitus. We are different, and the river has moved and changed. Sometimes the river is deeper than we expect, and we may be afraid of being dragged under even though we can still find our footing. What do we do? Changes will take place no matter how much we may fight to maintain a specific status quo.

What happens, though, when we get towed under and find ourselves getting pummeled furiously in the flow of Life? If we are to stay Earth-bound, we must breathe even when we feel we are drowning.

I believe we are supported by unseen forces and that everything coalesces by Divine intervention. One of my teachers, Richard Miller, PhD, who developed iRest® Yoga Nidra Meditation, writes that the Divine plays "hide and seek" while we as humans play lost and found. When we feel separate, we search, looking to find. You have picked up this book, and we are now meeting one another in a very sacred, exclusive place of kinship and understanding and are no longer separated. We may never meet in person in this incarnation, in the flesh, yet we are meeting now, and we are connected. I have survived my damaged rudders, and you will too.

I offer my hand and my heart in love and support and wish you the peace that you are seeking.

INTRODUCTION

The torment of precautions often exceeds the dangers to be avoided. It is sometimes better to abandon one's self to destiny.

—Napoleon Bonaparte

Often, beginning the work of becoming one's Self commences when one has suffered tremendous loss or has been challenged by the next cycle of samsara. Our perfect life or our preferred "perfect" world has collapsed. We are angry, and we are confident that our Creator has vanished. Our once well-rooted faith has been blotted out.

As *samsara* in Buddhism is the beginningless cycle of repeated birth, mundane existence, and dying again, I found myself in a prejudiced cycle of being, learning, and growing as I was, it seemed, contemplating weighty deaths of too many sorts and being erroneously blamed for the trespasses of others. After two incredibly challenging weeks of around-the-clock death labor with my father as his doula, I found myself navigating my mother's alcohol-muddled journey of my Faud's crossing. Less than three years later, her physical body passed, and so did the last real tie to my tribe of origin, people that I had moved away from decades earlier. The demise of my framework for my place in the world for me, as I knew it, paralleled my mother's hospice.

I had crashed in just about every way possible. After supporting my mom (from a distance of several hundred miles) through a lengthy illness, I was drained financially and faced with hostile siblings who believed otherwise. Saddled with the task of unraveling my parents' estate, which had no funds—during one of the worst economic meltdowns of this century—the hostility escalated as family secrets of substance abuse, theft, and deception surfaced. A minor example: I was financially assisting my mother; she was using credit cards, loans, and mortgages she had cosigned on (and she'd hidden from me) to support lazy, parasitic, adult children.

An egregious embezzlement by a trusted employee during my mother's illness had irreversibly destabilized a business that had taken my husband and me more than a decade, thousands of hours, and hundreds of thousands of dollars to build. I was grossly distracted and on the road much of the time; we had trusted this person, the two other cohorts, and the attorney peripherally involved who later was imprisoned implicitly. A perfect storm of financial ruin, this employee's blatant and nefarious transgression took away my livelihood, my credit, every shred of savings, and eventually, the home that my husband and I built as well.

Further, I chose to honor my word to other business partners and colleagues. Three of them committed suicide during this time; one of whom was managing a massive network of funding on our behalf, including millions of dollars in outstanding unfunded loans. The others did what they could with the means and understanding they had at the time and, in doing so, walked away from their financial promises and obligations to me. Every trace of income had vanished, our accounts were drained, all the credit lines were closed, and we lost the home we had built, as well as all our investments. My tax accountant disappeared, and I was told she was having an affair with one of my brothers. The high-profile attorney I'd trusted for years went to jail. A perfect storm. I was physically, emotionally, and psychically wrecked.

The dominos toppled; people lost money. I stood fast in protecting people when they chose not to reciprocate the same. People I considered friends took intimate knowledge, including my social security number, and turned it against me. People I thought of as family colluded with them.

Those who didn't know the facts blamed and publicly shamed me, and they did so viciously, ruthlessly, and seemingly without a shred of compassion.

All this was taking place as I was burying my mom.

Parts of me survived. My faith did not.

Firmly in the throes of middle age, my body fiercely revolted, and we had no insurance. By revolted, I mean it did everything it could to stop me: blinding migraine headaches, uncontrollable shaking, and allergic reactions resulting in hives, fevers, and acute exhaustion. I would sometimes stand up and blackout. Emotionally I was drained, and more significantly, because my trust and faith had been shattered, I was exquisitely angry. My husband, someone I'd been with for over two decades, retreated into his pain and "into the bottle"; another preternaturally complex, probably karma-specific, and excruciating matter entirely. How could all these things have taken place when I honestly was doing what I thought I could to live my life from a place of God-centered service, integrity, and compassion for others? I had never intentionally sought to harm others; there were those in my constellation who insisted I did.

My artistic creativity—my solace and best friend since childhood—abandoned me as well. Art was always my lifeline, and now it had vanished too.

Today I have a clearer understanding of the why. Back then, it felt as though the last shred of joy had been stripped away. Without being rooted and self-unified, our connection to Source—our conduit for genuine creativity—goes asunder.

Yoga, as a spiritual practice, came back to find me when I had quite nearly given up.

The yogic fundamentals of breathwork, meditation, and contemplation were all inroads to reclaiming my kinship with Creator. Those roads also led to extensively questioning the modalities of connection, interaction, and communication with Source. For me, the practices of yoga and exploring what author and the "father of firewalking" Tolly Burkan refers to as acts of faith and "Extreme Spirituality" became my "Let's See What Ol' God Will Do Now" experimentations with me as the test subject. The studies of hypnosis, hypnotherapy, and meditation surfaced in very tangential and oblique ways and became the modalities of communication with which I investigated what was unfathomable to me.

Are we ever really deserted by our Creator? Can we find or reassume channels of communication? Spirituality means something different to me than it does to many people, and it definitely is not that of cowering to a malevolent Sky Daddy. I believe our Source is always present, and that we are the ones blocking the connection. Some of us must take a longer detour to find our way back onto our paths and continue on our way to our truer home.

As I tell my groups, we all gestate at different rates.

In Buddhism and Hinduism, samsara refers to the continuous cycle of birth, death, and rebirth that all beings undergo. This cycle is seen as a result of past actions and attachments, and it continues until a state of liberation or enlightenment is achieved.

We're ignorant of this endless cycle sometimes, yet cycling through this infinite series is something we evidently must do. Yoga also teaches us that sometimes samsara is considered to be *dukkha*, or that which can be regarded as unsatisfactory and painful and perpetuated by desire and ignorance. That doesn't mean it is negative.

Thich Nhat Hahn counsels that "the potential for ignorance lives in all of us; it gives rise to misunderstanding, which can lead to violent thoughts and behavior. Although ignorance and violence may not have manifested in your life, when conditions are sufficient, they can. This is why we all have to be very careful not to water these seeds and not to allow them to develop roots and grow into arrows."

Genuine ignorance, to me, is also choosing not to understand, learn, or comprehend something that is of vital importance to our soul's journey when given the opportunity.

Thankfully, I embraced this tide of learning when it came back, even though this cycle, this samsara, was incredibly painful, and I was incredibly ignorant. That ignorance, in retrospect, has been an incredible blessing in a precessional sense: I would never have come to know and love the people that I have been blessed beyond measure to know now. People who have survived and thrived, people whom I've held hands with and cried with, and who have gone on to impact so many others in such a positive way from the deep, painful work of their healing journeys.

My existence, though, as I had known it at that time, had collapsed. I was livid at a Creator I was certain had abandoned me. Driving far too fast on mountain roads one afternoon, I was seriously contemplating disregarding the hairpin turn and launching my car and me over the railing.

I'd spent three days in interviews for a job that read like it was created exactly for me. The interviewers had all been so positive and excited for me to join the team. I, too, was happy and filled with gratitude that my husband and I would be able to make our way back up and out of the dark, a pain-filled abyss that had become our life. Rejoining the workforce after years of self-employment wasn't something I was planning, and for those of us who know, starting over again as an employee in midlife is challenging at best. I'd sent out hundreds of resumes and had gone to dozens of interviews. One interviewer noted aloud (as she clucked her tongue) that I was "much older than she expected." I'd gotten many of the "you're so overqualified!" remarks. Another high-profile hiring manager had stated that if I were hired, my coworkers would assuredly be half my age and quite likely twice as proficient with social media.

I was, however, ecstatic about the prospect of this new position.

They called. "You are perfect for the position... but..." the supervisor began. Ah yes, the "but"' the Big Ugly Truth: my once impeccable, hard-earned credit was the issue. We were deeply in debt; the attorneys we consulted at the time had said we were "far too broke to contemplate bankruptcy." Another likewise added, "... and it would appear that you've got a very long road ahead of you given the audacity, idiotic beliefs, and entitlement issues of your irrational siblings." The attorney had also said: "Your sister must go to jail for the harm she intentionally has caused."

The lynchpin: my mother had left me, unbeknownst to me, in the executor position of a bankrupt estate when she passed.

A frivolous, seven-figure lawsuit had been filed and illegally levied against me—by siblings—while I was living thousands of miles away. One sibling had stated flatly that I was dead to him before I'd moved away; another was resolute in her belief that I had gobs of cash hidden away somewhere and was insistent that I support two other full-grown, fully capable siblings because they "needed it" and because our parents expected me to and because I "must." The alcoholic brother was quite another issue.

The lawsuit had been filed—and the service was received on my behalf—all without my knowledge while I was living thousands of miles away. Someone who looked like me and knew much about me had said she was me; someone had forged my signature.

Legal counsel had suggested filing criminal charges against two of my allegedly normal siblings and legal complaints against a third that would "surely relieve him of his career." My extremely destructive alcoholic brother was part of the melee too, and "brilliant enough to convince everyone that his illness made him do it" per the attorney. I was told that the "alcoholic brother was hell-bent" on taking me down and "didn't give a damn about going to jail either. Where he's getting his money from, no one seems to know for sure. Your sister, well, she's a professional asshole thief who has sued several ex-husbands out of hundreds of thousands of dollars. And that other brother? He's definitely an asshole, just like that sister of yours. God help the medical system. If he's not above doing this to his own family, what would keep him from killing off a patient who may be struggling?"

Ah yes, family. I had chosen a doozy.

All sentient beings retreat to rest, to heal, and sometimes to die. I had moved three thousand miles away from my home state and started over from a personal ground zero at a time when many of my peers were enjoying their retirement, multiple homes, extended vacations, and "cabbage-patch" grandbabies. I did not understand how, when all should have been well and right with me and my world, everything could or would give way. I was broke; there was no safety net, no hidden caches of cash, nothing, and I had tens of thousands of dollars in outstanding debt and had lost dozens of properties to foreclosures. My credit would be crippled for years to come.

I decided I had to die as that iteration and start anew as I had done when I'd removed myself from the horribly abusive home I'd been raised in as a kid. When I left home, I did so with virtually nothing and lived off the coins I'd squirreled away by selling my artwork and by creating a small business that supported me. There were no safety nets then either.

At the point of giving up, my world overturned, and indeed, the analogy of the caterpillar and the butterfly became self-evident as I was ready to lop off the top of the chrysalis and yank myself out of—or into—being somewhere or someplace else.

The difference this time is that I had reached a place of utter exhaustion and given up hope. Many of us are finished with life when hope is exhausted.

Some might refer to this time as a dark night of the soul. I heard the most ludicrous statement the other day: that one can only be enlightened if they have experienced a dark night of the soul. I disagree. How is it that addicts hit "rock bottom"—a dark night—and relapse? Or a recovered addict goes willingly into a relationship with an abuser? The dark nights are a perspective. So is that of becoming enlightened.

For me, these are cycles of life and death, a samsara. Rock bottom is a sort of death, and there is a perilous grief concomitant to this place. Do we move sideways or stay immobilized in that grief? Some of us may fail to realize that it is not a permanent, concrete place. A relationship or a family or a tribe ending is a death, and we find that we must move away, lest we die too.

As noted, samsaras represent cycles. For me, as had happened so many times before, another cycle arrived shortly thereafter.

Just as I was regaining a modicum of bravery, a bit of momentum, and learning to breathe again, an additional set of salvos arrived: another frivolous lawsuit had been filed, delivered, accepted, and won by default, once again, while I was still living thousands of miles away. This lawsuit had been entered by an employee who was friends with my siblings—and was also someone my husband and I had considered a friend. She and another employee, whom I suspect she had been having an affair with, had access to my social security number, knew confidential details of my life and businesses, and, I later learned, had utilized my business credit, network, and resources behind my back and without my permission. When the bottom started falling out of the economy in 2008, they had both concocted a story that I had somehow, somewhere, protected a great deal of money and that I was hiding money in my own assets in some sort of Ponzi scheme. I had not done either. What I had done was willingly protect other colleagues by not disclosing private, legal information. Three of these people died during this time, and several others failed to follow through on contractual agreements as they, themselves, were crashing into their own financial ruins.

All of the people involved in filing this lawsuit had either been employed by me or supported by me at one time, were friends, or were related by blood. I was mortified by the story that had been woven and the avenues that had been illegally taken against me. There were hostile internet threats, emails, phone messages, and online character disparagements from them as well. I didn't have the resources or the energy to fight back.

As a therapist had said to me, "Leaders make easy targets. You, Laura, are a leader and far too compassionate toward those who certainly have not earned your compassion."

Concurrent with the discovery of the filing (another surreptitious and altogether staggering blast received via email from a bogus email address), I lost the functional use of my dominant side through a debilitating injury. We had no medical insurance. The use of my hands and arms was vital for my work at the time.

Damaged Rudders

The third doctor I spoke with had flippantly remarked that it would require a miracle to regain the use of my arm and shoulder; surgery "may or may not" help, he said, and would cost thousands. The constant dull roar of the pain could be prescription medicated, I was told.

I had believed in miracles as a child and had gleefully ventured out on my own as a very young teenager, knowing full well that the Universe would provide for me what my family had not. And the Universe had, quite willingly, assisted me all along my way. What had happened? Why had the Creator abandoned me? And not just abandoned me, why had the Creator beaten me down before doing so?

Things were a wreck in my home life as well. So, as I saw it then, the very last shreds of my hope and my resilience were destroyed along with the use of my arm. I was exquisitely tired and broken; I decided I was done with being a human.

The Creator had Plans as Creator always does. Sometimes we listen, and sometimes we don't. As one of my esteemed teachers Doria Cordova says, sometimes we get tapped and sometimes we get hit by a Mack truck.

Yoga—the meditative aspects primarily—had been a fundamental practice for me decades earlier, and I had strayed as mainstream yoga had become asana-based, more focused on physical exercise, and far less esoteric than I preferred. On the way home from the third doctor's office, unable to move my right arm, depressed, deflated, and angst-ridden, I found myself at a yoga studio. I didn't have the time, patience, or money to join a yoga studio. Besides, I couldn't move my arm most of the time and was in chronic, see-red-type pain when I could.

Why had I been pulled into *that* studio on *that* day?

Some would say that I landed there at that studio on that day by accident. I believe I arrived there by finally listening.

CHAPTER 1
THE WHOLE OF OUR LIVES

Learning how to be kind to ourselves is important. When we look into our own hearts and begin to discover what is confused and what is brilliant, what is bitter and what is sweet, it isn't just ourselves that we're discovering.

—Pema Chodron

I was always one of "those" kids. And it is quite likely you were too.

My mother, of course, attributed my unexplained "knowing" to an overactive imagination and deemed much of what I "knew" to be a byproduct of yet another prohibited foray through my father's *Encyclopædia Britannica* collection.

For me, everyone and everything had amazing, palpable colors. I boycotted Barbie dolls and tea parties; my world was more real and alive than all of that plastic and pretend nonsense. People didn't have different-colored skins in my world; they had different layers of color. Rocks were hot or cold or somewhere in between; flowers were friendly and full of various degrees of happiness. I would hug the watermelons my father grew because I loved them and felt they loved us too. I refused to eat meat because I knew where it came from, and my heart ached for the animals that had died. We would visit the ocean, and I would wander for miles on the shoreline, barefoot, simply to feel the energy of the Earth, giddy as the waves glittered and sang to me. The desert floor, where I was raised, reverberated in electric waves that I could see and feel. "Touch them! The waves are the same; the ocean used to live here," I would say to my parents, who promptly shrugged me off. Later, I would say that the mountains were calling me and that I needed to go home to them. My mom would shake her head and mutter something about me being burned at the stake in a former life, quite likely multiple times.

Yes, I was "that" kid.

Were you as well? You were. Have you forgotten?

When I was not quite five years of age, my dearly loved great-granddad—my best friend in the world at the time—told me he was leaving the planet the night before his physical body finished its job. My mother had picked up the phone the next morning, expecting news of improvement about her grandfather's stay in the hospital, and I had calmly said, as she was picking up the receiver, "Grampa Miller left. He told me last night." I had tried to explain to her that he was fine; it was just that his body was in an "icebox" (his words to me) under a building. She refused to listen. Instead, my mom, constantly startled, and always somewhat flustered by me anyway, dropped the telephone and promptly backhanded me for lying. My mom's mom confirmed that Grandpa Miller's body was in a hospital basement, the hospital morgue, hundreds of miles away, and had been since early morning.

This memory is as clear to me today as if the entire incident had just taken place this morning.

While I didn't stop communicating with other dimensions that day, I stopped sharing certain things with many others.

The teachers' remarks on report cards throughout grade school noted my refusal to participate and that I was "challenged" as a learner. The carefully folded report card retrieved from my father's belongings after he physically left this planet probably said it best. "All she ever wants to do is play. How this unique child can create straight As out of thin air is beyond my comprehension as a teacher."

Traditional learning seems to involve a great deal of effort, analysis, and mechanical memorizing for many of us, and countless creative children are traumatized early on as a result of either the system, attitudes, and behaviors of their caretakers with regard to the educational processes or the ignorance of their teachers.

Children, when allowed to flourish, play often and connect easily with their fantasies and with the Universe because they are still operating at different brainwave levels much of the time and thus are connected to and capable of living in a world of wonder. "Play is a kind of meditation for it takes us back to the Source of all things," writes Matthew Fox, "including joy and beauty. We ought to follow this path regularly... the more conceited a culture, the more it needs to revivify itself through play."

Dr. Paul Masters, the visionary founder of the International Metaphysical Ministry, imparted great wisdom about the nature of creative thought and inspiration. According to his teachings, a creative thought is not just a mental concept; it arrives with an incredible sense of inspiration that permeates our entire being. This inspiration is more than a fleeting idea; it carries with it a deep and unshakable Knowing.

In the realm of metaphysics, it is understood that our thoughts have the power to shape physical realities. Dr. Masters emphasized that each of us is a unique individual, and our existence itself is a testament to our special purpose in the grand tapestry of existence. He articulated that the core purpose of our lives is to unlock and manifest our innate uniqueness, allowing it to find expression and be shared with the world.

This concept invites us to recognize that we are not random beings in the Universe but rather intentional creations with a distinctive role to play. Our creative thoughts and inspirations are the seeds of this purpose, and as we nurture and bring them to fruition, we align ourselves with the greater flow of life. In doing so, we not only fulfill our individual destinies but also contribute to the collective evolution of consciousness.

Dr. Masters' teachings serve as a reminder that each of us holds within us the potential for untold creativity and purpose. It is through the exploration and expression of our unique gifts that we find meaning, fulfillment, and a deeper connection to the universal creative force.

> **As each has received a gift, use it to serve one another, as good stewards of God's varied grace —1 Peter 4:10**

If the Universe gives us a creative idea, will the Universe also guide us to the means to bring that idea to fruition in the physical world? Creation is said to be finished, and all that we are or ever will be exists right now. So yes, we really can have what we want. We are free to choose, and we can willingly alter the trajectory of our life. Many of us find this difficult to believe, and sometimes it seems it should be arduous work to create or obtain those things we want.

Author Julia Cameron beautifully captures the essence of aligning with one's true calling. She emphasizes that our deepest desires and passions are intricately connected to our life's purpose. When we wholeheartedly engage in what we are truly meant to do, a remarkable transformation occurs.

In this state of alignment, doors of opportunity effortlessly swing open before us. We find ourselves in the flow of life, where synchronicities abound, and the Universe seems to conspire in our favor. It's a sense of being in the right place at the right time, guided by a higher purpose.

The work we do in this state of alignment ceases to feel like a burden; instead, it becomes a joyful expression of our authentic selves. It feels like play because it resonates with our innermost being, and it brings a considerable sense of fulfillment.

Julia Cameron's insight reminds us that the pursuit of our true calling is not merely a quest for success or recognition; it's a journey toward self-realization and a life that feels purposeful and meaningful. When we heed the call of our deepest desires, we embark on a path where work and play seamlessly merge, and our lives become a testament to the power of purposeful living.

We, at every age, should play more, embrace our creativity, and follow where the Universe leads us, should we not? How can we do this easily, comfortably, and without allowing judgments from ourselves and others to disrupt us in such seemingly unsupportive times?

Creativity and spirituality, both deeply influential forces in human life, arise from an intangible transcendent capacity within us. They share the power to liberate us from self-imposed limitations, guiding us on transformative journeys.

When we heed their call and embrace these forces, we embark on a path of growth and evolution, advancing along our soul's journey. This journey allows us to bring forth hidden aspects of our authentic selves, revealing the depths within.

As Thomas Moore beautifully expressed, "Losing yourself in the Divine embrace of the creative process, you disappear. Your ego or limited sense of separateness vanishes, and you emerge into the vast ocean that is creativity . . . bringing forth something entirely novel."

This process is a boundless act of self-discovery and expression, allowing us to access the infinite wellspring of creativity within. Through creativity and spirituality, we transcend limitations, connect with our deeper essence, and contribute to the ever-evolving tapestry of existence.

That something novel or new that emerges may be an arrangement, a piece of artwork, or an idea that did not exist before. Is this not an innate need, something that is a basic necessity to our human nature, to create? Ellen Dissanayake, an anthropologist, suggests that it is and further describes creating as "making special." "Creativity includes the arts, yet truly encompasses the whole of our lives. Every act in which we 'make special' can be a creative one," according to Dissanayake.

Creativity, then, is *supposed* to encompass the whole of our lives.

And yet, so many people will insist they are not creative.

A "thousand unseen helping hands," as Joseph Campbell referred to the "lucky breaks," will appear as if by magic along our way when we are in that synchronous and sometimes deliciously supernatural place of creativity and spiritual flow. Is this not a normal state when we are honoring our Self? Children naturally seem to sense this Divine assistance and expect these unseen hands along the way.

Where do we, as responsible adults, lose our connection to this Divine understanding, and why?

Psychologist Carl Jung's insights shed light on the nature of the Self and its connection to the broader Universe. According to Jung, the Self transcends the individual "me" and encompasses the Divine, the Spirit that binds us to the cosmos. It serves as the cohesive force that unites conscious and unconscious aspects of our being, forming a harmonious whole.

Jung, widely regarded as one of the twentieth century's preeminent psychologists, introduced the concept of individuation. This process involves bringing the personal and collective unconscious into consciousness, revealing the entirety of one's personality or Self. In Jung's view, the images we create serve as expressions of our unlimited human experiences and reflections of our genuine, authentic selves. These images act as clues to the unexplored aspects of our lives, yearning for outward expression. Jung encouraged individuals to approach these symbolic images with a discerning eye, uncovering deeper meanings and embracing their fuller, truer selves.

Furthermore, Jung believed that creativity springs forth from the realms of play and fantasy. These imaginative realms hold the keys to unlocking our creative potential and accessing the wellspring of innovation within us.

Jung's insights into the transformative power of creativity serve as a philosophical testament to the journey of self-discovery and self-expression. In this realm, creativity is not just an outlet but a mirror, reflecting the depths of our innermost selves. It is often in these depths that we encounter the contrarian nature of creative individuals—those of us who thrive not just in the creation of art but in the art of living differently. This inherent contrarianism, a hallmark of creative minds, subtly lays the groundwork for resilience. It speaks to a unique capacity to see the world through a different lens, to challenge norms, and to find strength in the unconventional. As such, those who engage deeply with their creative selves are often unknowingly nurturing their resilience, building an inner fortitude that prepares them for the complexities and unpredictability of life.

BECOMING RESILIENT

Resiliency, it is said, can be learned, but it cannot be taught. Paradoxically, resilient people are not rule bound. We may be duty bound; we are not, conversely, rule bound. A good thing since many of us who are resilient are contrarian by nature.

And many of us contrarians naturally seem to upset those around us just by being ourselves.

According to journalist Anna Quindlen, "The thing that is really hard, and really amazing, is giving up on being perfect and beginning the work of becoming yourself."

For us contrarians, however, oftentimes we find that we must "go along" to "get along" with others in our lives from the time we are children lest they cut us from the herd. Later, we acquiesce in trust. Finally, the circle completes, and the real work of becoming our true selves begins again—a samsara—and we find ourselves voluntarily removing ourselves from our selected communities.

Are we all legitimately exceptional? Do we have a specific purpose? One of the most insightful statements from Dr. Masters' work was that we are to "remember daily" who we are:

"You are a child of the Universe, with a right to be free of discord and negativity. You are a Divine heir to the riches of your Divine Father's Universal Kingdom. The essence of your True Selfhood is One with God and Eternal Life."

When I was younger, I always used to reply with "I'm a child of the Universe!" when queried about where I lived, was born, or had traveled from. My gram said so.

What happened?

Upheaval is a part of life, especially for those who are on a bumpy toll road of growth, and while compassionate states of mind, including those of heart-centered kindness, happiness, and trust can be developed with practice, it takes an inordinate amount of work for some of us to expand past our set points of understanding and tolerance. Were we born this way? Some people insist we are, and set points are not that easy to budge. "Apart from a growing 'positive psychology' movement... Western scientists are still largely oriented toward healing the mentally ill, rather than improving the lives of the functionally OK. Recollect Freud's humble goal: to transform hysterical misery into common unhappiness. Western science is content to believe that each of us has a more or less genetically determined set point for well-being—and that happiness and love happen to us" (Ellison).

Being "functionally OK" was something I, like so many others, was great at, along with having a mediocre set point for ordinary personal contentment. Many of us also know quite well that it is far more than happiness and love that "happen to" us.

"I stand in the way, and things just happen to me. I don't understand!" laments my neighbor.

We forget how to breathe; our health begins to fail. We learn what unmedicated depression means and feels like from a personal standpoint. We drift. We fall. We fail. We blame others when we are too fearful to recognize opportunities for growth. We believe others when they say they love us and forget that real Love is not controlling another person or being controlled by someone else. Truly loving ourselves is also not pushing ourselves until we cannot breathe another breath.

For most people, change happens slowly, over the course of time, as an accumulation of smaller alterations—to routine, to diet, of thinking. These shifts may seem trivial within the moment, and therein lurks the predicament. Much like termites, these seemingly insignificant changes can substantially erode exceptionally durable areas.

For some of us, a "problem" may be the complete disintegration of life as we once knew it. Those horror stories of devastation always happen in the movies or to other people. The stories consistently and unequivocally belong to someone else. They cannot be real; they are exaggerated and boisterous and ugly and too loud to be real.

"Well, it wasn't a matter of Life or death, was it?" some may posit.

Indeed, it may be.

CHAPTER 2
OBSCURE LESSONS

I am not what happened to me; I am what I choose to become.

—Jung

We're here in Earth School for our Soul's lessons, lessons that are meant to evolve us to higher places of being, understanding, and compassion for ourselves and others. We were put here to learn, to grow, and to evolve into the exquisite beings we are, and whether or not we like it, lessons will come.

Each of our lessons brings with it a new level of awareness, and with awareness new choice points are possible. Whether we choose to embrace the newfound awareness remains a conundrum for many of us. I believe we are destined to repeat those lessons we didn't master the first time, subtleties and all.

Trauma, for example, can be characterized by a complete lack of immediate choice *in* the moment when accidents, abuse, neglect, or crimes are committed against us. Some disassociate and lose all connection to themselves and, often, humanity. Some of us have endured intense and chronic deprivation as children, from nourishment to the safety and support of trusted guardianship. We had no one to embrace us, to shield us, to protect us from all the real or imagined terrors the world might hold for us while we evolved into autonomous little beings.

Damaged Rudders

Bessel van der Kolk, MD states that trauma is the opposite of complete communication. Yet ... is it?

Our bodies hold on to somatic memories, our brains entangle those experiences, and we fire reactions together from a neurological standpoint. Experiences buried deep within our childhood surface in ways we don't understand or comprehend, and we find ourselves crushingly confused. Disturbing events take place—seemingly randomly in the implicate order of Life—that perplex us in the moment and leave us feeling alone, frustrated, bitter, angry, and marginalized. Why me, we ask, and why now? We think we have no control, and we struggle to decipher cryptic messages about our responses. Something shattered our sense of safety, and this fear and a sense of helplessness permeated our lives. Many of us stop participating, and we sit things out.

Or, as I share in my retreats and workshops, some of us find that rock alongside the path in life and promptly sit our asses down. We may appear to be the innocent bystander, or in this case, rock-sitter; we nonetheless surreptitiously judge ourselves and others as they continue on their way.

Undeniably, some people remain consciously unaware well into what might be considered the adult years. Others happily languish in their own, time-honored, composting heaps of pessimism, hatred, anger, bitterness, sadness, laziness, or lethargy—because it's known and comfortable—rather than working through the roadblocks or breakdowns that may lead to breakthroughs. Breakthroughs are a birthing process of sorts and can be uncomfortable.

Avoiding the discomfort of growth can become a generational pattern as well.

Nonetheless, we are still taxed with the responsibility of learning what we've been put here to learn and to help lead each other home. I believe we meet others for their lessons and for ours; it is part of the mandatory lesson plan here in Earth School. There are no coincidences. Sometimes we are a conduit; other times we are the one on the hot seat.

Laura Weber Garrison, PhD

Maintaining one's trajectory and forging ahead can be a formidable challenge at times. Yet, the choice remains ours to make. I firmly believe that we are not fated to meet our end on a mountain we've scaled for some time, alongside some fellow traveler. We have the agency to descend from these metaphorical peaks—be they mountains of sorrow, disappointment, despair, or anguish—armed with faith.

Staying on the path and continuing to move forward, though, can sometimes be quite challenging. Do we have a choice? I believe we do. I also believe and know in my heart that we are not destined to die on a mountain we have climbed with one of our trail mates. We can find our way off the mountains—of sorrow, disappointments, despair, and anguish—in faith.

What we don't always realize, however, is that faith can be elusive, slippery, and sometimes indistinguishable from our "knowns"—the beliefs we harbor that run amok in the background of our consciousness. We may think we're moving in a certain direction in faith only to fall into a deep, dark chasm of disillusionment. We feel hurt, we're mad, and we're bitter. Moreover, we feel victimized by our Creator and by those we believe the Creator has provided for our protection. We believed we were moving forward in faith only to be backhanded into a dimension we don't understand.

Do we choose the lessons? As one of my group members so eloquently lamented: "The love of my life turned out to be a pathological liar and a predator. I thought I knew him. I gave him my heart, we promised to love, honor, and protect each other, and they counseled us through our Church. Why did God allow *me* to do this to me? What good can possibly come out of me breaking my own heart through being with this psychopath?"

How easy it can be to forget that we are spiritual beings here to learn essential lessons via a physical, human-form experience. And somehow, we must learn to be at peace with both the perceived positives and the perceived negatives in our relationships with ourselves, others, and the world in which we live.

Survivors of prolonged or recurrent abuse also often experience tremendous difficulties managing their own emotions and negotiating and maintaining healthy, viable relationships. Persistent feelings of shame, worthlessness, and intense self-blame are concomitant to viewing the world at large from a fractured state of distrust and hyper-vigilance. This often includes self-loathing to some degree.

We are wounded, so we further self-inflict: "You hurt me, I kill me." We self-inflict through addictions and abuses, self-destructions of too much work and not enough self-care. We do for everyone else and not for ourselves, and we are burned out when we could, instead, be growing ardently, wildly, and with abandon.

We do not trust others easily; we find we do not trust the world we live in either. We're so busy being on guard that we do not allow others to get close to us. Our patterns of rejecting ourselves, our existence, our gifts, the world, and other people have been hardwired into us thanks to our addicted, traumatized, fucked up families. . . .

How, then, can we regain our sense of equanimity and grow wildly once again?

PATIENCE

> In this far corner of the Universe
> I exist serenely,
> With quietness in my heart,
> Humility in my soul.
> For I know the grandeur
> That awaits me.
> I know a time is pending
> When I shall slough off
> This mortal illusion,
> When I shall leap from plane to plane,
> When I shall live
> Within the breast of all things,
> When I shall fill up all Creation,
> When I find my way home at last

Laura Weber Garrison, PhD

To the ultimate God. (Doss, 1979)

CHAPTER 3
YOGA ARRIVED

Listen. Are you breathing just a little and calling it a life?
—Mary Oliver

"You can heal your *Self*," Yogi Doug said to me as I stood there in the studio on the first day of this next chapter of my new life.

Me? Heal my Self? My mind did not understand how yoga could fix anything as broken as I was then, even with some prior yoga-based experiences. Why was I even there? At that time of my life constant pain, debilitating exhaustion, and indescribable heartache were habituated, unkind passengers I carried with me most days.

Checking out permanently—death—had seemed a more straightforward solution. I had decided I was essentially done with being a human anyway.

While most of those around me had no idea of my challenges, my vital life force, my *prana*, Doug explained, was short-circuiting. "Your heart is broken. You've got to start breathing again. Your life force is depleted."

"And, perhaps, you've turned the anger inward," Doug remarked.

I remember smirking. How did he know? I was doing my best to stand there in my power: shoulders squared, poised, and calm. I had kept my dark glasses on to cover the purple-black bags under my eyes and had deliberately not disclosed anything remotely personal. I had quietly asked about class schedules and fees, nothing more. This barefooted ex-Marine who looked more like a kindly Irish grandfather than a yoga master continued: "Prana. You can and must heal your Self. No doctor can do it for you." He fascinated me, and I appreciated the tone of his voice as much as the noticeable field of energy that surrounded him. I had overheard someone mention that he'd walked the Camino de Santiago, a 500-mile pilgrimage across Spain, a goal I had also plastered into a vision book some decades earlier at a more optimistic time in my life and wondered how he had evolved on his Camino. Knowing he was ex-military, I was confident that he had endured trauma.

HOLDING SPACE

When you hold space for someone, you bring your entire presence to them without judgment and without trying to rescue them or somehow fix the situation. You are entirely present and work from your heart, for them, from a place of unmitigated support.

A dear friend and colleague, Joy Anderson, LPC-MH, PPC, QMHP leads grief therapy groups and notes that her sessions are filled with laughter as well as tears.

"One way I knew I wanted to be a therapist and knew that I could do this work was because of some experiences I had before returning to get my master's degree. First, I had the experience of being present with a couple as they learned their teenage daughter had died in a car accident. Though this was utterly heartbreaking, what I found was that I was able to be present with this couple and hold space for them."

How many of us are willing and able to be present when faced with someone who is grieving, and further, are we honestly able to hold the necessary and much-needed sacred space?

Joy continues: "What I have found is that many people are unable to be there for others in the deepest depths of despair, often due to their own unconscious death anxiety (fear of their own death) or fear of losing their own loved ones." Indeed, grief creates deep and intense pain, along with a confusing array of emotions.

"I learned that I could do this thing that other people had difficulty with, and I could be there with others with compassion. I also found that the act of holding space, of being with a bereaved person, of witnessing the pain, helped to ease the pain. More than that, I was immensely impressed and humbled by those who found the courage to face this deep, blinding, gut-wrenching, every-minute-of-the-day kind of unrelenting pain. They faced it head-on and moved towards it to find some peace, some comfort, some glimmer of hope so that slowly the pain would fade. I saw this pain turning to joy, to growth, to beauty. So yes, I hold space for my clients as they re-encounter the depths of hell. And yes, I feel with them. Though, also, at the same moment, I feel hope and gladness because I know this process will bring them healing." Joy owns and operates Joy of Healing, LLC.

MOVING THROUGH THE STAGES

Everything of this world—and others—is composed of energy in one form or another, and when the energy that we consist of—whether body, mind, or Spirit—is blocked, we consequently suffer imbalances. Yoga addresses those shortcomings, and we fully employ and utilize the breath in yoga. Breathing always regulates, increases tolerance, and lowers the intensity of the reaction. We have an intrinsic, hard-wired need to feel safe; breath establishes this bridge of safety.

Most of us do not breathe with conscious awareness, yet our breath is intrinsically linked to our experiences. Our breathing patterns, unlike those of contented animals or people in deep sleep, are often disrupted by our emotional attachments. According to Alexander Lowen, natural breathing involves the entire body; every part is affected, though not all are engaged. Learning to control one's breath involves effort and attention to improve respiratory movements and psychological functioning. Breath is both voluntary and involuntary.

In yoga, the practice of pranayama is not just breath training but a transformative bridge, seeking self-awareness, health, and spiritual growth by harmonizing mind, body, and spirit without disrupting the body's natural rhythms.

Yes, it is yoga, and yes, it is learning to breathe. Breath is life; no breath, no life. It is not yoga in its totality.

Pranayama is a Sanskrit word translated as "extension of the Prana (breath or life force) or breath control." The word is composed of two Sanskrit words: prana meaning life force, and either *yama* (to restrain or control the prana, implying a set of breathing techniques where the breath is intentionally altered in order to produce specific results) or the negative form *ayāma*, meaning to extend or draw out (as in extension of the life force). Breath is a bridge between the mind and the body.

What's vital to understand in the context of healing is that there are dramatic health benefits from what may be deemed a very simple practice of focusing on the breath in conjunction with acknowledging one's thoughts.

Pranayama, while not intended to control the body directly, significantly impacts metabolism and oxygen consumption. This practice shifts the autonomic nervous system away from its excitatory state, promoting a balance beneficial for overall health. Pranayama has demonstrated positive effects on immune function, hypertension, asthma, and stress-related disorders, highlighting its broad therapeutic potential. Through its influence on the autonomic nervous system, pranayama emerges as a key element in holistic health and wellbeing.

The autonomic nervous system, or ANS, is the primary mechanism in control of the fight-or-flight response and the freeze-and-dissociate response. A division of the peripheral nervous system, the ANS regulates our critical involuntary physical reactions and bodily functions that remain primarily unconscious, such as our heart rate, digestion, respiratory rate, and pupillary responses.

To be brief, the autonomic nervous system has two main branches: the sympathetic nervous system and the parasympathetic nervous system. The sympathetic nervous system is often considered the "fight-or-flight" system: it accelerates the heart rate, constricts blood vessels, and raises blood pressure. The parasympathetic nervous system is often considered the "rest-and-digest" or "feed-and-breed" system and is responsible for slowing the heart rate and increasing intestinal and gland activity. In many cases, both systems have opposite actions, where one system activates a physiological response and the other inhibits it.

RESILIENCE AND THE DYSREGULATED NERVOUS SYSTEM

When the autonomic nervous system does not send or receive messages as it is designed to or the message is not clear, a person may become dysregulated and thus experience a variety of symptoms and medical conditions. This miscommunication can wreak more havoc than you may think.

In short, dysregulation generally refers to the lack of equilibrium between the two branches of the ANS. The branches, the sympathetic (SNS) and parasympathetic (PNS), have complementary functions, and they normally work to compensate for each other's activation. Dysregulation is what happens when the nerves in the ANS do not communicate as they are supposed to under routine circumstances.

The umbrella term for this miscommunication and subsequent malfunction is *dysautonomia*. Over 70 million people worldwide are reported to be living with various forms of dysautonomia, and people of all ages can be affected, albeit in varying degrees. Dysautonomia is also known as autonomic dysfunction or autonomic neuropathy. Dysregulation and overstimulation are not the same in this sense.

A person is dysregulated when they cannot find ways to manage behavior and mood, is unable to feel emotions, when the emotions overwhelm the person, and when the emotions remain unresolved and unmanageable for a prolonged period of time. Dysregulation is also the inability to manage the intensity and duration of negative emotions.

Here's a quick, albeit brief, way to distinguish between the SNS and the PNS:
- The SNS branch is in charge of moving a person into action, like a gas pedal.
- The PNS is the one that calms a person down, like a brake.

When there's dysregulation, it means that the two branches have lost their coordination, and the system has lost its equilibrium. You are out of equilibrium, out of stasis, and yes, out of balance. Dysregulation is impactful far beyond the emotional component.

The expression of toleration of changes in emotional states is known as resilience. Resilience is what regulates our tolerance to affect and its vacillations.

When there is a loss of equilibrium, the emotions can easily spin out of control, and we are less resilient to changes, stress, and for many of us, less able to cope with what may be considered ordinary and everyday life.

AFFECT DYSREGULATION

Affect is the part of a person's emotional experience that is felt; it's the physiological manifestation in the body of having an emotion.

If the emotion is anger, for example, the affect could be that of intense involuntary shaking, sweating, having a bright-red face, and the sensations that those changes in physiology feel like. If the emotion is sadness, the affect could be seen as tears, choking, flushing of the skin, and an inability to catch the breath. The affect is the external reflection of what is happening internally.

Affect dysregulation is defined as problems in managing or recovering from extreme emotional states, including maladaptive overregulation or under-regulation of elevated affect states. Affect dysregulation is one of the most important characteristics of Borderline Personality Disorder (BPD) and Post Traumatic Stress Disorder (PTSD).

First, it may be useful to know that trauma is a disorder that develops from the dysregulation of the ANS after experiencing constant stress, fear, confusion, and strong emotions that feel overwhelming and impossible to manage.

Consequently, people may feel out of control. This is because they lack affect regulation.

Under-regulation involves limited access to strategies that could reduce intense affect states and associated difficulties with impulse control and goal-directed behaviors. For example, anger that escalates into rage or anxiety that ramps up into an unmanageable state.

Over-regulation involves limited awareness or clarity of the experience of emotions.

LEVELS OF AROUSAL

When we refer to affect or regulation, we are referencing some of the functions of our nervous system—the ANS in particular. The ANS oversees all the automatic functions of the body and of supplying energy to the internal organs, including the blood vessels, stomach, intestine, liver, kidneys, bladder, genitals, lungs, pupils, heart, and salivary and digestive glands.

The sympathetic nervous system (SNS) branch is constantly active at a basic level to maintain equilibrium or homeostasis within us by ramping up the heart rate, widening bronchial passages, constricting blood vessels, causing dilation of the pupils, and raising blood pressure. It causes goosebumps and perspiration too.

It is also responsible for the fight-or-flight response—preparing our system to keep us out of danger.

The other branch, the parasympathetic nervous system (PNS), does its part in maintaining equilibrium by conserving energy as it slows the heart rate, increases intestinal and gland activity, and relaxes muscles in the gastrointestinal tract. The PNS is also responsible for defensive actions, sometimes called faint, collapse, immobilization, or submit. When overactivated, it is responsible for the dissociation of the experience or of the memory.

A quick segue here: It is often noted that the PNS is responsible for "freeze." This is a misunderstanding. Freeze is a defense that uses both the SNS and PNS branches at the same time.

Once you understand that those forces are at work, you can better understand their relationship to affect dysregulation. Affect dysregulation means the two branches of the ANS lose their coordination. When this happens, the entire system loses its equilibrium, and the emotions can then easily spin out of control.

A person is considered to be emotionally dysregulated when they have the inability to feel emotion(s) or cannot find a way to effectively manage moods and behaviors. Emotions, which are energy in motion, remain unresolved and unmanageable for a sustained period of time and can become overwhelming for the person, both mentally and physically.

Ordinarily, people with dysregulation will feel it in their bodies. Conversely, they may feel nothing at all. While that may seem contradictory, it is important to understand that both states create distress. This is also known as affect (recall that affect is the physiological manifestation of emotion within the body and reflects the changes that our nervous system is going through).

When a person has been exposed to extreme amounts of stress or has been traumatized, the ANS can deviate from normal functions and manifest states of:
- Heightened activity of the sympathetic nervous system—also known as hyper-arousal.
- A predominant activation of the parasympathetic, in this case, hypo-arousal.
- A pervasive heightened activation of both—this is a Rigid-Stuck or "Freeze" state.
- A constant parasympathetic activity with the withdrawal of sympathetic activation. This is known as Tonic Immobility.
- Parasympathetic surge—known as Collapse Immobility.

We all require a certain level of arousal—a state of increased physiological activity—to function in the world. We move between activity and inactivity to balance the use of energy of the brain and system. The activation of the ANS goes up and down in a way that is similar to the way our heart rates oscillate.

Hyper-arousal is a state or condition of physical and emotional tension produced by hormones released during the fight-or-flight reaction. When the stressors activate your sympathetic branch, you will experience emotions like anxiety, anger, fear, or disorientation, and your level of arousal could go up to levels that go beyond what you feel you can manage. Hyperarousal outside the window of tolerance feels like overwhelm or helplessness.

When the stressors cannot be managed by the sympathetic, the parasympathetic will get activated in an extreme way in order to solve for the sense of helplessness, leading to feelings of numbness, confusion, low energy, disengagement, and despair to the point of hopelessness.

While this state of numbness and confusion may seem innocuous at first, there can be serious medical and mental implications. If left unchecked and unresolved, this state can create consequences such as dissociation, shutting down emotionally, and shutting down physically.

So as I mentioned "automatic" with reference to the nervous system earlier, it may help you to think in terms of the ANS being the "automatic" nervous system—because most of our responses are unquestionably automatic. We teach our bodies how to respond via our repeated thoughts, and we can habituate into unbalanced responses.

If a person is emotionally dysregulated, these states can become their automatic reaction to what may be considered mundane or everyday "somewhat stressful" situations—such as traffic, noise, or deadlines—independent of the initial trauma or stressor. The body has reacted in a certain way and gotten stuck in that response pattern.

For some of us, a loud boom or even a slamming door may send us into an extreme reaction. The sound of a ringing phone or a knock at the front door in the middle of the night can send some of us into an outright panic attack.

ADAPTATIONS

The term resilience was first introduced into psychology and psychiatry from technical sciences and, afterward, through medicine and healthcare. It represents a complex set of various protective and salutogenic—meaning able to cause human health and well-being—factors.

Salutogenesis is the origins of health and focuses on factors that support human health and well-being, rather than on factors that cause disease (pathogenesis). Resilience is defined by PubMed.gov as a protective factor that makes an individual more resilient to adverse events that, in turn, lead to positive developmental outcomes.

Resilience is a positive adaptation after stressful situations, and it represents mechanisms of coping and rising above difficult experiences and the capacity of a person to successfully adapt to change, resist the negative impact of stressors, and avoid the occurrence of significant dysfunctions. It likewise represents the ability to return to the previous, so-called "normal" homeostasis or a healthy condition after trauma, accident, tragedy, or illness.

And the higher the resilience, the lower the vulnerability and risk of illness.

Good resilience facilitates many aspects of good health and well-being. Resilient individuals tend to be optimistic and see everything as a useful experience and will focus on personal strengths and qualities. They also develop close relationships with others, have developed social skills, and are emotionally conscious.

Resilience experts believe that anyone can strengthen their resilience and thus contribute to the advancement of their own health. I believe this to be true as well.

INCREASING AFFECT TOLERANCE

If you have read my work, or have worked with me, you know I spend a considerable deal of time on creating safety, exploring beliefs and how they may or may not serve us, and on patterns.

In my work, we "play Jenga" with the habituated ways of being—patterns—that have been adopted that currently drive automatic behaviors. Patterns dictate many of our reflex reactions, and when we disrupt outdated belief systems, question the automatic responses that we have created in our bodies, and work to bring the ANS back into stasis, we can better heal holistically. Beliefs, which are simply repeated thoughts, drive behaviors. Patterns thus develop from and through these beliefs and we, in a very real sense, teach the body how to respond automatically under various circumstances.

Behind those patterns are the deep-seated, hardwired, primal responses such as the fight, flight, or freeze in response to danger. I discuss patterns in much greater detail in my forthcoming book, *Going Rogue: Healing in Spite of Your Traumas*. For now, just know that once we are aware that we have a choice and comprehend, rather than simply "know," that we are greater than our bodies, we can better modulate our reactions.

Two other "primals" I work with in my practice are flop and fawn.

When one is fawning they are essentially people-pleasing, with the thought behind this response, from a trauma-based perspective, being that of "if I can appease this person, I can be safe from conflict or pain." Is it a pattern of avoidance? Yes, in a sense, just as the more commonly used term of "going along to get along." Flop is also known in my practice as "playing possum." More on these later.

Automatic reactions to danger have evolved over thousands of years as a key survival tool. The response is there to help keep you alive by preparing your body to react to danger in a split second.

The challenge is that of dysregulation, wherein literally just about anything can and oftentimes is considered a threat. When we become dysregulated, something as innocuous as an unrecognized sound can trigger us into a state of physical panic that leaves us quaking or exhausted long after we identify the cause.

Recall that resilience is a positive adaptation after stressful situations and it represents mechanisms of coping and rising above difficult experiences—the capacity of a person to successfully adapt to change, resist the negative impact of stressors, and avoid the occurrence of significant dysfunctions.

Recall also that resilience also represents the ability to return to the previous baseline after trauma, accident, tragedy, or illness and the ability to cope with difficult, stressful, and traumatic situations while maintaining or restoring normal functioning. To increase tolerance, and thus resilience, the body must feel safe.

Seems rather daunting and unobtainable for some of us who idle at high speed most of the time, right?

SAKSHI

One of the tools I teach my clients to use is to simply notice in their bodies what is happening within the various reactions or responses they have. This is *experiencing* from a somatic place. This can be difficult when the world is perceived as threatening and our own body does not feel like a safe place. Yoga comes to the forefront here. Yoga means to yoke or connect with a Source beyond ourselves, and one of the most important functions of a yoga practice is that of being the witness of our own minds and thoughts. The Sanskrit term for witness is *sakshi*. It is a combination of the words *sa*, meaning "with," and *aksha*, meaning "senses."

In my practice, we begin with affect. I teach clients to recognize the affect as it is taking place in their bodies without expressing any need to control or change what is happening. It becomes a matter of pausing, noticing, breathing, resting awareness on the reaction or response, and just being with the emotion. From there, we move to sensations and the detached noticing of what is taking place within the body.

Being with that emotion may only be a fleeting instance of pausing, and that's okay.

Here's why this works: Pausing is a signal. We need to develop the awareness around getting triggered by something and, further, recognize that it is necessary to listen to and notice the emotion before it becomes too loud or even overwhelming. Remember that emotions are energy in motion. We can address this energy, and the motion it is causing within us, with awareness.

When we are attentive to what is happening in our body, the brain understands that we are participating in the decision of how to manage that reaction. If you ignore your affect, then the brain goes into an automatic mode without your conscious will. When this takes place, it becomes quite easy to feel out of control.

By noticing the effect, though, the brain activates the part that it's in charge of, regulating the emotional response.

And just by noticing and becoming aware, you are creating more tolerance.

When you feel hyper-aroused, the first line of defense is to lower the intensity of this arousal. Again, this work is about creating safety.

Some things to do when hyperarousal surfaces:

- Reach out to someone.

  Recall that hyperactivation means that you feel like you're in danger. Is there someone you can reach out to that you trust and feel safe with?
- Release some of the excess energy by moving your body in an intentional and intense way.

If you exhaust your energy in something physical, your brain will assume you were able to defend yourself, and it will go back into equilibrium sooner.

When you are hypo-aroused—the opposite of hyper aroused— you must physically move. The brain must be signaled that you are not defeated—and that defeat is not imminent—and that you will keep fighting rather than submitting. The point is to have the sympathetic activation compensate for the excess of parasympathetic.

The ANS can be retrained or "reset," and this retraining or resetting is the impetus and at the core of the work I do with the people that come to see me.

A person who has been traumatized, abused, or continually overstimulated to the point of failure or exhaustion can gain a much more balanced response and exponentially better resilience through the interconnectedness of the practices of yoga, creativity, and the subsequent reconnection to their own Divinity. I call this "crossing the chasm" in my work because, quite often, a person is doing just that. Depression lifts, the world becomes a safer place, being human becomes more worthwhile, and life, with all its challenges, is better tolerated. Once things are stable and safe, happiness, growth, and new possibilities emerge.

RE-REGULATING THE AUTONOMIC (AUTOMATIC) NERVOUS SYSTEM

Something I'd like to reiterate here is that the autonomic nervous system has widespread innervation to nearly every organ system in the body.

Here is a quick science-y deviation in regards how the stress response system works:
- The locus ceruleus in the brainstem is the "Let's Go" button or the "On Switch "for the fight-or-flight system. It releases norepinephrine/noradrenalin any time stress of any kind is detected. All of this takes place in a part of the brain called the limbic system.
- This triggers the amygdala, which triggers the hypothalamus. The amygdala prompts feelings of anxiety and fear.
- The hypothalamus then releases Corticotropin-releasing hormone (CRH), which stimulates the pituitary.
- The pituitary releases ACTH—adrenocorticotropic hormone—to stimulate the adrenal glands.

- The adrenal glands release adrenalin and cortisol. Although norepinephrine is crucial for our survival and proper brain function, it becomes toxic when it is in excess.
- Elevated levels of norepinephrine in the brain result in fear, anxiety, panic attacks, insomnia, and the inability to relax, while adrenalin triggers the liver to dump its sugar reserves into the bloodstream.
- High levels of sugar in the bloodstream alert the pancreas to release high levels of insulin.
- Elevated levels of insulin in the bloodstream on an ongoing basis lead to many degenerative health conditions, like insulin resistance, obesity, type 2 diabetes, and heart disease.

During this process, other neurotransmitters like dopamine, GABA, endorphins, and serotonin are summoned up repeatedly to modulate the excess stress, which eventually leads to depletion.

A brief note here about neurotransmitters: Neurotransmitters are the body's chemical messengers, and they are governors—they govern our moods, thoughts, feelings, behavior, memory, and cognitive function. If neurotransmitters become depleted, then many other psychological symptoms may develop.

Additionally, neurotransmitters are needed to modulate the autonomic nervous system and restore the body to the parasympathetic state, so if they are not available in sufficient numbers, the sympathetic nervous system may run rampant.

Cortisol helps to counteract some of the negative effects of stress and keeps things in balance. It enhances digestion and metabolism, restricts insulin, and is a crucial player in blood sugar management, glucose metabolism, immune function, and the inflammatory response.

However, the excessively high levels of cortisol that may occur when the demands of stress are disproportionate can result in elevated levels of anxiety and fear and disruption of the hormonal system.

The adrenal glands will no longer be able to produce enough cortisol if the demands for cortisol remain high and incessant. Adrenal exhaustion is an exquisitely challenging type of exhaustion (noting the same from personal experience here).

Since the primary root of dysautonomia and autonomic nervous system dysfunction lies in an overactive sympathetic nervous system (or activation of the fight-or-flight system), the definitive goal in recovery is to restore balance to the ANS.

The process of restoring balance to the ANS requires a multifaceted and inclusive approach that addresses the contributing chronic stress factors that exist for each person. This requires a variety of techniques and lifestyle changes that encourage the activity of the parasympathetic nervous system and oppose the elevated levels of norepinephrine.

HABITUATIONS

We are habituated *into* the ways we act, react, and respond to stressors. Remember the equation of E+R=O:

The Event + (your) Response = (your) Outcome

We do have a choice and can effectuate healing. Does it take awareness and work? Yes. Is it easy? No. The key is understanding your own, unique, and personal stress loads and the contributory factors that you do have a modicum of control over. Diet, environment, the work we do, and the people we choose to associate with—all are impactful on our health. We can and must "control the controllables" with awareness.

It is imperative that you work to reduce your total stress load, and this looks different for each person. This includes nutritional deficiencies, candida, heavy metal toxicity, emotional stress, hypothyroidism, hypoglycemia, Lyme disease, low serotonin, or structural stress—or a combination of the aforementioned. Each of these stressors is contributory and simply addressing one, such as emotional stress, is not going to heal you if you are, for example, also nutritionally depleted, sleep deprived, or constantly bombarded with negativity from those you choose to spend time with.

What we focus on expands. We can help to minimize the impact that stress has on our lives by the way we choose to respond to it.

PRANAYAMA

Breath is one area that we can have both involuntary and voluntary or conscious control over, and fundamental to this is that our full, controlled exhalations can trigger the parasympathetic nervous system resulting in a relaxation response in the body.

Dirgha pranayama is known as the Complete or Yogic breath in yoga and utilizes the full capacity of the lungs. We pant when we are frustrated or emotional, and some of us drag on cigarettes to breathe more deeply and thereby relax. Most of us don't breathe deeply, and we must for many reasons. While the utilization of the full capacity of the lungs may sound complicated, three-part dirgha pranayama is among the easier-to-learn and more fundamental of pranayama techniques.

In the practice of three-part dirgha pranayama, the approach to breathing is methodical and deliberate. The technique involves a slow inhalation, filling the lungs from the bottom up, using the diaphragm, and then expanding the rib cage. This inhalation extends to the upper part of the lungs, near the shoulder blades, and is briefly held. The exhalation process is equally precise, beginning from the upper lungs and progressing downward, concluding with a gentle contraction of the abdominal muscles to expel residual air. This systematic approach ensures a deep, thorough breath cycle.

Dirgha pranayama is thought to increase overall energy, renew the entire system, improve digestion, and keep the lungs and chest flexible and relaxed. Five to ten rounds are completed, and it is a recommended breathing practice for use before meditation. We utilize this breathwork in virtually all the group work I teach. I also teach this technique to my clients for their use at home. The methods are easy to learn and incorporate.

Uijayi pranayama is another deeply relaxing and very soothing breath practice for many people. Breathing through the nostrils, one slightly engages the glottis and constricts the back of the throat so that the air creates a light sound of rushing wind as the air passes through the throat.

Ujjayi pranayama, often termed the "victorious" or "conquering" breath, also emphasizes a harmonious and rhythmic flow of breath. In this practice, both the inhalation and exhalation are maintained at equal length, creating a steady, soothing rhythm. The focus on this balanced breath helps in reducing mental agitation for many, as the mind becomes absorbed in the sound of the breath, facilitating a state of calm and centeredness. Likewise, meditation can be induced by utilizing this breathing pattern. Uijayi pranayama is also thought by many who practice it to heighten awareness and enhance creativity.

Nadi Shodana is also known as "alternate nostril breathing" or "channel purification breath."

Here's how to practice this breathwork:
- The right thumb and ring finger (you are welcome to use your pinky finger if that works better for you than the ring finger) are used as clamps for the nostrils and are placed at the dips on the right and left sides of the nose.
- After the right side of the nose is closed with the thumb, exhale through the left nostril, and then slowly inhale through the left nostril. Yes, exhale through the left, then immediately and slowly inhale through the left.
- The left nostril is then closed with the ring finger; exhale through the right nostril.
- The completion of this round is inhalation through the right nostril, the closing of the right side with the thumb, and exhalation on the left side.

Nadi Shodana is purported to stimulate and synchronize the hemispheres of the brain. It also strengthens, calms, and regulates the *nadis* (an energetic system in the body, more on that momentarily), increases the assimilation of energy, and helps to eliminate waste.

If 70 percent of our body's wastes are removed via our breathing, why do we give our breath so little attention most of the time? Further, if deep breathing also stimulates the relaxation responses, why isn't it second nature for us?

Instead, many of us stop breathing in response to inundation and somatically go, sometimes directly and automatically—into a flight mode where breathing becomes shallow and laborious. We do this reflexively, without conscious awareness.

BREAKDOWNS

Undeniably, some people covet codifying their collective waves of panic and happily languish in their own, time-honored, composting heaps of sadness and lethargy rather than working through the breakdowns that may lead to breakthroughs. "It's comfy in my bed till noon and beyond; I like it there, so that's where I spend most of my time," stated a young woman in one of my groups. When queried further, I found that I was confused as to whether she was simply lazy and spoiled or weathering a bout of depression. "Why bother," she had gone on to explain. "I like ruminating. I'm really smart, and I don't have to work or anything, so why not?"

"Are you feeling stressed or depressed?" I had asked, noting from intake paperwork that she was already seeing a therapist and had not been diagnosed with depression.

"Nope. I just like to stay in bed."

Baffled, I kept quizzing her about why she would spend her precious life worrying and cocooned in her bed, especially if she were as smart as she stated. Her consistent reply was "I don't know."

"What if you *did* know, then what?" I would ask.

"I don't know!" she would insist.

I've since seen a number of teenagers and young adults who have said the same thing to me; it's almost as if there is a secret society of those who have chosen to stay in bed or on the sofa, instead of participating in life.

They've effectively planted their asses on the rock on the side of the path.

Is that any real way to live?

Some of us prefer to face life and stress head-on. We barrel into it, wallow around in the anguish, dive in deeper if we find a pocket, and come up, exhausted and covered in misery, and we keep on going. Depression can quickly loom much too large, though, when one is exhausted. My depression and exhaustion also led to syncope or fainting.

For me, learning not to faint took real effort. My body would collapse, and I would find myself slumped over my desk or contorted into potentially compromising positions on the floor.

One outcome of learning breath control is that a person can use these practices to ease stressful or challenging conditions. Yoga teaches us how to maneuver through our lives and work without disruptions through mindfulness. The work of our yoga includes the use of our awareness to return the focus of our attention back to the breath, which for me and countless others serves as an anchor within the chaos. Taming our monkey-mind to stay focused, even for a moment sometimes, can be a slow and frustrating learning process, especially for some of us admittedly Type-A individuals.

Those of us who regularly practice pranayama know that it has a very distinct balancing effect on the nervous system. The work of yoga can, and will, become a doorway.

SUBTLE STRUCTURES

Yoga teaches us there is an energy network in the body known as the nadis that corresponds to the nervous system. Stephen Cope explains this beautifully in his book *Yoga and the Quest for True Self*:

> Yogis discovered beneath the physical structures of the body an interpenetration and underlying subtle sphere of reality, which they call the energy body or

the pranamayakosha (literally, the sheath of vital airs). The very nature of this subtle structure is movement, flow, and change. Over the centuries, and particularly after the advent of hatha yoga in medieval India, adepts developed a precise anatomy of this energy body. Yogis found the pranamayakosha to be replete with thousands of invisible channels, or nadis, through which prana flows, energizing and sustaining all parts of the physical and energy structure. Most of the fascinating yogic diagrams of the energy body make the Nadi system look like a much denser version of our circulatory system or nervous system. While Western science has mapped out about six thousand nerves in the nervous system, yogis generally agree that the prana body contains at least seventy-two thousand nadis. This astonishingly detailed description of the nadis was apparently mapped out in deep states of meditation and was confirmed over and over again by Hatha yogis." (203)

Energy is said to be absorbed and flow through these nadis, and as the "nasal passages have more nerve endings than the oral cavity, more prana is assumed to be absorbed by nostril breathing" (K. Weiss).

Breath, once again. So is breath yoga, as some insist?

The word yoga is derived from the Sanskrit root *yuj*, which means to unite, join, harness, contact, or connect. In more common usage, the word yoga often means any method by which an individual is brought into a "yoke" or a union with God.

For me, this means reconnection or a reunion with Source.

"Yoga consists of observances, abstinences, posture, control of life force, turning the senses inward, concentration, meditation, and super consciousness or reintegration" (White). Dr. Masters taught that meditation was our connection to Source. Stephen Cope also explains that "in practicing yoga, we're training our awareness to attend to the flow of thoughts, feelings, and sensations in the body—and to be with these different states without self-judgment or reactivity."

Reactivity is a concern for most of us. Author and Holosync founder, Bill Harris, explains that we "become stressed and reactive when we receive more input than we can handle or when our internal map isn't adequate to negotiate the challenges of our environment." Dysregulation ensues.

Our thoughts and feelings are trained by our habits to flow in predictable patterns, which determine whether our life fosters a sense of ease and happiness or a sense of frenzy and chaos. These patterns are so ingrained that even the hint of a possible directional change is incomprehensible for many people, and it is the constant identification with these patterns that forms our belief system, which, in turn, is a blueprint for our lives.

This grand plan, or our internal map, dictates how we act and react in the world as well.

Understandably, then, there are times we may involuntarily resort to the use of various coping mechanisms we may have learned as children. The brain is unquestionably organized to reflect what we know in our environment. All of our personal experiences are cataloged within the networks of cells that make up our brains and are likewise held somatically within our physical bodies.

The brain can be rewired in a sense since it keeps changing, growing, and regenerating throughout our lives. "What wires together, fires together" is a familiar axiom. When we make mental associations, we form critical pathways in our nervous systems that create clusters of thoughts and physiological states. Research tells us we can rewire the pain, stress reactions, and physical weaknesses that may have been wired together in our brains and body, even if they occurred when we were children. We aren't born with negative feelings, for example; those are learned behaviors that we have adopted as truth. Other behaviors stem from stress or trauma that we have or continue to experience. Our bodies become encoded with memories, and not all of these memories are pleasant for us upon recall.

YOGA AS A MENTAL CONSTRUCT

Einstein said that "we cannot solve our problems with the same thinking we used when we created them." Similarly, we are bound to our same, ongoing realities if we stay in the same consciousness that created it.

How then are we to change our consciousness if we are bound by our beliefs, our reflexes, and our same thinking?

What I have found through my practice is that our authentic yoga seeks us out, just as experiences and people do that are meant for our evolution. "One of the significant bonuses of Hatha yoga is that it acknowledges the interrelationship of body, mind, and spirit. What happens within the body affects the mind, heart, and spirit—and the reverse is equally true" (White 27). While many people begin yoga, for example, as a new exercise routine, the outcome is that they will inadvertently encounter a much more united and self-realized state if they are willing to face themselves and stay with the practice. Some of us refer to this as the magic of yoga: you are not doing yoga; yoga begins doing you.

It seems that here in the West, the word "yoga is nearly synonymous with Hatha yoga. This is not so, for example, in India, the birthplace of yoga, and where, many are often surprised to learn, thousands of yogis and yoga lineages have no physical or asana practice at all. The focus instead is on meditation, devotional and philosophical practices as some believe that attention to the physical body detracts one from a spiritual life and creates an inappropriate attachment to the physical body" (White). Yoga is a practice, and consciousness can directly affect our reality.

NOBLE SILENCES

Everyone seeks peace and harmony because this is what we lack in our lives. From time to time, we all experience agitation, irritation, and disharmony. And when we suffer from these miseries, we don't keep them to ourselves; we often distribute them to others as well. Unhappiness permeates the atmosphere around someone who is miserable, and those who encounter such a person also become affected. Certainly, this is not a skillful way to live.

We ought to live at peace with ourselves and at peace with others. After all, human beings are social beings, having to live in society and deal with each other. But how are we to live peacefully? How are we to remain harmonious within, and maintain peace and harmony around us, so that others can also live peacefully and harmoniously?
—S.N. Goenka in Berne, Switzerland

One of the most challenging courses I have voluntarily encountered was that of sitting in *vipassana* meditation for ten days. Jack Canfield, author of the Chicken Soup for the Soul series, commented that sitting vipassana was the "hardest thing he'd ever done." It surprised me that he would say this, and when I questioned him, he responded with encouraging words about his own humanness and how "the sit" facilitated spiritual growth. I knew sitting for ten days in silence and stillness would be a transcendent leap for me that was lodged somewhere between rebellious and life-altering along my path as well.

Ten years later, in Nepal, with more than 250 other meditators, I made that leap.

The Nepal Vipassana Center, Dhamma Shringa, was founded in April of 1981 and is located in the lower foothills of the Himalayas at approximately 5,200 feet above sea level. The center covers almost four acres, overlooking the Kathmandu valley, approximately 12 kilometers north of Kathmandu City. The property is covered in greenery, with a modest set of facilities furnished with remarkably simple amenities. Sparse and clean, it is not classifiable as a cozy, modern, retreat center by Western standards.

One of India's most ancient meditation techniques, vipassana means "to see things as they really are." Rediscovered by Gotama

Buddha more than 2,500 years ago, vipassana was taught by him as a universal remedy for universal ills, and today, many practitioners still believe in its curative powers. It is a non-denominational technique and a superbly tough mental training. We are taught that, just as we use physical exercises to improve our bodily health, vipassana can be used to develop a healthy mind. Our group had representations from many faiths, and dozens of countries, and the participants ranged in age from fifteen to over ninety years of age.

The days are sixteen hours long, beginning with the bells at pre-dawn and ending with a class after our daily sit. We sat, motionless, on an uncomfortable personal cushion, with others of the same gender less than an arm's length away, for hours at a stretch in the big meditation hall—men on one side of the building, women on the other. We were in Noble Silence, not speaking, nor even acknowledging one another throughout our time at the Dhamma Shringa. Break times were brief; mealtimes consisted of a cafeteria setting with ample portions of simple, vegetarian, Nepalese food. Men and women are separated at all times, even if married, and dorms had up to sixteen beds each. There is no charge for the course or the lodging, and voluntary donations are made at the end of the sessions as scholarships for incoming students.

Sitting with more than 250 people from around the globe in meditation was an intense and immensely growth-inducing experience, especially on the final day for me, when we all focused on sending healing through our meditation.

Students are encouraged to practice for two hours daily, an hour in the morning and an hour at night, once we return to our daily lives.

One of the women I spoke with after the program shared with me that she had taken part in this ten-day sit each year for five years and had a brief daily practice of "maybe ten minutes." I asked her why she didn't simply practice twice daily as we were being taught. She said she wasn't willing and that it would take too much of her time. She is a busy professional that travels around the world for work, and she uses the "sit" as a complete retreat and reset. The even more extraordinary facet of meeting her was that she had a sister whom she was en route to visit who lived not twenty minutes from my home in the United States. She had traveled from Washington, DC, specifically to be "in the glory" of the Dhamma Shringa, which is considered by many to be a uniquely energetic and extraordinarily powerful meditation center.

The ten-day vipassana hadn't cured me of the underlying leitmotif of "something is still missing." It did give me, however, a set of tools that helped me to refocus and release many of the tensions I had. I recall sitting in Nagarkot at the base of the Himalayas several days after the vipassana, full of sadness and conflict that I could not justify on a conscious level. I sat vipassana at 4 a.m. for an hour and wrote most of the day. Oddly, I stayed up all night, something I never do under normal circumstances, working on books for children. Where the concept came from for those two books that manifested over the course of the next few days is still elusive to me.

Alas, there is much work that must be undertaken to untie those pesky knots.

THE PRACTICE

A fundamental aspect of embracing new learning experiences involves being open to the space for comprehension and growth. How frequently do we obstruct our own progress with the automatic response of "I know!"? This automatic reaction eliminates the opportunity for fresh insights. Furthermore, adults frequently hinder their own advancement with statements like "I can't," "It's too difficult," or "I don't know." But why do we readily fall into this pattern? It's because it's a learned and familiar behavior, and there's a fear of change lurking beneath it.

Primarily, we must confront our deeply ingrained habits. The process of learning something new demands a commitment that goes beyond our typical daily routines. It challenges us to shift our usual ways of doing, existing, and being. And just like any other transformation we aspire to achieve, we need to overcome various factors, such as time constraints, environmental influences, the opinions of others, and our own physical limitations.

We must also embrace the possibility that, with our newfound awareness, changes are possible.

Once we realize that we do have a choice, invariably we as humans must begin to ask the more critical questions of the "How?" Our ability to overcome these factors of time, space, and Self is hinged upon our understanding that we must now think, act, and become greater than our present reality. This is "Matter to Matter" thinking as defined by Joe Dispenza.

Our answers don't necessarily reside in our internalized, ingrained beliefs about the world as we know it. We must be willing to go beyond what we think we know, what we have been taught to believe is "real," and what has been normalized as "what is" within the confines of our own life experience.

Hence, I believe once we get back in touch with the life force of our breath, only then will our mind, heart, and body, and Spirit begin to cooperate.

Change, though, is extraordinarily terrifying for many people.

And many of us assiduously avoid change on a subconscious level, even if we insist we are in the process of change. We have our opinionated friends and family, the "knowns" of our familiar environments, and ingrained patterns that we're up against as well.

Sometimes we do everything we can to launch ourselves, a product, an idea, start a new relationship, end one that isn't serving us, or otherwise attempt to make a move... and we still find ourselves stuck. Why? Do we pay attention to the signs? Do we heed the little salvos or shrug them off as synchronicities? Or what of the bigger "stop now!" signs from the Universe? Nope. Most of us bully through and continue on our way, blaming each other for our choices and staying in that stuck place of stagnation.

My maternal grandmother, whom I dearly loved and who saved my life when I was a toddler, left the planet in her early seventies. I was angry at her for leaving; she, however, was done. She despised my step-grandfather, stifled her personal sense of Self and creativity to get along with him, and sought solace with her "titty-balls," a rather smelly concoction of (mostly) whiskey and milk, and paired the drink with cigarettes. "Why do you stay with Pa Pete when he is so mean and you hate him so much?" I would ask. She would tell me that things were "just the way they were." My mother repeated the scenario, sans the cigarettes, with my father. She, too, died early from complications borne of alcohol abuse. She was also angry and depressed.

Why were they self-grounded and unable to rise to their God-given potentials? "Some folks are born waiting to die, and they'll do almost anything they can to make that happen no matter what we do, think, or feel," according to one of my colleagues.

I left home at an early age, traveling to Europe with earnings I had squirreled away from babysitting, selling seeds to neighbors from plants I had grown, and doing needlework for others. My father scoffed when I asked if I could go, mumbling something derisive about me not having the money to go, him not paying, and the stupidity of the idea. He rejected my request for parental consent and shooed me away with the flip of the newspaper he was reading.

His dismissals were frequent, harsh, and thorough. However, on that day, I persisted, and I told him I was going, knowing full well he would get angry. And he did in a big way. He stated that if I thought I was old enough to make my own decisions as an adult and thought I was ready to take care of myself, then I might as well move out.

I did just that upon my return.

Knowing what I do now, I know that I went because I had to; I was called, and the call felt like an enormous magnet across the continents. My future Self was on the other side of the Atlantic Ocean, and I knew that I had to go and join her there. Was I running away from home? No, I was ready, quite able, and very willing to go and was intentionally seeking refuge from an incredibly hostile "home" filled with rage, addictions, dysfunction, and abuse. The thoughts of going were all I could think. Going to Europe meant my first time on an airplane, leaving the state where I was born, and flying halfway around the world, alone.

When I returned from Europe, I left my tribe of origin, not even old enough to obtain a driver's license.

Part of my mission from the time I can remember cognate thoughts was to see the arcane sites of the planet in person. I'd pore over my father's encyclopedias, rummage through his metaphysical books, and question my gram, his mother, who was part Cherokee and well-versed in the roots of the worlds beyond the world. I would question incessantly.

My father would have none of me traveling abroad and had sought to ground me in virtually every way possible once I was old enough to voice my own opinions. He was rather spiteful toward his own mother too. She was a strong woman, a contrarian. They were estranged for many years.

THE BANE OF GIRLNESS

I was born a girl in this incarnation and was therefore considered "less than" in my father's generation on every level: less smart, less durable, less worthy, and in many respects, much less important. My father was operating from his paradigm of understanding and, at that point in his life, hadn't yet evolved to the place of comprehending that while we are all at different places on our path of growth, we are all worthy.

My father had toured Europe on foot as an infantry soldier during World War II and had returned, one of six left alive, of a company of 150 under Patton's command. Profoundly traumatized, the experience wracked him with karmic luggage and heavy *dharma* his entire existence in this incarnation, and it took him most of his adult life to reconcile many things. He left the planet without ever having taken proactive steps to work through his C-PTSD, and generationally the traumatic responses still linger.

He tested at genius level and was raised by a single parent, my gram, during the Depression. A resentful, bitter survivor, he had gone to war as a child, well before he had an actual intellectual capacity for understanding the implications it would have on his entire life and the karmic impact it would have on his offspring. Decades after the war, and thousands of miles from where the event took place, I would meet the nephew of a man whose body had shielded my father during a night of hellfire. Some would say that the meeting was a coincidence. I believe that, in the quantum field, nothing is coincidental. The nephew shared the astonishing nuances of mind-boggling survival with my father. My father rarely discussed the war; he had no choice but to disclose things that day, and it was then that I began learning about the malleability of time and how we somatically—and sometimes irretrievably—hold onto memories and events.

DHARMA

Present in the present moment, where and when one is supposed to be. Is that humanly possible?

Stephen Cope talks about the "just-rightness" of dharma in his book, *The Great Work of Your Life*. Cope writes that it is our job to make a choice that creates the right conditions for dharma to flourish. Dharma, at least for some of us, is filled with karmic baggage, and thus, making those just-right choices requires assistance beyond our current level of understanding and participation beyond what we may be capable of at the moment.

Karmic baggage can be quite cumbersome. And it can be odd, scary, and way too heavy sometimes.

Why is it that we encounter dharma that is not of our preference and co-create realities that we don't think we envision? The place I referred to as "home" devolved into a rather cold and uncomfortable environment when I would have preferred that my home was a sanctuary of comfort, respect, and kindness. Disease and unrest, exorbitant bills to pay, and too much chaos to manage instead found their way into the hoped-for haven. Did I choose this intentionally? Yes, I let my devious and incredibly-resourceful-when-he-wanted-to-be alcoholic brother in when he "had no place else to go." I hadn't consciously asked for specific outcomes; my choices delivered me there nonetheless when I failed to hold boundaries for my own wellbeing.

We learn or choose not to. We grow, or we choose to stagnate. Change is inevitable, nonetheless.

A young woman who had been part of my practice before she fired herself insisted she was anxious and stuck and was feverishly "shining the light on all the seedlings of growth" she had planted without avail. She further lamented—and advised others via social media—that perhaps it was time to do any number of avoidant things since she "wasn't getting anywhere" in her life.

The reality was that she didn't want to take personal responsibility or to be held accountable. She expected others to do, answer, and fix things for her, and contrarily, was quick to rebuff anything that wasn't known to her. "There is no reasoning with her. She has an absurd rebuttal for everything!" was an observation another group member noted.

When queried one night during group as to why she wasn't making any progress toward building a business of her own (which is what she was there to do), she nonchalantly told the group that contacting potential clients or working through other key components necessitated by a business plan did not "spark joy." She recoiled when it was noted by one of the group members that she was acting petulant and undisciplined and flared when I questioned her follow-through and demonstrable commitment to any of the promises she had made to me or to the group.

She likewise became defensive within the scope of our final sessions together when I flatly refused to collude with her stance of being a victim of her circumstances, which were, in her opinion, a lack of time, lack of knowledge, being concerned about family members, and working "so much."

All viable concerns, certainly. However, the critical questions: who and what had she continued to surround herself with and how many hours (daily) was she continuing to troll or doom scroll on sketchy dating apps and social media?

An articulate and witty girl, she was used to navigating her world through clever duplicity, triangulation with others, verbal judo, and sidestepping the necessary work, frictions, or uncomfortable self-created problems at hand. When I challenged her, for example, about completing vital group-required homework, she attempted to justify her literal months of failing the requirements with a haughty, "I am reading other books.... I read slow," and claims of "It's hard" and "I don't know how."

She works part-time and has a college degree. She has no partner and no children. She found time for vacations, naps, massages, yoga classes, and time at the beach. She found time for over five hundred non-monetizable posts on a personal Instagram account. She routinely hung out at the bars and stayed out late.

She had the time and had access to the tools. While the business-building group was not a support group, per se, they were supportive and incredibly patient with her, as was I. Patience only goes so far when there is no recompense. Her excuses and failure to follow through on promises, commitments, and yes, homework, were, for her, a conscious, evidenced, deliberate, ongoing series of easier choices.

Much like the alcoholic who chooses to continue to frequent the familiar bar wondering why he still struggles with alcoholism, she was emulating, co-regulating, and entraining with those idlers she kept around and with those who would collude with her.

Undeniably, she had openly eschewed making the required commitment to necessary separations from the knowns in her world. Instead, she made excuses and chose to remain true to "her" people, the places, and to the familiar in her current world. She further perpetuated and substantiated her stories of being the victim through her unwillingness to take the appropriate, necessary actions toward ownership of her actions, remedial course corrections, and real growth.

Thus, it wasn't a matter of her not knowing how to implement the significant changes she professed to desire; rather, she was unwilling to relinquish what was familiar, known, and easy. She sought to continue her usual behaviors, those she had always managed to escape consequences from, yet expected a different outcome.

Our response to life's challenges serves as our rudder, steering us through the often turbulent waters of emotion, circumstance, and relationship dynamics. Just as a rudder guides a ship through currents and winds, our responses dictate the direction our lives take. They determine whether we drift aimlessly, crash into obstacles, or navigate toward a life of purpose and meaning. By mindfully choosing our responses, we exercise control over our emotional and mental states, which in turn influences our actions and their outcomes. This continuous and conscious steering empowers us to align our course with our goals and values, ultimately guiding us toward a fulfilling life.

Navigating the road to personal development is a journey of considerable effort, though, and it demands genuine commitment to confront and tackle tough challenges. This is a truth I share with all my clients. And this a process where it's important to recognize and respect individual limits or thresholds, as there are moments when one might feel overwhelmed. While I approach these situations with compassion, I maintain a clear stance of not tolerating any form of evasion or dishonesty. My practice involves holding individuals accountable, establishing firm boundaries, and providing supportive guidance to foster genuine growth.

When I established a decisive, final boundary with her, her reaction was one of indignation, not humility, and she refused to accept personal responsibility. She blamed me, positioned herself as the victim, and attempted to garner support from the group. On social media, she quickly and openly reverted to the "fun" lifestyle, reassociating with the same self-destructive individuals and habits she had previously declared she had moved on from.

In her story, you might see elements that mirror your own experiences, especially those times when subconscious blind spots or entrenched patterns have kept you in a state of perceived victimhood. Similarly, there might have been instances where you placed responsibility on a previous counselor or therapist, not yet realizing that your choices and the unacknowledged patterns in your decisions were, in fact, hindering your journey toward substantial personal growth. An exquisite form of self-sabotage, is it not?

The truth is that we become the sum of those people, places, and circumstances with whom we invest the most time and energy. We do not rise to the level of our own expectations when we are surrounded by underachievers, slackers, or addicts; we will, instead, sink to the lower levels of those we choose to be with. If those people or situations are toxic, they will cripple our growth as well as drain us energetically. Expecting otherwise is much like ingesting tiny amounts of poison over an extended period of time and expecting our physical body to maintain optimal health. Depletions of any sort, be it emotional, physical, or mental, drops us to our more primal ways of reacting as well. Thus, we automatically and subconsciously regress to our known habits, patterns, and behaviors because they are familiar and somehow, we have decided, help keep us safe.

Change requires active and committed participation, not just showing up half-heartedly for therapy sessions or for a class wherein you make endless postulations about your inner saboteur or karmic contracts or excuses about why you didn't have time to do your homework. In my world, if someone says, "I don't have time," what they are really saying is, "I really don't want to."

We have to take the steps and we have to take committed actions.

And, like it or not, we are inevitably forced into changes in the natural, implicate, and progressive order of our incarnation here in Earth School if we fail to honor the required participation and adulting in our own lives.

The aforementioned woman made conscious choices to maintain stasis in her world, to stay in the knowns. Thus, her ingrained habits and patterns took over, much like toxic weeds in an untended garden, and she slid quite willingly back into her own subconscious versions of safe and familiar.

THE TENSION OF OPPOSING FORCES

Some of us have studied for decades in professions that may have either run their course for us or were never genuinely a fit in the first place. Stephen Cope acknowledges this in his discussions about the emergent third way, which unites and transcends two opposing forces, the third way being the one that usually comes as a surprise. He refers to holding this state of tension, this gestation, as "psychic utero."

And we all gestate at different rates in this incarnation, and there can be a great deal of tension around this for many people. It's a structural tension, the closing of the gap between a version of a current reality and the visions you might hold. It's a nebulous and confusing space between The Here and Now of what you've been training, learning, growing, doing, or being and the "There" of where you want to be. This is what I call the Liminal Space.

You can lose the material things; however, one can never lose the mastery of what we have learned and who we have become in the process of achieving something.

Remembering what we have learned, especially if the lesson was very painful, may be another paradigm entirely.

CHAPTER 4
INTO THE TRANCE

Thank you, Lord, for bringing me where I did not want to go.
—Nikos Kazantzakis

The fundamental beliefs behind the religious system of Eckankar, the ancient science of soul travel, for example, cite everyday contemplation of the world as a way 'in,' with the "simple explanation of contemplation being 'completely interested' in a subject" (Steiger). This is meditation, though, is it not? The Tibetan word for meditation "Gom" means "to become familiar with" and has the inference of training the mind to be familiar with states that are positive and beneficial, namely, concentration, compassion, correct understanding, patience, humility, and perseverance.

When we meditate, we are engrossed, we are unaware of the peripheral experiences, and we meld with that one, particular contemplation. "The way by which each person can regain the original mastership of his own 'Garden of Eden' is by use of the faculty of imagination which God has endowed each of us as His Divine gift to all men. Eckankar teaches that we can have solace in the higher states of consciousness ... such as those which were common in the lives of the old Christian saints and the lives of the Eastern adepts" (Steiger 132) and that it is neither religion, philosophy nor metaphysical in nature; instead, it is a 'path to God'. The path to God, to our Source, we find, can be a somewhat convoluted journey for many of us.

"We cannot manage our worldly difficulties successfully unless [the] soul is able to live again in the spiritual consciousness of itself. In seeking this state of experience, then, we must first seek self-recognition or self-realization. The more that [one] practices the art of self-recognition, the greater the awareness of the God-state of realization" (Steiger).

Eckankar—or ECK—holds that Westerners are not suited to the requirements of heavy concentration and extended periods of silence necessitated by meditation. It is alleged to be too intense of an experience, and we, as Westerners, are thought to be just not capable of what Easterners have known how to do for generations.

Meditation, however, can be a simple act of awareness and congruence on some levels. When we are mindful, we are in a meditative state. The levels of awareness can and do vary, however, and the act of being 'present in the present' moment may look and feel completely different for you than it does for me.

OUR "OTHER" SELVES

And we are not alone. We all have more than one 'self' inhabiting our personal space.

There is a definite part of each one of us that seems to always "know better," do things automatically, is excellent at spontaneous reactions, and occasionally complicates our life as we might consciously view it. Many of us suspect that this part of our being has far more control over us than we give it credit.

A simple overview: Why do we blush when we are embarrassed, cringe when someone runs their fingernails across a chalkboard, or suddenly shriek or catch our breath when startled?

Every shift in our physiological condition is mirrored by a corresponding shift in our mental and emotional states, and vice versa. This phenomenon is driven by the "inner Self," which operates independently of conscious thought and readily engages well-established behavioral patterns in response to mental, energetic, or physical triggers. Moreover, our subconscious Self plays a pivotal role in regulating vital bodily functions, including heart rate and blood pressure, accounting for approximately 90% of our continuous physiological processes.

Thus, to understand and develop these interactions more fully, we must first address our subconscious as the source. Our automatic pilot who is running the show for us always assumes it knows best.

Serge King emphasizes that our primary conscious ability is the capacity to 'direct our awareness and attention in response to thoughts or experiences.' At times, it may seem as if we are constrained by a larger and occasionally contradictory 'self,' but King argues otherwise. He underscores that the subconscious eagerly seeks guidance and readily follows previously embedded directives when allowed to operate independently. Essentially, the subconscious exhibits 'complete and unquestioning obedience' when effectively engaged and provided with guidance. The key lies in understanding how to establish effective communication.

METHODS OF COMMUNICATION

Meditation and self-hypnosis, while remarkably similar, are intrinsically different forms of communication. These techniques, not new in the context of self-improvement seen in methods like "The Silva Mind Control Method" and "Dianetics," share a common foundation: the discipline of oneself and achieving harmony and balance among the various aspects of our personality.

While meditation and self-hypnosis are comparable in methodology, they differ in actual practice. Both do involve entering an altered or 'trance state.'

A trance state implies an inability to function or of being in a state of daze or stupor. Many of the uninitiated also frequently confuse meditation or self-hypnosis with the deeper trance states of hetero hypnosis, wherein a person may only have limited contact with his or her surroundings and may be unable to recall what went on during the trance.

"Light trances are daily, commonplace occurrences for all of us. Our attention becomes focused on one or a few objects, events or thoughts and because of this narrowing of attention, our generalized orientation in our environment and our awareness of our surroundings" (Carrington) begins to alter.

HYPNOSIS AND HYPNOTHERAPY

Hypnosis, in a clinical therapeutic setting, is a "treatment intervention comprised of the professional inducing the client into a relaxed state and then offering post-hypnotic suggestions during that time to the client for the client's ultimate goal of relief from symptoms. Hypnotherapy is the process of psychotherapy with a patient who is in the hypnotic altered state of consciousness" (Zimberoff). Yes, psychotherapy.

According to David Hartman of the Wellness Institute, in hypnotherapy, we have "access to being in the subconscious state (theta brain waves) while retaining a link (alpha brain waves) to the conscious mind (beta brain waves). The framework of hypnotherapy provides an especially useful vehicle for accessing the altered state necessary as a catalyst to receptivity to the unconscious imagery" that one may be harboring.

Clearer vision *into* one's true Self, I believe, can best be obtained by coherence between the mind, emotions, body, and Spirit and the trance state is an instrumental gateway to that unity. The tricky part is that we must get out of our own way to allow our healing to commence.

In my work, I will often guide clients or participants into a light trance state within the context of accessing the subconscious to obtain answers and information that may lie dormant, be hidden behind emotions such as guilt or shame, or that may be lurking in the shadows. It is an altered state; the participant is in control and aware of the surroundings. We're essentially moving from a beta brainwave state into an alpha brainwave state, a deeper state of mind.

Altered states are often called trancework; meditation and prayer are also a form of trancework according to many sources. Working one on one with patients, we can go quite deeply and heal places through this work that only a portal such as clinical hypnotherapy, can access. In group work, for example, I teach participants to lean into this work, feel safe in doing so as they learn to trust themselves and to embrace the healing that the process excavates rapidly and easily. The work we do together is intense; the environment that a group of open, loving people working together to effectuate positive changes and growth is intensely laden with magic and wonder.

We all—each and every one of us here in Earth School—have so much to excavate and process through. Just brushing up against some of those memories, which are all cataloged in the subconscious and stored away somatically in the body as well, can be distressing for some of us. Exploring this healing modality in a container of safety and trust, however, puts the experiences into a much different light, and thus a much different perspective can be had.

Consider this for a moment: There are experiences that may trigger you that I may find commonplace and have no issue with. I, conversely, may be alarmed by something you are good with or may even find annoying or amusing. Snakes and spiders don't bother me although I've had several medical doctors insist they might. Raised in the desert, I was bitten by a rattlesnake in my teens and had a severe reaction to a black widow spider's bite in my late twenties.

Some people love shopping for meat. The smells found in the meat aisles of the grocery store, and those of formaldehyde, chlorine, and a rotting animal corpse render me lightheaded and nauseous. I recall riding in a car with a friend one lazy autumn afternoon when he spotted roadkill. It was a large deer, mostly intact and covered with blood and flies. My friend was intent on taking it home with him. My eyes were filling with tears as he insisted the doe may still be viable for consumption and he was reflexively agitated at my reactions. He simply could not comprehend why I was emotional and repulsed.

Our perspectives are undeniably shaped in relation to our view of our individual experiences, and we all work from different paradigms.

We all have some complicated glitches in our personal software; it's a matter of becoming aware enough to grow past the challenges and work through the knots or samskaras.

The world we live in is inundated with propaganda and promotions that are skewed—organic produce, for example, is not necessarily without pesticides, and while monosodium glutamate (MSG) might enhance a food's natural flavor, it is most assuredly not a natural flavor enhancer and is quite toxic for many people.

Most of us are running on autopilot or dropping in and out of a state of shock much of the time, and there are those who capitalize on those altered states, from Big Pharma to commercialized businesses. We're inundated with billboards and advertisements, commercials, and publications. Learning to be in the moment, to be right here, right now, in our heart center rather than in our monkey mind, is our monumental task as the observer or witness to our own experience. If we can step back and look at the situations as observers, though, we can work from a higher place of our inner knowing.

CHAPTER 5
OUTDATED ATTACHMENTS

> *Yoga is the journey of the self, through the self, to the self.*
> —The Bhagavad Gita

The trance or altered state of consciousness provides "access to, and activation of, the somatic unconscious through implicit memories, using the dominance of theta frequency brain waves" (Hartman), the same state as our dreaming REM sleep or deep meditation. This access to the somatic elements is crucial as much of our reflexive behaviors are stored in the personal energetic realm of our "biocomputers": we run programs and are driven by programs that we already know neurologically.

Having trained extensively in the clinical applications of hypnotherapy, my position is that gaining access to—and compliance from—the underlying 90 percent of our mind, the unconscious that is responsible for running so much of our lives, is imperative if one is to effectuate lasting changes. "Clinical reports demonstrate that the most common problem in deep psychological work, which doesn't engage the deeper subconscious conflicts, is blocked imagery" (Zimberoff). Talk therapy alone, while quite helpful for some, can be less than beneficial for many people. Accessing the unconscious can help us through those blocks.

The ability to judiciously modify one's blocks and automatic responses to the things that take place in life is central to overall well-being. The challenge is that we are operating from a conscious place and often, getting in our own way of healing.

Another aspect of healing hinges on refusal and rejection. When we judge experiences as good or bad and seek to control them accordingly, we are in conflict. When we refuse to accept what *is*, we repress, and suppressed emotions often become toxic. Moreover, whatever is harbored in the unconscious will always be projected outwardly in some way. I liken this to trying to hold a beach ball under the waves in the ocean.

Trauma, abuse, and concomitant trauma, for example, can leave a person hyper-vigilant and over-sensitive to environmental signals, thereby overwhelming their capacities to handle and adapt to the stressors successfully. More than 70 percent of the US population has experienced some sort of trauma—that's over 223 million people. Trauma can stem from a multitude of situations and occurs when a person is overwhelmed and responds with intense fear, dismay, distress, and helplessness. Extreme stress overwhelms the person's capacity to cope, and each of us has a different precipice when it comes to a point of breakdown. Bill Harris explains that we each have an "upper limit to the amount of input we can handle, our 'personal threshold,' and that this limit is based upon how much chaos or entropy we as a system can dissipate" (Thresholds of the Mind 133). The effects of too much stress on any organism are well known.

What can transform over time, nonetheless, is a person's baseline response to those stressors or how they automatically or physiologically respond to a given stressor. This is an essential aspect of the work: a person's resilience and flexibility to circumstances and challenges in life can be altered.

Harris explains: "Chaos is an essential part of the growth process and should be welcomed rather than resisted ... if chaos continues to build, the system will eventually reach a point that the system can no longer hold itself together. The system breaks down, ceasing to exist in the old way."

Ah yes, we are ceasing to exist in the old way. Why is it, then, that many of us cling to our past, to outdated and possibly detrimental ways, to antagonistic situations, and to less-than-supportive relationships that may no longer serve us? There are many and varied reasons and each of us does have the capacity for change.

The challenge for many of us is that we do *not* want change.

MOVING FORWARD

I could, at various points in my life, fall over just from standing up too quickly if I was distracted or otherwise not mindful. With solid rooting in authentic yoga training, most of which has not been *asana* or the physical practice, I can now easily navigate heights and stand at the edge of the trail at the top of tall mountains without my mind insisting I will plummet to the valley floor below. I am deaf on one side (with severe inner ear scarring), which has also left me without the physical balance and proprioceptive abilities that most of the population enjoys. While some may consider deafness a "problem," I now consider it a tool and a blessing. It wasn't always that way for me.

We have all witnessed people convince themselves of something. More often than not, though, doesn't it seem that the manifestation is that of something negative? Or that something is wholly irrational that may be to their detriment?

Not long ago, a coworker, upon learning that four of her immediate circle of cronies had suddenly developed breast cancer, insisted that she, too, must be sick. How could she not be sick as well, she would argue. After numerous visits to multiple doctors, she was finally diagnosed with a "possible malignancy" that consequently required multiple surgeries and protracted rounds of chemotherapy. Yes, she had good insurance, and no, she had no prior health concerns.

She convinced her body that it was damaged and working improperly. It dutifully complied.

I believe we can absolutely do the same in reverse. I believe fully that we can heal our bodies and our lives using our minds. Is it always easy, fast, or exactly as we envision? Perhaps not. As Joe Dispenza states, "There will be initiations."

What is challenging for someone may, in fact, be impossible, either emotionally or physically, for someone else simply because they believe it to be so. Why is this? Some authorities insist that it could be that we are just too attached to the outcome of something, and that, alone, is enough.

Is the attachment of a physical, mental, or spiritual nature or a combination of all three? And why do some people, such as one of my clients who was abused more than four decades ago continue to cling wholeheartedly and with their entire mind, body, and Spirit to their stories of past hurts?

For my patient, Kay, it is, as she describes "who she is," and while she claimed she wants "to be well and is sick and tired of being fat, sick, and tired," she continued to self-sabotage. She initially presented with great insistence that she "cannot change" certain things, such as her weight or blood pressure or heart problems, and that she is a "naturally angry person." Her general practitioner insisted that she lose weight and "get a handle on the stress that is killing" her, hence the reason she showed up in my practice. During her first visit, she flared when I asked her if she had sought treatment for post-traumatic stress.

During the first group session, she was lightning-quick to defend her toxic opinions (which she asserted to be facts), openly violated the safety standards of compassion and kindness that we held within the container of our group setting, and mocked other patients at the clinic with a quick, "I'm just teasing to lighten things up." She was condescending, maladroit, and domineering to the point that others asked if I would remove her from the group, and if I did choose to work with her, to please do so outside of the group's container.

A successful and wealthy woman in the business world, she would loudly barge into meetings and was consistently late for appointments, as evidenced by mutual colleagues. She was also more than one hundred pounds over her ideal weight, was on a plethora of medications, and told me she could not remember the latest time that she had slept through an entire night, even with prescription sleeping pills.

In my offices, I allow three chances before someone "fires themself," and here is why: The first digression may be a misunderstanding; someone says something that triggers another, and the remark was truly made from a place of blamelessness and nonharm. The second faux pas may be a mistake or another innocent misunderstanding. We're human, we all make mistakes. The third time, when we are aware of the boundaries, of each other, or when something is done with intent, there is no excuse. Such as with the young woman I noted earlier who failed to take personal responsibility for participation.

Kay broke into a fit of anger when I explained there would be no further work together if the disrespectful behaviors continued after her second group meeting and her second private appointment. Instead of apologizing, she threw a tantrum. I turned her away from further appointments and took her out of the group. She then resorted to sobbing, and she asked me for one last chance, promising to do her absolute best to participate and to heal.

As we progressed through treatments, Kay explained to me that she suspected she had been abused as a child and that her mother had denied any knowledge of any whatsoever. They had stopped discussing anything that had to do with "anything personal" years before, according to Kay, and had virtually no interaction. Kay's body would show me symptomology in support of abuse each time we met. She remained in denial.

What we did find out over time was that there was horrendous abuse within the constellation of her birth family.

The assaults began when Kay was a toddler and went on until she was a pre-teen. The incidents were many and varied, levied by an uncle and an older brother, who had, we later discovered, repeated the patterns of other male relatives, including the grandfather on her mother's side.

During a momentous hypnotherapy session one afternoon, she recounted an out-of-body experience wherein she watched a small, helpless girl being attacked. She indicated she was watching from the ceiling and, "try as she might," was unable to help the child. She moved past this scene quickly and described playing with her toys all alone in the front room of her mother's house while her mother was away.

"Where is your mother?" I'd asked her.

"She went out. She always goes out. Goes out all the time," she'd answered.

"How old are you?" I asked. She acted startled and began crying.

"Little. I'm three or four...."

She began screaming and nearly convulsing. And then she stopped moving altogether.

"Where are you now, Kay?"

"I'm hiding. Shhh," she said quite softly.

She then squealed and began flailing her arms. "He's in the hallway! He sees me! I have to run and hide someplace else!" She could not tell me at that time who "he" was.

During the following session, Kay was able to move off of the ceiling and back into herself almost immediately. She was the young girl, unable to fight her much larger male assailant, and he had assaulted her with his fists repeatedly before brutally raping her and tossing her down a flight of stairs. That attack had rendered her unconscious, broken, and close to physical death.

Her mother had taken her to the hospital and left her there, alone, overnight.

My patient had consciously blocked this memory for decades, and when we unlocked it during her session, she regressed fully, reliving the event in horrifying detail. She screamed for her mother repeatedly and moved her body in ways that seemed physically impossible. She fought; she went into shock and fought back hard, this time winning. Angry, purple, and bright red welt marks surfaced on her wrists, arms, and legs. Her throat looked as if a set of large hands had left red imprints; her upper chest area flared with what appeared to be scratch marks. Her eyes were bulging, and she was gasping between the screams.

I held her hands, assured her she had survived, and we brought the little girl back.

This time we were able to help her to the place of being the observer, someone who somehow survived. Once the session was over, the welts subsided as well. What was crucial was that she was able to finally identify that the attacker was her brother.

She explained that it was as if an enormous weight had been lifted off her chest, and she felt she could finally breathe and tossed her inhaler into the trash. She reported that she slept most of the afternoon and all the following day after the session.

When she confronted her mother with the information, her mother insisted she didn't believe the attacks ever happened. She rationalized every wretched detail Kay brought up with a seemingly well-rehearsed set of denials: Kay was clumsy and had stupidly fallen down the stairs, and that her big brother was wrestling with her because that is what brothers do. Kay's brother had a thing for tickling people; Kay was a daydreamer and given to exaggeration ... the list went on. Kay had become pregnant during the last assault, and her mother insisted the pregnancy never occurred, or if on the absurd chance that it had, it was the result of Kay "playing doctor" with a neighbor boy. Kay miscarried at the beginning of her second trimester, alone in a bathroom at junior high school as an overweight pre-teen. Her body had developed early. "No one even knew I was pregnant because I was already fat," she said. "I knew I was, but I could not figure out how it happened at the time. I could not remember being penetrated." Kay explained she knew, though, without a doubt, the child was a girl. We would explore the loss of the baby and the grief she felt in later sessions.

The past and current abandonment by her mother is an even larger tragedy than most practitioners will acknowledge. Abandonment feels raw and painful. Abandonment is traumatic because it is trauma.

Many who experience abandonment also often feel intense shame, depression, and confusion—all elements of grief. Some of us likewise experience panic attacks and intrusive thoughts that become darker and darker over time.

I believe that a person can change her present responses and reactions to events that happened earlier in life through cognition and awareness. We're not changing what happened; we're changing how we would respond to it if we were stronger, more aware, or had loving assistance. It is our perception that defines the experience we have or had, and we respond accordingly thanks to the beliefs we've embodied.

Our response is our rudder, and those rudders do become damaged.

In Kay's case, the experiences were witnessed and processed through the eyes and maturity level of a very young child, a child who had been forsaken by her mother and devastated, physically and emotionally, by others she knew as family. Kay's coping mechanism was one of going into shock and "checking out."

Later in life she became the consummate bully and created a massive wall of flesh—she was classified as morbidly obese when she first joined our program—around herself to keep others at a distance. The weight was her blanket, her insulation layer, her armor.

When she first came to see me, she explained that she was often riddled with inexplicable pains, suffered from chronic insomnia, and had health challenges that routinely confounded Western medical practitioners with conflicting symptomology. She was, by her admission, "way too fat with a heart that couldn't keep up." She was also "insanely angry" at her mother and "hated [her] brother beyond reason," though could not provide a clear explanation as to why.

"It is confusing, and I don't understand," Kay began one afternoon in session. "Everyone loves my mother," she noted. "She's such a people-pleaser. My brother is a Big Wig, a highly successful businessman. My Uncle is like Santa, always giving people gifts and such. It must be me. Everyone in my family said I did things for attention and that I made up stories."

What's disconcerting is that she would often willingly cause some of those around her to agonize when she told her story. She seemed to intentionally "smear her ugly on us" is how another patient explained the phenomena of the energetic transferences and the subsequent resonance or entrainment individual members of the group felt. Other patients in our clinical group setting had grown weary of hearing the same complaints each week; others were openly dismissive.

Why were some members able to shield themselves—to sympathize or witness—rather than engage with her?

This is a dance of energies I continue to find fascinating from a perspective of my growth and, now, detachment, and this patient has unquestionably been a teacher for me and countless others in many ways.

Kay has since become a softer, kinder, more loving individual over the course of the past few years, and she genuinely feels compassion toward the child she was. The transformation has been and continues to be quite beautiful.

What I contend is that, ultimately, her suffering—her need to obstinately defer to and depend upon her story—was her choice, and this need was not only stunting her spiritual growth but damaging her body as well. She was willing to do the work she needed to do to heal. "I wasn't ready to die," she said, "but I couldn't go on living the way I was."

We can let the hurt or frictions be a part of our story or the whole story of our life.

She's let the old stories go, and her past no longer defines her or her future. Kay has since released over seventy-five pounds and enjoys mobility she hasn't known in years. "My relationships are so different now, so much happier and full of love."

She is also a welcome and cherished member of our group work.

CHAPTER 6
PATHWAYS OF FIRE

The function of prayer is not to influence God, but rather to change the nature of the one who prays.

—Soren Kierkegaard

How do we bridge the gap and reconnect with our Source?

According to Dionysios Farasiotis, "Prayer ... is a relationship between two persons, God and man, who move toward each other." Self-hypnosis, meditation, and hetero hypnosis are other modalities of communication and, while less commonplace, and often entirely misunderstood, are more similar than not to prayer. Andrew Newberg, MD, maintains, "From the neurobiological perspective the same biological chain of events is triggered by the contemplative techniques of religious mystics as they strive to clear their awareness of any thoughts other than God when one's thoughts become repetitive and mental focus grows more narrow and intense."

How can we access our Higher Self when our heart has been broken, our resilience has been thwarted, or we do not have the energy, intrinsic stamina, endurance, or perhaps even the desire to reconnect?

Where and how do we find our resilience? What qualities make one person more resilient than another? Can we learn to become more resilient or is our inherent resiliency set point innate or unchangeable?

Author and educator Bill Harris maintains that all suffering and discomfort result from our resistance to something. Our internal representations—pictures, words, dialog, and other interpretations of sensory experiences—according to Harris, are essential. Again, our perceptions shape our reactions.

Harris stated that when we are resisting something, we are making "internal representations of what we do not want." He likewise elucidates that if we can let go of our need "for control over the uncontrollable" and change our requirements to preferences, we will no longer suffer. Harris also posits that we will escape suffering only to the degree that we "are willing and able to let whatever happens be okay."

As iRest Yoga Nidra teaches us, welcoming without trying to fix, change, or get rid of will eventually lead to change. Emotions are cognitive and conceptual. Feelings are somatic; the emotions are the messengers.

Many of our experiences in life are undeniably steered by flurries of negative feelings, however. Because feelings are somatic—held within and felt by the body—they are also often tied to our beliefs, which we allow to torture us without the emotion being intrinsically linked to an experience. Feelings and emotions are constantly providing us with valuable feedback, which can assist us in surviving and thriving if we can step back and allow them to.

When physical depletion or motor impairment, loss of hope, and/or shattered faith get whirled into the equation, the feeling-emotion matrix can and often does become volatile and potentially life-threatening. I know this from personal experience. Perhaps you have wondered if it is worth staying Earth-bound too, and if you are currently at this juncture, I implore you to reach outside of the box, even if it is tenuous and only for a brief moment at a time. There are those of us willing to hold space for you if you allow us to do so; people you may not even realize exist yet are available and willing.

You have been blessed with this precious life, and you have bigger work to do; please don't make a permanent decision based on your current, temporary circumstances. Seek out those who will support you through these dark hours and entrain with that energy.

ENTRAINMENT

When we lose sight of our bigger why in life, the negative energy we emanate can and will draw more of the same people and situations to us. This is also known as entrainment.

Entrainment refers to a natural phenomenon in which one entity resonates synchronously and rhythmically with another in response to the dominant frequency of vibration. Think for a moment about how you feel in noisy, chaotic, demanding environments versus a slower-paced, quiet, and more tranquil setting. Your heart rate goes up, your breathing is likely faster, and you may feel agitated. Our heart rate will demonstrate how we entrain to the rhythms around us, even though we remain unaware of it most of the time.

Whether we like it or not, we are also responsible for the emotional energies that we project. Whereas feelings are somatic and based *in* the body, emotions are energy in motion. Our emotions can, and markedly do, affect others around us. We have a responsibility to help keep the peace and to bring each other up, do we not?

"Negative emotions are so distressing, studies show, that given a choice many people would rather endure great physical pain," (Ellison). Many of us sense angst, sadness, anger, rage, and various other emotions well before a person comes into our proximity. "I can walk into a room and know that there has been an argument," says one of my colleagues, who insists that he doesn't believe in human energetics or that we are built, as humans, out of energy and frequency. "It actually makes me feel differently when that happens. I can't stand it when someone is mad, and I melt when someone is in pain," he further notes.

And what do so many of us do with these emotions?

"If I'm hurting physically, that's all I can think about," stated a man that had come to see me for an intake appointment. "I like my pain. It's my friend." His pain is not *my* friend, however, nor is it friendly toward others. You'll likely not be surprised to learn that this man also has chronic, long-term health issues and has made a career for himself out of surgeries, doctor's visits, home health care, and investing in Big Pharma. When I asked him why he came to see me, he said his doctor wanted him to seek alternative methods of pain control and was hopeful to reduce the numbers and impact of the prescription drugs. He could not walk more than a few feet at a time, even with the aid of a walker. He was absurdly negative in his patterns of speech.

He informed me that the doctor's requests were moot: he liked how the pills made him feel and that he would rather "endure clinical hypnosis" to figure out other things if he was required to attend sessions. He also noted he liked my "vitality" and that he liked "plugging into" my energy. He had just begun smoking again after having a tracheotomy and a section of his lung removed.

My chest ached when he was in the office, and I recognized that while I was fascinated by his stories, I had to shield myself from his plug-ins and the draining effects of his actions. His presence has been a gift though. He was a teacher of another dimension, and he is a medical anomaly; that he is still on the planet at all is a miracle.

Negative emotions are part of our human experience, and our thresholds about those feelings and experiences dictate our level of resiliency. Vis-a-vis, our body complies—it becomes a mind of its own—and physical health, our external environment, and what we are capable of physically are all impacted.

My journey through loss and heartache has been paralleled by many; I know this. I survived, I'm thriving, and yes, I continue to be faced with initiations. I'm also doing what I can to stay centered in the present moment so the pain, when it comes, is manageable. For me, this also means continuing to learn and grow and surrounding myself with people who are conscientiously working to grow and heal. While our level of resiliency may vary, we all feel and experience pain, and sometimes the pain is that of necessary growth. How we handle that pain and progress or regress in life, spiritual growth, or participation in the human consortium is another matter entirely.

Severe pain can be managed on a moment-by-moment basis, it really can. While this may feel and look different for each of us, it is entirely possible and leads to a deeper level of healing and to a much more sincere sense of inner peace if we allow ourselves to embrace the lessons.

When we're in the midst of our own stories, we tend to forget that others may be in acute distress. I recently found out that my first boyfriend, Scotty, from third grade, who grew into an incredibly talented musician and athlete, took his own life unexpectedly a few months ago. I was stunned and greatly saddened by the news, even though we hadn't seen each other in many years. Upon learning of his passing, I instantly remembered so many things as if they were very recent memories, and that, too, surprised me. The most poignant remembrance: we were going to run away to live together at my granny's house together, and my granny had said she was happy to help us.

Scotty and I had ended up in the principal's office together one too many times because we were passing scribbled love notes back and forth during prayer time in class. And then the touching... we thought kissing meant sitting with our foreheads and noses pressed together. Putting us at opposite ends of the class hadn't solved the teacher's dilemma, nor had placing either one of us in respective corners of the classroom for time out. What was she to do with a blonde-haired set of eight-year-olds that believed God wanted them to love each other? So running away together to live with my grandmother two hundred miles away was our solution. Running away together never happened. Scotty ran away in his own way a few months ago, decades after our time together, and physically left this incarnation.

Damaged Rudders

It was a permanent solution to a temporary set of problems.

My nephew also committed suicide. A few days after his fortieth birthday, he hung himself while the world around him was in awe of his achievements as an entrepreneur and photographer. His sister had his name tattooed on her inner arm. His mother remains in her own state of shock; people that never met him still openly mourn his passing. Dan and I still invoke his memory with fondness, and our great-nephew—a miracle child who bears an uncanny resemblance to Sean—serves as a bittersweet reminder of him. The impact of Sean's decision reverberated through a far wider network of people than he likely ever realized. I can't help but think that if he had truly comprehended the sweeping emotional aftermath of his irrevocable act, he might still be with us today.

He'd spent a summer many years ago as my assistant in a medical practice where I worked and had been such a pleasure to be around, even though he was a very opinionated sixteen-year-old at the time. Watching him draw was intriguing and seeing how he so openly and lovingly contemplated the vastness of the Pacific Ocean after being raised in the desert areas of California was breathtaking from a spiritual standpoint. He was a cherished little brother to so many more people than he knew.

Another friend, also a gifted artist and entrepreneur, ran away in a similar fashion. The last time I saw him in the flesh, he kissed the back of my hand, asked about my "butt-headed" dogs (I had two English bull terriers at the time), and hugged me while saying he'd see me for brunch the next morning. I sensed something was troubling him; when I asked, he denied anything was amiss. When I showed up to meet him at his work the next morning at our agreed-upon time, his coworkers explained he had severed his carotid artery with a power tool the night before. Hundreds of people were present at a vigil for him the next day; the wave of sadness that ran rampant through the small town was stifling.

While our level of resiliency may vary, we all feel and experience pain. The pivotal issue herein is that we forget that there is a precessional effect—the pain we feel and act on ripples out and affects many, many more people than we can ever imagine. Thus, how we handle our pain and either progress or regress in life, spiritual growth or participation in the human consortium takes on another dimension entirely. A statement of "I just can't cope anymore" may mean exactly that. Please listen if you hear someone say they cannot cope or if you are feeling that way yourself. We all have a unique threshold to our upper tolerance levels, a tipping point of having our nervous systems go into overstimulation and overload, of entropy, and ultimately, of a shutdown.

EMBRACING THE ARCANE

As one doctor noted: "For me, what I had expected to be a wonderful season of my life turned into a nightmare that I still don't have words to describe. This situation pummeled and distracted me for years, until [...] I finally came out the other side. There were all sorts of layers of loss associated with this experience, some of which continue to reveal themselves" (Biali). If doctors, with all the education, tools, support, and prescription remedies so readily available to them, are subject to this sense of torment, what about us, the mere mortals?

Why is it that we allow ourselves to tolerate this suffering at all?

Robert Sapolsky, a neuroscientist at Stanford University, "calls this 'adventitious suffering'—the pain of what was, what will be, what could be or what someone else is experiencing" (Ellison). Sapolsky has also "shown that this type of suffering can damage the parts of the brain involved in learning, memory, and the immune system" (Ellison).

Another excellent reason for us to cultivate the sort of mind that, as Dr. Masters taught, can "see good in even the darkest of temporary conditions and circumstances."

For some of us, like me, who have been raised in highly dysfunctional families, a behavioral paradigm shift is required, and that takes desire and belief-changing work that oftentimes collides with the opinions of those in our circles of influence.

Our brains are wired for human bonds. Conversely, trauma rewires neural connections for protection, thereby compromising our abilities and desires to engage with people because we do not feel safe. We may also find that those around us who are similarly traumatized are incredibly resistant to us doing our work and may thwart our progress if given an opportunity. My mother used to say that "if everyone else around you agrees, you must be the one who is wrong." As I grew to understand that we entrain with those around us, my mother became evermore defensive. When I would seek substantiation from her as to the rightness of what I referred to as the "delusional stance held as an unverifiable truth by the masses of asses," she would remind me I was the black sheep of the family and a boneheaded one at that.

So what do we do? We replay a response from our subconscious repertoire of coping and often stay stuck in old ways until we have a near-death experience, an epiphany, or an awakening.

I can recall a situation wherein I was attempting to take a loaded gun away from my drunk alcoholic brother, much to my mother's dismay. "He'd never shoot any of us!" she'd insisted, angry at me for even suggesting he was dangerous. The fact he was unable to stand (and was prone to blacking out) meant nothing to her under the circumstances; I was the one who had escorted him in and out of rehabilitation facilities several times. When he verbally threatened my life, my mother said he didn't know what he was saying and was "just joking." My mother also insisted that my new "friends"—my instructors at the university and the people I befriended at Al-Anon —were brainwashing me.

Having my angry, inebriated brother pull a loaded gun on me was irrefutably an awakening of sorts, and I thank the Creator that those people did help wash my brain for me.

The work we must do is unique to each of us, and it can be increasingly demanding as we become more aware. The work does not get easier either. Our experiences as damaged, interrupted people, people without sound governors, are likewise vastly different from those of others. We've learned to adapt to—and live with—highly charged, stressful realities from a trauma-based set of responses. These are wired-in, autopilot reactive measures—reflex reactions—that we learned in order to keep ourselves alive.

We will also repeat these patterns spontaneously until we can holistically and successfully change the mapping of our brains.

The wonderful news is that it can be done.

TAKING THE LEAP

"No one who has lived on earth in the human consciousness has ever been successful at resolving problems [...] we must dwell in the spiritual consciousness before true success begins to come to us" (Steiger). Spiritual consciousness can be elusive and differs for each of us. Again, the desire to change is a fundamental aspect herein. Many people would rather not step into the darkness of their inner world to explore the arcane because they are terrified of what they might find. Quiet time absolutely frightens some people. Think for a moment: What's the first thing you do to create external noise in the morning? Do you turn on the television? Do you get into your car and turn on the radio? Why do you do this? "The noise distracts me so well and so much," says one of my clients. That noise drowns out the whispers from your Higher Self as well.

In today's fast-paced environment, we are constantly assailed by a barrage of external noise—ranging from the incessant chirping of social media notifications to the hum of traffic or even the chatter of a busy workplace. This overwhelming auditory stimulation does more than distract us; it creates a level of sensory overload that can be emotionally and physically taxing. For me, the impact is not merely distracting but outright disruptive to my overall well-being. It's crucial to understand that sound is more than auditory stimuli; it's a frequency that interacts with our bodies and minds. Some frequencies can unsettle our natural equilibrium, leading to stress, discomfort, and even physical ailments. Recognizing this interaction is the first step toward mitigating its toll on our well-being.

Everything is frequency and energy.

INTO THE FIRES

I keep a U-shaped piece of carbon-steel construction metal—rebar—on my office wall as a reminder that all things are not as they may seem energetically. Have you ever tried to bend rebar with your hands? It's nearly impossible. Rebar is manufactured to support concrete, among other things. And one of the most astounding feats and tests of belief I have participated in thus far in my life was that of bending rebar with another person, without using our hands or other tools. In a decisive display of energetic displacement and trust, Dan and I bent a six-foot piece of half-inch steel rebar into that stunning *U* shape in a way that could have killed or maimed either or both of us.

We were at a workshop where we had done other momentous things; this challenge was a leap of faith for many of the participants and a true test of belief in our power to transcend circumstances in ways that were seemingly unattainable. We faced each other and placed the bar between us with the blunt ends at our fifth chakras, the soft, extremely sensitive area spot where the neck meets the chest. We stated personal intentions, then walked toward each other. Simple, quick, without consequence. Neither one of us even had an indentation in the flesh; the bar bent easily and almost instantly. This experience stands as a tangible lesson in the realms of intention, trust, and the malleable nature of both energies and perceived boundaries. It remains a vivid symbol of the untapped potential that resides within us all. And it was a test of extreme belief systems, of spirituality, and of the densities of energies. Disclaimer here: do not attempt to do this at home.

Another test of belief for me was the Sweat Lodge. Unlike the rebar test, I've done this a number of times over the years.

Over the years, I have sat for hours with total strangers in the dark, smoke-filled, *inipis*, also known as "sweat lodges," communed with shaman elders in the highlands of Peru, and hung from ledges on the trails in Machu Picchu during symbolic death and rebirth ceremonies. The temperatures in the inipis exceed what is supposedly possible for humans to endure at approximately 180 degrees at times. Many elders say that the temperatures go even higher and may exceed 300 degrees.

According to some, the sweat lodge ceremony is older than recorded history and is practiced in some form by every culture in the world. The sweat lodge is a contemporary religious ritual also used by Native Americans throughout the Great Plains.

The ceremony generally takes place in a circular, domed-shaped structure constructed of pliable saplings (often willow) with a single entrance. The entrance will face a specific cardinal direction depending upon the ceremony. The structure is tightly covered with blankets and tarps, and in indigenous cultures, animal skins are also sometimes used. A pit is dug in the center of the lodge as a fireplace to receive stones that are heated in a fire outside. The lodge is considered to be a symbol of returning to the womb and the innocence of childhood; the lodge is dark, moist, and hot.

The ceremony consists of "entering the lodge, filling the pit with hot stones that are reverenced as ancient and spiritual in nature, pouring water on the hot rocks, praying, singing, speaking from one's heart, closing and opening the door a set number of times, and emerging from the lodge. Important elements in the ceremony that vary in emphasis from group to group are communication with the spiritual realm, moral and/or physical purification, the humbling of oneself, healing of Self and/or others through the physical and/or spiritual agency of the sweat, and voluntary suffering to achieve a specific need or to fulfill a pledge for requests already granted" (Wisehart).

Variations in the ceremony and the structure of the lodge vary by demographics, area, and by the ceremonial leader.

The sweat lodge ceremony is typically broken down into rounds or sessions with each session lasting approximately fifteen to twenty minutes. In special sweats, these sequences may vary from three to seven. Each round will embrace a specific spiritual energy or theme depending upon the leader.

The four elements may be called upon, the stages of spiritual development may be addressed, or perhaps a specific invocation may be utilized depending upon the season. The intention of the ceremony is essentially that of purification.

Most of us emerge fatigued, though, more often, we are emboldened and conclusively moved in spiritual ways by what we have encountered. In one ceremony I took part in, my paternal grandmother appeared with messages of warning, of praise, and of community. Thinking the heat had caused some sort of distortion or hallucination, my skepticism was entirely replaced by words of kindness and courteous reverence uttered by my *inipi* sitting mate, who addressed the essence of my grandmother as "Mother Indian Gramma" who appeared for her as well. I was stunned. Later, these messages would help steer me through some of the most challenging times I have known to date.

The elder who leads the ceremony may choose to perform healings, invoke the spirits or ancestors, lead a meditation, or ask for some participation from each of the members who are present. Singing, chanting, or drumming may also be included in the ceremony. Conversely, many ceremonies are conducted in complete silence. There is no light other than the fire, the air is dank and heavy with moisture, and it can be exceptionally difficult to breathe, especially when various herbs or tinctures are added to the flames. The door flap to the inipi is typically opened during a break of several minutes between the rounds to allow for those who find the need to leave or to get up to do so. When the participants leave the lodge and enter the outside world, we understand it to represent their rebirth.

No one I have ever sat with in inipi has been physically harmed by participating in ceremonial sweat lodges. I do not expect to be injured, nor expect to witness anyone being injured, in future participation either. While people died in Sedona (and dozens were hospitalized) after a sweat lodge ritual organized by James Arthur

Ray took a very tragic turn in 2009, I believe there is more to the story of how and why those people succumbed.

Peruvian shamanic practitioners, also known as elders, noted that my presence alone during the times that I was visiting them in Peru, especially as a Rubia (blonde) woman, was a calculated risk of what the outside vote may have allowed. The country was also on the brink of war. "You have big work to do in the world, so you must stay," I was told. Was I afraid? No.

On the contrary, I was inspired. The word *inspire* is Latin, and the word *inspire* means to breathe in. I have visited Peru frequently since then, lived with the indigenous peoples, was shepherded by Peruvian elders, participated in a multitude of spiritual ceremonies, and worked on secretive, baffling archaeological digs that would astound the lay public—all in sacred places where "foreigners," and oftentimes women, were forbidden.

What the Peruvian elders chose not to include was, "And it will severely test you." I knew, however, that I had lessons to learn there. I was held in safety, even though, for example, the American Embassy was bombed during a brief visit I had made from Cuzco to Lima. Insurgents were raiding buildings, and roads were being closed; many felt a small-scale war was imminent, and foreigners were being detained. My passport was taken from me by the officials; I spent the night in the Congressional Building alongside a hundred plus other foreigners and detainees, huddled in a strained, terrified silence while the bombs and sirens went off around us. I had my faith and knew that things would be as they were supposed to be. Others there did not. I sat with children and the elderly, holding their hands and consoling them. A bomb hit the building next to us; many people were injured, and while the newspapers may not have relayed the information, dozens of people died.

People do perish visiting sacred places, traveling where they are not allowed, and in practicing acts that test their faith. Pilgrims and others have died at Huayna Picchu, Machu Picchu, and the Pyramids; wisdom keepers in both Peru and Egypt acknowledge that intent is a very fundamental determinant of outcome. "We are all part of the Wheels of Life, and we have wheels of life within our bodies," my elders would say. "Wheels must be honored and respected."

That noted, what constitutes, for example, a ceremonial sweat lodge? I believe that the essential, sacred integrity of protocols and practices must be recognized, and this veneration is a mandatory component of participation in feats, tests, or leaps of faith.

Anything exposed to fire is inexorably altered. Thus, in faith, I have also walked, collectively, on more than a mile of burning embers, barefoot, without being burned, and have participated in many shamanic fire ceremonies. I will do so again soon.

THE CHAKRAS

The word chakra is the Sanskrit word for "wheel" or "vortex" and refers to each of the seven centers (nine, according to shamans) that comprise our energy system.

The first written references we have for this concept were given to us by the ancient Hindu writings, although the concepts of energy centers and circuits in the physical body are repeated with slight variation in nearly every religion and spiritual belief system throughout recorded time. Translated from Hindi, the word chakra means "wheel of spinning energy."

The *Vedas* are the oldest written tradition in India, (1,500–500 BC) recorded from oral tradition by upper-caste Brahmins, who may have been descended from the Aryan stock which entered India from the north. The original meaning of the word chakra as "wheel" refers to the chariot wheels of the rulers, called *cakravartins* (the correct spelling is *cakra*; pronounced with a *ch* as in church.) The word was also a metaphor for the sun, which "traverses the world like the triumphant chariot of a cakravartin" and denotes the eternal wheel of time called the *kalacakra*, which represents celestial order and balance.

There is some mention of the chakras as psychic centers of consciousness in the Yoga Upanishads (circa 600 BC) and later in the

Yoga Sutras of Patanjali (circa 200 BC). Most interpretations of Patanjali read a dualism between *purusha* (pure consciousness) and *prakriti*. In Hinduism, prakriti (also spelled *prakrti*) refers to a primal creative or natural force and denotes the natural or original intended state of something or of an individual's being. The term is derived from the Sanskrit *pra*, meaning "beginning," and *kriti*, meaning "creation."

The implication was that the goal of yoga was to rise above nature for the realization of pure consciousness. The word yoga, however, means union or yoke.

The main text about chakras that has come to us in the West is a translation by the Englishman Arthur Avalon, in his book *The Serpent Power* published in 1919. The *Sat-Cakra-Nirupana*, written by an Indian authority in 1577, and the *Padaka-Pancaka*, written in the tenth century, also contains descriptions of the centers and related practices.

In these traditions, there are seven primary chakras that exist within the subtle body which overlays the physical body. Other traditions believe there are nine major chakras, and energetically speaking, there are hundreds of minor chakras throughout the body. Through modern physiology, we can see that these seven chakras correspond exactly to the seven main nerve ganglia, which emanate from the spinal column. The chakras are thought to function as regulators for the flow of energy through and around us. While they are not physical, the apex of each vortex connects to our spine and endocrine glands.

Every being and every thing is created of energetic frequencies, and the chakras are energetic facets of our consciousness. While not as dense as our physical bodies, they are still energetically part of who and what we are. I believe we all share the same radiant anatomy, which includes the chakras and the acupuncture meridians. I'll go into more detail about the energetic frequencies of who and what we are in later chapters. Chakras are said to affect the mind and thought processes.

The most important thing to note here is that we can and do get stuck energetically. If our chakras are not balanced, or if the energies are blocked, it will slow the vital life force down, and they may also affect the mind and thought processes.

Here is a brief description of the nine chakras:

First Chakra—*Mūlādhāra*

> *Mūla* = Root, Origin, Essence
> *Ādhāra* = Basis, Foundation

The first chakra is located at the base of the spine and is also known as the root chakra. It is also a gateway to the feminine of Mother Earth. When we become disconnected from the Earth, we begin to seek nourishment from the surface, and it is taught that we become like a tree whose shallow, widespread roots cannot keep it from being uprooted during a storm. We lose our stability. We have no foundation. We, too, become uprooted.

First chakra drives are also primal and instinctual.

The Mūlādhāra chakra forms the foundation and starting point for our spiritual development and is the root from which we receive the sustenance for our spiritual development. The color associated with this chakra is red.

Second Chakra—*Svadhishthāna*

> *Svā* = Self
> *Adhishthāna* = Seat, Residence

The second chakra is located approximately four fingers below the navel and is linked to our subconscious and tribal flaws and connection. Also known as the sacral chakra, it is here that a valuable opportunity to develop our human consciousness to a higher level is offered. Through work on the Svādhishthāna chakra, we can bring our baser instincts under control, transform them, and ultimately transcend them. This chakra marks the second stage of our human evolution, and the color is orange, the color of fire.

Third Chakra—*Manipūra*

> *Mani* = Pearl, Jewel
> *Pūra* = Place, City

The third chakra is located at the solar plexus, about two inches below the breastbone. Its associated color is yellow. Imbalance or blockage in the Manipūra chakra is thought to obstruct and destroy our energy and likewise may produce various physical and psychic problems. If we are unable to think clearly, to express our thoughts and feelings, or if our mind is foggy, there is often a disturbance in the Manipūra chakra. Various ailments are also attributed to third chakra imbalances such as diabetes, skin diseases, cardiovascular diseases, gout, arthritis, rheumatic diseases, and allergies.

The third chakra is the power center in the luminous energy system. Its power can be used constructively to manifest our aspirations in the world. When used destructively, it can repress our primary nature or libido.

The feminine power of the first chakra and the primordial sexual energy of the second chakra are transformed into a fine fuel that the third chakra uses for the fulfillment of our dreams.

When we awaken the power of this chakra, we experience fearlessness and a resolve that cannot be deterred by adversity. Obstacles in our path crumble.

The function of the third chakra is to translate vision into reality.

Fourth Chakra—*Anāhata*

> *Anāhata Nāda* = Unlimited, infinite sound

The heart chakra is located at the cardiac plexus in the center of the chest and is considered the center for love, compassion, and spirituality. This is also the chakra connecting body and mind with spirit. The color associated with this chakra is green.

The love of the heart chakra is not that of affection nor romantic love; it is the love of Creation. It is impersonal and not sentimental. Realization of all-embracing, Divine love, free from the impulsiveness of Earth-bound emotions, is the spiritual goal of an open fourth chakra.

Christian theologians refer to this love as agape. The Inka call it *munay*. This kind of love is not a means to an end; it is considered an end in itself.

Fifth Chakra—*Vishuddhi*

Visha = Impurity, Poison
Shuddhi = Purification

The fifth or throat chakra is located at the hollow of the throat at the larynx.

The color associated with this chakra is blue, and it is a center of physical and spiritual purification and of balance. The yoga technique of Prānāyāma (conscious guidance and regulation of the breath) exerts a strong influence on the Vishuddhi chakra, at both the physical and astral levels.

The fifth chakra is also our psychic center, responsible for clairvoyance, clairaudience, clairsentience, and the ability to communicate without words.

The fifth chakra gives us the ability to envision possible futures and to act on our vision and is said to give voice to the feelings of the heart.

Sky Chakras

In the sixth, seventh, eighth, and ninth chakras development becomes transpersonal.

Sixth Chakra—*Āgyā*

Āgyā = Command, Knowledge, Wisdom

The sixth chakra, brow chakra or third eye, is located at the upper end of the spinal column, at the point of transition from the spine to the brain. Its radiation is, according to some of my teachers, in the center of the forehead between the eyebrows. One of my mentors teaches that we are activating the pineal gland, and that this gland is a transmitter, our third eye, to and from other dimensions. The color associated with this chakra is indigo.

In the Hindu traditions, it is thought to be the third eye of Shiva who grants knowledge of perfect truth and nonduality. We express the Divine within ourselves, and we see the Divine in others. We realize that we are an eternal being housed in an earthly body.

Seventh Chakra—*Sahasrāra*

Sahasrāra = Thousand, Infinite

The crown chakra at the very top of the head is our portal to the Heavens, in the same way that the first chakra is the portal to the Earth. The halo depicted in paintings throughout history is purported to be the manifestation of a fully unrestricted seventh or crown chakra, and luminous threads from this center are thought to reach up to the stars and to our destinies. The Earth protects us and nurtures us with her life force, and the Heavens propel us toward our Becoming. The color associated with this chakra is violet or purple.

The crown chakra is the center of spirituality, enlightenment, dynamic thought, and energy. It is also considered to be the center of connectedness with the Goddess (God), the place where life animates the physical body. When this chakra is unbalanced, there may be a constant sense of frustration, no spark of joy, and destructive feelings. Illnesses may include migraine headaches and depression. Balanced energy in this chakra may include the ability to open up to the Divine and total access to the unconscious and subconscious.

The lesson of the seventh chakra is said to be that of mastery of time. When we break free of linear, causal time, we are no longer in the tyrannical grip of the past. Today is no longer the result of an earlier incident, and we experience freedom from cause and effect. Whereas in the sixth chakra, the healer gains knowledge of past and future events, when s/he awakens the gifts of the seventh chakra, s/he is able to influence those events.

Eighth Chakra

The eighth chakra is known by the Inkas (the term Inka means "ruler" or "lord" in Quechua and was used to refer to the ruling class or the ruling family) as the *wiracocha*, or "source of the sacred."

It is said to be our connection with the Great Spirit, the place where our creator or God holds space within each of us. When our physical being dies, the eighth chakra is thought to expand into a luminous globe that envelops the other seven chakras in a vessel of light. According to various teachers, this chakra is demonstrated as the light surrounding Christ and as the fire that descended upon the apostles at Pentecost when they received the gift of the Holy Spirit.

The eighth chakra's source is the ninth chakra, Spirit. The ninth chakra resides outside our Energy Field and extends throughout the cosmos. It is the heart of the Universe, at one with the Great Spirit.

Ninth Chakra

The ninth chakra resides at the heart of the Universe; it is outside of time and space, and it extends through the vastness of space and connects to the eighth chakra by a luminous cord.

While the eighth chakra manifests in time, the ninth chakra is present in the timeless now, a point without time. It is said to extend through the vastness of space and is connected to the eighth chakra by a luminous cord.

The eighth chakra is where God dwells within us, and the ninth chakra is the part of us that resides within the Creator.

The eighth chakra corresponds to the Christian concept of the soul, which is personal and finite. The ninth chakra corresponds to Spirit, which is depersonalized and unbounded.

The High Heart Chakra

I also teach, as my elders have taught me, that there is another chakra that resides between the heart chakra and the throat chakra. This energy center is known as the high heart chakra and the feminine center. This area is also known as the thymus chakra and the etheric heart, and sometimes as the seat of the soul. This is the area where intent is purported to originate.

This chakra connects the emotions of love, truth, compassion, and forgiveness, with language and intent, allowing a person to speak from the heart. Ever notice where a person's hand or hands will go when they are feeling a wave of deep emotion or connection?

CHAPTER 7
WHEN OTHER LANDS CALL

Nothing in life is to be feared. It is only to be understood. Now is the time to understand more, so that we may fear less.

—Marie Curie

My father made a bust of Queen Nefertari while he was still in medical school that now sits on a shelf in my office. I still have no real answer as to why my father had carved it. The statue is made of solid, polished concrete, stands approximately fourteen inches high, and weighs about thirty pounds. It is hand-carved and quite beautiful, with great attention to detail. The headdress he'd carved is different, more of an elongated skull cover, and quite different than most the Queen is shown wearing; the eyes appear heavily lidded. The bust was an object of my curiosity as a child.

Just before my father's passing, the bust fell and broke at the neck. No one saw it topple, and it had been sitting in virtually the same place in my parents' home for decades. There was conjecture that my father had sent some sort of message from another dimension and given the bust a good shove while he was being held hostage in the intensive care unit.

My mother had started to dispose of it, and as synchronous timing would have it, I intervened. The bust came home with me.

Nefertari was also known as Nefertari Meritmut and was the first of the Great Royal Wives (or principal wives) of Ramesses the Great. Nefertari means "beautiful companion," and Meritmut means

"Beloved of [the goddess] Mut." One of the best-known Egyptian queens, next to Nefertiti, Cleopatra, and Hatshepsut, it is said that she was highly educated and able to both read and write hieroglyphs. She used these skills in her diplomatic work, corresponding with other prominent royals of the time. Visiting Egypt wasn't on my top priority list. There are numerous other places I'd have preferred to visit first. I believe we go when and where we are called if we choose to listen.

Our group was on a pilgrimage and had followed a set of synchronicities that led to taking the trip during a time when travel was not advised. When we arrived at the airport, we were met by a military escort armed with machine guns, and several members of the group decided, at the airport after flying all night, to return home.

Here I was once again, a *Rubia* in a prohibited land, at the wrong time, in a sea of dark-haired, dark-skinned people.

Egypt is a complicated place, and there were several quite weighty experiences that shifted my perspectives from that of skepticism to the curiosity, trust, and wonder that I had enjoyed as a child. One experience was visiting a heavily guarded shrine that was not open to the public where an ancient statue of Sekhmet, the lion-headed goddess associated with Upper Egypt, was secretly housed. Our guide purportedly had privileges extended by not only the locals but by the Wisdom Keepers and the national government as well.

Our guide gave us a brief background on the statue and said it was intentionally hidden by the government and guarded by men who were generationally assigned the task of doing so. Housed in what looks from the outside to be a somewhat dilapidated wooden shed behind a simple wooden fence, the sculpture stands approximately six feet tall and is exquisite, perfectly preserved, and appears to be carved out of a dark-green granite or possibly diorite. The stone felt as smooth as silk and looked to be laser-cut.

Our guide, who explained she was a medium and believed in God, seemed to immediately go into a trance state as we entered the shrine. Though immensely skeptical, I was fascinated when she began channeling information that was complex, otherworldly, and beyond comprehension. She said she had a special connection with this deity, who was also called the "Terrible One," "She Who is Powerful," and the "Eye of Ra" when she was in her protector form. Sekhmet was also considered to be a mighty solar goddess of destruction, war, power, and fire; legends say it was she who used her breath to create the deserts of Egypt. She is also believed to come to the aid of those who are respectful of her power. Our guide explained that she was seeking aid from this realm for our group as we were traveling on the cusp of times that could quite realistically erupt into war in Egypt. She also noted that she was assured that we would be protected while we were in Egypt.

CONNECTIONS ACROSS THE CONTINENTS

Another exceptional incident for me was touching the sacred geometry carved on the walls of the Temple of Osiris in Abydos, Egypt. The place was too familiar; caressing the granite monoliths took me to my knees, knocked the breath out of me, and caused my eyes to tear up for reasons I could not describe to others.

Our Wisdom Keepers, people (always men) who are bound generationally to pass down the teachings through the eons, explained that the largest of the carvings at Abydos was completely submerged under water that once covered the plains of Egypt for thousands of years.

After seeing the flower repeatedly in parts of Peru that were restricted to foreigners in the early 1990s, I had returned stateside looking for a gold charm of the symbol that I could wear around my neck. I had wanted to purchase a gold charm in Peru and had only found them in silver.

During my stay in Egypt, I wandered into a tiny shop while the others I was with were making their way into the building next door for lunch. The elderly shopkeeper motioned to me to come to him; I presumed this man might merely have wanted me to buy something and to have a real foreigner with whom to practice his English. What piqued my curiosity was that he seemed to glow. The little shop was filled with exquisite articles of jewelry, stones, and ethnic items; it was clean and tidy, well-stocked, and beautifully organized. I asked him if he spoke English. Shaking his head, he merely smiled at me from the other side of the counter. Somehow, I felt that I knew this man from some other place and time, and I felt genuinely safe.

He patted me gently on the wrist and gestured for me to turn my palm up. He then placed a gold flower of life disk, a charm about the size of an American quarter, in my hand and folded my fingers around it.

"A gift," he stated in broken English. "Welcome home."

Home? This, I pondered, was probably among the very last of places I would want to live. Even a big salaried job with a surplus of perks could not convince me otherwise.

A strange, familiar, serene sense of kinship washed over me at that moment. I knew that I knew him. We stood for a long while just looking into each other's eyes; he smiled and patted my arm, not saying a word.

THE FLOWER OF LIFE

Sacred geometry, also known as the flower of life, Genesis pattern, or creation mandala, can be found in many places around the globe, and the symbols depicted on the wall of The Temple of Osiris in Abydos are estimated to be 6-10,500 years old by some authorities. The local people contend that the artwork is much, much older. Some authorities also say that the symbols were etched into the stone; still, others say that they were burned into the granite in a sort of branding fashion. Either way, the glyphs are precise and quite large. What's intriguing to me is that temple walls had been submerged underwater for thousands of years, and yet the symbols remain very clear. I had seen the exact replica carved or burned into granite pillars in the highlands of Peru in places forbidden to the general public. They, too, had been submerged at some time or times.

HAKIM

One of the more special and most unexpected of experiences I had while in Egypt was that of being graced with Hakim's physical presence. Meeting Hakim created the space for a better understanding of what apparently brought me to Egypt in the first place.

Born and raised in the village of Nazlet El Saman at the periphery of the Giza Plateau, Abd'el Hakim Awyan—Hakim—was a Wisdom Keeper of the oral traditions in Egypt. One could see the Sphinx from the small, square window opening of his modest home, and he often spoke of sleeping on the large block protrusions on the outside of the Great Pyramid. He told us of various dignitaries who had visited and of others, such as the Grateful Dead, who had spent time with him at his home smoking the hookah pipe and learning about Egypt. Virtually everyone in the surrounding areas knew him. One had only to tell a taxi driver to "Take me to Hakim's" to find their way back to the Giza Plateau.

The original name of Ancient Egypt was Khemit, meaning "The Black Land." The discipline of Khemitology was developed by Hakim. Hakim decoded the origins of ancient Egyptian symbols through tracing the linguistic roots of words.

When he was quite young, Hakim, whose name means "the wise one" or "wise healer," embraced an interest in the true origins of the many monuments and artifacts of ancient Egypt and had a much different view of Egypt's past than many traditional historians. He embarked on a lifelong study and used the knowledge gained from acquiring degrees in both archeology and Egyptology throughout his fifty years of fieldwork and had a sincere love of people and of Egypt. He, like many other contemporary indigenous Wisdom Keepers around the world, believed that a new age was dawning and that the time had come to share this sacred information with the "outside" world. Those of us who were fortunate enough to spend time in Hakim's presence were introduced to an entirely different version of Egypt's biography, cartography, and history and to an altogether different understanding of the shifts that are occurring in our world today.

I first met Hakim at a lecture in Cairo and had no prior knowledge of who he was at that juncture. Listening to him speak was surreal and elicited that intense and unsettling sense of Knowing. I knew him; I understood his words as if I had already experienced the lands he was speaking about, and his words made crystal clear sense to me.

After the lecture concluded, I went up to him and placed my hands on my heart center in greeting. He did the same, his black eyes twinkling as he smiled widely, and then he reached out to me, arms outstretched, beckoning me to come closer. This was at a time when women were expected to be out of sight and covered from head to toe in hijab and burkas. Women are much like chattel, as several of the ex-pats explained, and no touching of the opposite sex was tolerated. Nonetheless, I kissed him lightly on the cheek as he had done with me and said, "I am so grateful and honored to meet you. Thank you for your work in the world."

He replied, "It is so very good to see you again, my dear."

And I hugged him despite being earnestly instructed not to do so by the others I was traveling with. He hugged me tightly, as if I were someone he was quite fond of and as if he hadn't seen me in a very long time.

Women, the guards harshly reminded me, were to know their place: women are subservient and subordinate to men. They reprimanded me for touching Hakim. He bowed his head in my direction and placed both hands on his heart center. "Be well until we meet again," he said as they led me away. That would be the last time I saw him in this incarnation.

GIZA

The Great Pyramid, also known as the Pyramid of Khufu or the Pyramid of Cheops, is the oldest and largest of the three pyramids in the Giza pyramid complex bordering what is now El Giza, Egypt. Constructed of more than 2,300,000 limestone and granite blocks, the average weight of a block is about 2.3 metric tons (2.5 tons). The sheer size, weight, and resonance of these monoliths defy comprehension, even more so when one stands next to the structure.

Many of the enormous casing stones and inner chamber blocks of the Great Pyramid fit together with an extraordinarily high level of precision. Based on measurements taken on the northeastern casing stones, the mean opening of the joints is a mere 1/50 of an inch. Do you know anyone alive today that can draw or cut fifty straight lines within the space of an inch on a piece of granite and do so with less than a tiny fraction of deviance over the span of several feet? No, probably not. I share this information as a subtle reminder of how tiny we seem in contrast with our physical world sometimes.

While some authorities maintain that the pyramids were burial chambers, nothing has been documented that would indicate anyone or anything was ever entombed within the pyramids—there are no inscriptions on the walls, no evidence of burials, and no artifacts.

Specialists such as Hakim teach that the pyramids were power centers and that the Great Pyramid, specifically, was used to convert the Earth's vibrational energies into energy to power Egypt. What astonished me were the burn marks deep inside the pyramid that, according to our Wisdom Keepers, were caused by an explosion within the pyramid—yes, inside—which ultimately shut down the entire operating system and left Egypt without a source of electricity.

Findings and conclusions about the waves of electromagnetic energies flowing through the Earth and converting those energies into free electrical energy for power were documented by Nikola Tesla's experimentations in Colorado Springs, Colorado during the late 1800s. In the 1890s, Tesla invented electric oscillators, meters, better lights, and the high-voltage transformer known as the Tesla coil. He also experimented with X-rays, gave short-range demonstrations of radio communication two years before Guglielmo Marconi, and piloted a radio-controlled boat around a pool in Madison Square Garden. Together, Tesla and Westinghouse lit the 1891 World's Columbian Exposition in Chicago and partnered with

General Electric to install AC generators at Niagara Falls, creating the first modern power station.

Having experienced the very real energy within the pyramid and witnessing events while there that defied ordinary understanding, I agree with the theory of the monuments being power stations.

The King's Chamber within the Great Pyramid measures 34.4 feet from east to west and 17.17 feet from north to south. It has a flat roof that is an inch over 19 feet above the floor. There are shafts connecting the various chambers within the pyramid, and a great deal of speculation surrounds the purpose of these shafts. Egyptologists long believed these were air shafts designed for ventilation; others think they were designed to accommodate the ascension of the king's spirit to the heavens. As one of our indigenous leaders noted, "Sing. Anyone who sings when in the pyramid sings in harmony with the Earth and knows the truth." The shafts inside the pyramid are lined with granite, and the acoustics are simply phenomenal. One of the people in our group noted that the reverberations of the crystal singing bowl our Guide was playing while we were inside the Chamber literally made her body sway against her will.

The giant obelisks made from solid pieces of granite that surround Egypt are said to "sing" from the core of the Earth. And they seem to; I tapped on every obelisk that I could touch, and the tones they emit are breathtaking.

The King's Chamber is entirely faced with solid granite, and the only object in the chamber is a rectangular coffer comprised of one solid block of granite. One corner is broken. The supposed sarcophagus is slightly larger than the entryway (known as the Ascending Passage), which shows that it must have been placed in the chamber before the roof was put in place. Microscopic analysis of the coffer reveals that it was made with a fixed-point drill that used hard jewel bits with a drilling force of two tons. Historical notes indicate the jewel bits were made of sapphires. How were the sapphires cut? Carving this coffer would have also required saws that were eight, nine feet in length. Advanced sources of power would have been necessary to conduct this type of drilling, sawing, and polishing.

It's well documented that the granite blocks that comprise parts of the pyramids were originally encased in limestone; the limestone could have, in effect, functioned as insulation. The stone blocks used inside the pyramid were made of another form of limestone containing crystal, which is an extremely high electrical conductor.

If superconductive materials were installed where the coffer is, Wisdom Keepers tell us, the pyramid could—and did—manufacture enough electricity for all of Egypt.

Relief carvings show that the Egyptians used hand-held torches, which appeared, from the carvings, to be powered by cable-free power sources. The arc lamp used in the Lighthouse of Alexandria, for example, is another evidence of electricity in ancient Egypt. The energy required to power the Lighthouse of Alexandria for twenty-four hours a day could only have been supplied by a regular electrical source.

This superconductor is also thought to have been the Ark of the Covenant, which was known to have been in Egypt in ancient times, and whose dimensions would have fit inside the stone chest. In addition to its other properties, there are various references that the Ark of the Covenant served as a capacitor.

The Ark of the Covenant, as described in the biblical Exodus 25:8-10, 16; 31:18, was a sacred chest crafted by the ancient Israelites as per Divine instruction. It served as the repository and guardian of "the Testimony," which consisted of the Ten Commandments inscribed on two stone tablets. Beyond its religious significance, some theories suggest that the Ark may have symbolized early experiments with electricity. There are historical accounts of sudden deaths associated with contact with the Ark, resembling fatalities caused by high-voltage electrical discharges. It's proposed that such a charge could have resulted from the accumulation of static electricity, a phenomenon that occurs rapidly in hot, arid climates like the Middle East.

The Prophet Moses was adopted by Pharaoh and, according to historical records, was raised as an administrator. One of the phases in leadership training in ancient Egypt was that of learning all the secrets of Egypt. When Moses fled Egypt, he was said to have taken the Ark of the Covenant with him. This is likely one of the more pivotal reasons the pharaoh was so intent upon chasing Moses as he fled.

Perhaps Moses used the Ark to part the Red Seas?

Historic references also show that the Egyptian civilization reached its peak during the reign of Ramses II, who lived at the same time as Moses. Those civilizations collapsed less than ten years after Ramses II, and Giza, once the center of the civilization, was abandoned.

Did Moses remove Egypt's source of electricity?

INTO THE GREAT PYRAMID

I have been blessed to have spent time in a sacred ceremony in the King's Chambers of the Great Pyramid, a place where both Jesus and Buddha were said to have meditated, studied, and had spiritual initiations. Egypt had declared a veritable shutdown of international travel as the country was faced with great unrest, and the mere fact that we were inside the Great Pyramid was against the law at the time. The military was hugely present while we were there, and they directed machine guns at people with the most minor of provocations. Bribery—baksheesh—was commonplace. Yet there we were, a group of us, for more than six hours, safe and protected.

A tiny fraction of people on the planet have been inside the Great Pyramid; an even smaller number have spent time in a ceremony within the chambers. For this, I am grateful.

Was I afraid?

Yes, quite frankly, I was.

Those of us who have been within the confines of the chambers, and those that will do so in the future, are called to do so, according to Hakim. It is not luck or a matter of money or of time; it is a matter of circumstance. The same month I was in the Great Pyramid was the same month the entire structure of my life at the time was collapsing. The money was all but gone; I had paid for this trip months ahead of time. My infrastructure of work was imploding, and so was my marriage. It was a time of a new Genesis of sorts. The magnet from around the globe pulled me as it had done when I was a teenager; the same as it had done every other time, I felt that absolute requirement that I must go.

TARYN

There was a young woman in our party, Taryn, who was on the pilgrimage to Egypt to better understand the antiquities and found, concurrently, that she was also there finding a resolution to awkward conflicts in her life. She was a beautiful pixie in her early twenties who confided in me much as she would have a trusted older sister, and we spent a great deal of time talking, laughing, and walking in meditation together. While in Cairo, she had purchased an exquisitely clear quartz crystal point and was wearing it as we entered the Great Pyramid. We had both noted that the crystal seemed like pure water in its clarity. It was a stunning, single-terminated point, not quite an inch and a half in length.

After our ceremony, one that exceeded several hours (and felt no more than twenty minutes) Taryn and I exited the pyramid with our group and took turns taking pictures. It was well after dark; the sky was a black velvet blanket filled with stars. We noted that orbs were showing up in all our pictures—and in virtually every photograph taken by our group—and commented that our stateside friends would likely blame the cameras or the operators for the circles. Orbs were seen moving in video recordings made by some of our group.

Orbs are masses of energy that show up in photographs. Some claim they are spirits or ghosts. Others believe the spheres are a phenomenon caused by dust, water, or low-resolution cameras.

Dr. Gary E. Schwartz and Adjunct Research Professor of Optical Sciences Katherine Creath at the University of Arizona published a study on orbs in 2005. They said most orbs can be explained by the reflection of the camera's flash off of objects in the scene, or off of dust. However, Schwartz and Creath acknowledged that some orbs seem to defy conventional optical explanations. An orb captured in a BBC documentary, filmed with top-of-the-line videography equipment, drifted before disappearing. Schwartz and Creath write: "It is not possible to explain orbic objects such as these that move in dynamic and unpredictable paths as being caused by stray reflections. It is also not possible to explain many of them as being caused by dust particles in the air."

How can one explain lightning when the skies are clear and stable?

Taryn showed me the pictures she took of the pyramid. There was, without a shred of doubt, a lightning bolt that was coming out of the sky and touching the top of the pyramid in her series of pictures. It was breathtaking and raised bumps on our arms.

Her crystal now had a solid inclusion, a full demarcation line running through it. The inclusion, which was jagged and running from end to end was an incredible reminder of how energy flows and morphs and disrupts and reorganizes through all things, including each of us.

CHAPTER 8
INTO THE HEART

You gain strength, courage, and confidence by every experience in which you really stop to look fear in the face.

You must do the thing you think you cannot do.

—Eleanor Roosevelt

As you know by now, I've been traveling since I was a teenager and have always taken the local's road, gone where I wasn't supposed to, have been in community with those who live there, and have participated in indigenous ceremonies whenever possible. I plan to travel the rest of the time I'm here on the planet and experience as much of the world as I can as part of my evolution, not in a Bear Grylls-survivalist sort of way, but in a testing-of-faith way. Am I often terrified? Yes. And I will continue to readily enroll in "acts of extreme spirituality," to quote author Tolly Burkan.

Why did I—and do I—feel compelled to test myself? Maybe I was esoterically invited to do all of this so that I had the physical memories and neural pathways of being able to do these things again and share my experiences with others who may be fearful. For me, these experiences have been real acts of trust and faith; acts of commitment and confidence in a Higher Power. Other times, I have found myself trapped or barricaded by my lack of faith and the apparent need for a wake-up call of a higher order.

One such time happened several years ago on a suspension bridge across a raging river at night, in the rain, thousands of feet above sea level in the Himalayas. I had no conscious intention of the circumstance transpiring; swollen rivers, mudslides, and an uncompromising and incredibly immature travel companion who childishly abandoned the group all collided to land me right there at that moment in time. The porter, a boyish eighteen-year-old, who had been assigned to stay back and be my guide, had jackrabbited ahead to find alternate routes. The trail we were on was completely washed out in several places and strewn with fallen trees, debris, and unstable rock in others. Rushing water made some crossings impossible, and we had to double back many times. The next village, the one where we were supposed to stay for the night, was still six hours away even under optimal conditions, and we were both soaking wet. Neither of us had eaten, and while there was water everywhere, potable water was nowhere to be found. I hadn't seen him for several hours. The last words he'd said were "Go forward," so I did. The rain was sheeting down; the mountain crossing was very steep.

There are many long suspension bridges in Nepal, and I crossed many more of them than I wanted to on that trip.

This bridge was different; I could see less than twenty feet in front of me. Getting safely across the bridge and finding my way in the dark, in torrential rain on unfamiliar trails, meant having absolute faith. I asked for a sign assuring I would be staying Earth-bound that night; the Creator sent fireflies and the familiar sense of Knowing.

Alone in the crossing, I blacked out at the belly of the bridge, at the lowest point, which was approximately two hundred feet lower than the landings on either side of the canyon. I was outside of my body long enough to realize I had a choice.

I'm not sure how long I lay there until I felt the bridge sway, and I was finally able to feel my legs and hands. Inexplicably, I had held onto the miniature flashlight I was carrying and was somehow able to make my way on my hands and knees to the other side. I curled into the fetal position at the landing of the bridge, tucked up against the railing in the rain, and waited for the porter. He still had not returned an hour later.

I managed to compose myself and got moving again. I do not remember the rest of the trail between that bridge landing and meeting my Sherpa.

What I do remember is that it was another six hours before the rain finally subsided and nearly nine hours before I met my Sherpa. I do also know that I fell many times evidenced by the numerous cuts and bruises I had; I'm still astounded that I didn't slide all the way down one of the steep embankments.

I developed acute mountain sickness, also known as AMS, about three days into the trek. AMS is an affliction that even the local people who live at high altitudes sometimes mysteriously develop. Some of those whom I'd been trekking with trivialized my symptoms as that of a cold; I suspected differently, but we were miles into the mountains on trails and without cell services. I had no choice but to keep moving.

AMS can be a severe illness and is one that can claim lives. Breathing took monumental effort; I was experiencing migraine headaches, nausea, and was dehydrated. The blackout I experienced on the bridge was one of several.

There were maybe a dozen houses at the plateau; how I knew to knock on his door in the early morning hours can only be attributed to being guided by a Higher Power.

Geljun Sherpa is an angel incarnate, an absolutely wonderful man. He and his family operate one of the obscure teahouses in a village on a lesser-used trail at more than eleven thousand feet in the Himalayas. The area is only accessible by foot or air services; there are no vehicle roads. Supplies arrive via horseback, by pack mules, or by air to villages such as his. "Some trekkers use this trail on the way to Base Camp; not many though," he had said.

He sat with me for some time, talking with me and holding my hand while insisting I drink some earthy herbal concoction that smelled of fusty mud, garlic, and ginger.

Geljun had left the door open and the light on to watch for the porter and had assured me that the porter would find his way, even if the trail completely disappeared. "They just know how to talk to the mountains; they are born here and part of them," Geljun said. The porter showed up about an hour and a half after I found my way to Geljun's home.

The porter told Geljun that he had circled back and had been unable to find me in the rain and darkness and had hoped I had found a place to hide for the night. He explained to Geljun that he had taken an alternate mule trail through the rocky areas to reach the village and was bewildered to see that I was already there. At first, he thought I had died and that what he witnessed in Geljun's kitchen was my ghost.

He asked Geljun if I was dying. Geljun sternly reprimanded the boy for leaving me in the first place, requested he make himself something to eat, and then find a bed in one of the spare rooms. It was important that the porter leave the two of us alone, Geljun said. Geljun's wife stood guard.

"Today is not the day you will die," Geljun assured me. He told me stories about his sons, who were in college in the United States, stories about his time as a Sherpa and as a porter on the trails, and about how our God had brought us together at that place and that time because we were meant to meet in this lifetime. He was kind, and he was delightfully bilingual, bantering with me until the first rays of the sun shone through the mist.

"You have survived the night," he declared. "Now you rest and know that God has work for you to do on the Earth."

Ah, yes, that. More work to do. Of course.

He explained he would arrange for air transport later that morning. A helicopter would cost nearly $5,000 US in cash and the hospital visit would likely require another $2–$3,000. The trip in and out of the mountains at altitude by copter is risky at best, and the area was shrouded in cloud cover, making the journey even more hazardous. I had travel insurance that might potentially reimburse the trip, but I was not carrying $5,000 cash on me. I asked him what the alternative was; he stated flatly that people in my condition usually died. He said that he would not let that happen and had friends he would call in Kathmandu that would help.

"The porter is a stupid, stupid young boy; he does not understand how sick you are. The woman who left, her heart is not good. *She is not good*," he said, referring to the travel companion who had left several of us behind as she sprinted up the trails without informing us. I misinterpreted for a moment; "She's on her way to Base Camp; she's an athlete who is training for Mount Everest," I said. She was a "self-absorbed child," he said, clearly disturbed.

"She is evil, a deviant, not a good heart," he continued. "She was here only to bring all of us together for our lessons. That is a good thing. She is not a good person; her heart is not good," he said. "She has failed this test and will continue to fail." He shook his head somberly. "How could she leave like that if she were of a good heart? You may die if we do not take you off the mountain. I fear greatly for the others who are traveling with her." I was deeply worried about them as well.

I spent three days in a hospital in Kathmandu, the first time in my life that I had ever been hospitalized. Ever. My father had delivered all his children at home, and though I had been quite ill as a child, he was the one who administered the medications. As an adult, I routinely see an acupuncturist-chiropractor and don't see a general practitioner.

The doctors at the hospital in Nepal were dismayed at the severity of my condition. My lungs had begun filling with fluid, a precursor to the final stages, and I was dehydrated. No bones had been broken, but I had numerous strains and sprains, and I couldn't feel several of my toes. They said I only survived because I'm as "strong as a mountain mule."

They argued with the insurance carrier on my behalf, who had steadfastly refused to pay for emergency evacuation off the mountain or for mandatory hospitalization. The insurance company supervisors claimed they were a "reimbursement carrier," even though I had checked and rechecked the policy prior to my departure concerning emergencies.

The transport and my stay were inexplicably covered.

A German woman who lived high in the Alps was in the room next to mine there in Kathmandu and explained how she had fallen on the saturated trails after developing AMS. Her leg was broken in several places; she'd been in the hospital for over a week. "Germans do not get mountain sickness, and I know I died. No one believes me when I tell them that I was out of my body and could see my leg bone sticking out or hear what they were saying," she stated. "My travel mates say I am delusional, but I knew exactly what they were saying."

CYCLES

Some Masters teach that we cycle through our lives in a series of samsaras, a wandering through and moving on that is intended to take us higher with each cycle.

Tolly Burkan sent me a signed copy of one of his books in response to a note of kinship and respect that I had sent to him. His book had arrived concurrently with meeting Doug, my kindly Irish granddad of a Yogi. Tolly's signature contained a heart and a smile. That had moved me greatly; I, too, had signed my name with a heart and a smile before depression had reared its obnoxious head.

Was the arrival of this book merely a gift, or was it so much more?

Burkan, as noted earlier, is also affectionately known as the "father of firewalking" and has trained hundreds of firewalking instructors since 1977, including the maverick motivational leader, Tony Robbins. As of this writing, Burkan has retired and states that "over five million Westerners have firewalked" with virtually no injuries. Having been involved in the building of firewalking lanes, I understand, firsthand, how real the possibility of serious injuries can be. In all the times I have firewalked, I have never been burned (and I sunburn quite easily) and have only witnessed one participant sustaining a minor injury to his hand when he tripped. According to Burkan:

> Typical firewalks open to the public involve coal beds ranging from 1,200 to 1,500 degrees Fahrenheit. Dr. Ron Sato, a faculty member of Stanford University's Medical School and director of a nearby hospital burn unit, says that human flesh momentarily exposed to 1,200 degrees Fahrenheit should sustain third-degree burns to the epidermis and dermis, charring the entire thickness of skin to a blackened carbon residue. Dr. Sato has treated people who have accidentally stepped on glowing coals and were so severely burned that they required skin grafts. When asked about people who voluntarily firewalk without injury, Dr. Sato says, "There's no logical explanation."

Harvard-trained physician and medical researcher Dr. Andrew Weil comments, "There is no way I can be convinced that mental state is not the key variable in firewalking." Our mental state is remarkably determinant of what manifests our outer world. He continues, "To overcome external circumstances, you must first overcome your internal world." Dr. Weil has personally experienced several firewalks.

Within the Vedic tradition, the route to liberation and joy is found in releasing attachments.

That also means letting go of the outcome.

Yoga can be this gateway of detachment for many of us. In my search for authentic personal peace, I felt, and still do feel, compelled to test my human, physical limitations through extreme acts. A teacher referred to my exploits as my "vain anxiety." I always thought of these types of feats as leaps: leaps of faith, leaps into the unknown, and the proverbial leaps without a safety net.

Chögyam Trungpa Rinpoche (1940-1987), one of the early Tibetan Buddhist teachers to come to the United States, played a pivotal role in establishing Naropa University in Boulder, Colorado, and Shambhala International, a global network of over two hundred meditation centers. He shared valuable insights, including a phrase I deeply appreciate: "Strive to remain open, cheerful, and courageous simultaneously. This demands a continuous willingness to take leaps of faith." Achieving both cheerfulness and courage necessitates ongoing stability and an equanimous mind.

As found in the "Bhagavad Gita," which is also known as "The Song of God":

> Yoga is perfect evenness of mind. Seek refuge in the attitude of detachment, and you will amass the wealth of spiritual awareness. Those who are motivated only by the desire for the fruits of action are miserable, for they are constantly anxious about the results of what they do. When consciousness is unified, however, all vain anxiety is left behind. There is no cause for worry, whether things go well or ill. Therefore, devote yourself to the disciplines of yoga, for yoga is skill in action.

Vain anxiety, indeed. How many of us fully embrace our anxiety as who we are, as an integral part of our daily existence? Chemical signals in our body create the impulsive reaction of anxiety response, and the results are real. Is that a healthy way to live our lives? Are we supposed to live in a constant state of hyper-alertness or chronic unrest?

How do we unify our consciousness, then, when so much of what we do comes from those involuntary places of reaction? Many of us well know that unconscious, automatic responses create our suffering. Bill Harris states that we often "tenaciously hold onto them."

According to Harris, there are six stages of conscious change:
1. Awareness

2. Identification
3. Focusing
4. Expansion
5. Resolution
6. Reintegration and Reprogramming

Thich Nhat Hanh teaches that "the secret of creating peace is that when you listen to another person, you have only one purpose: to offer him an opportunity to empty his heart. If you are able to keep that awareness and compassion alive in you, then you can [...] listen even if the other person's speech contains a lot of wrong perceptions, condemnations and because you are already protected by the nectar of compassion in your own heart." This preeminent teacher continues: "Keeping your awareness keeps you safe."

With awareness, real changes can become plausible.

Looking within, then, is the way to understand and shift our internal baseline, and moving this set point is something we must do in the conscious embrace of real change.

Spirituality, creativity, and authentic yoga can help take us there.

And what better way to communicate than through our hearts?

According to Jung, "Your vision will become clear only when you can look into your own heart. Who looks outside, dreams, who looks inside, awakes."

PSYCHOPHYSIOLOGICAL COHERENCE

The University of Pennsylvania Medical School documents that "the search for spiritual, or unitary experiences is intimately interwoven with human biology [and] hard-wired into our brains [...] what Buddhists call 'oneness with the Universe,' and Franciscan nuns call 'being in the presence of God,' are not the result of delusory or wishful thinking, but rather the result of a sequence of clear, discrete, observable and recordable neurophysiological events."

"I always ask my heart what is right, true, or correct," states counselor and teacher John McVay. "Our thinking mind gets in God's ways sometimes." And I agree. Sometimes our damaged software—

and the damaged rudders we are working with—create more friction than is necessary.

Several years back, I attended a workshop that delved into the power of heart-centered energetic interactions. The facilitator aimed to prove a captivating thesis: not only are we deeply interconnected, we also have the ability to influence each other's energetic states from our heart-center. The evidence presented was so compelling that even the most hardened skeptics among us couldn't brush it aside.

One fascinating demonstration involved the simple act of hugging. We discovered that hugging another person from the right to their left—instead of embracing in a "heart to heart" alignment—had a draining effect on our energy levels. This was more than an exercise; it was an experiential revelation about the energetic subtleties of human interaction.

Further insights emerged as we formed chains of people, some of whom weren't even in physical contact with one another. Astonishingly, reactions manifested at the opposite ends of these chains. For instance, a person at one end would focus on a negative or hostile thought and energetically "send" it down the line. No words were spoken; it was a silent transference of thought energy. Muscle testing at the far end of the chain consistently revealed weakened energy fields. Conversely, when thoughts of love, kindness, and acceptance were "sent," muscle tests exhibited bolstered strength—every single time.

For skeptics in the room, this was a groundbreaking moment. Those of us who are more intuitive—often labeled as Empaths or empathic individuals—already recognized and embraced this form of energetic communication. Our perceptive filters are less conventional, and we often process feelings and sensory information in ways distinct from the general populace. In this workshop, our intuitive experiences were corroborated with empirical evidence, reinforcing what many of us have sensed all along: the tangible impact of heart-centered energy.

Information of all sorts can be communicated between biological systems, and studies support the idea that energetic transferences do have more of an effect on other living beings than we may have previously understood. Some of us cannot, for example, tolerate being around certain people or environments, or we are plagued by the sense that something isn't right in various situations.

Is it paranoia or intuition? Paranoia implies a disconnection from reality, often based on fear or excessive anxiety about perceived threats that may not be grounded in fact. In contrast, intuition is a form of knowing that bypasses logical reasoning, often tapping into experiences, observations, or innate sensitivities. For Empaths or those with highly tuned intuitive skills, distinguishing between the two can be a significant challenge. Both can feel similar, producing an emotional or physical response that urges you to pay attention. However, the nature of the information and how you use it differ vastly. In a setting like the workshop, designed to demonstrate energetic interconnectedness, intuition could emerge as a powerful tool for understanding the experiences. It may allow participants to "sense" the energy shifts in a nuanced way, validating experiences they have had elsewhere. Paranoia, on the other hand, might manifest as an undue concern about the potential consequences of such energetic interactions, perhaps even projecting malintent where there is none.

Recognizing the difference often involves a combination of self-awareness, mindfulness, and rational thinking. While intuition might nudge you toward something that feels deeply true or resonant, paranoia is more likely to push you away from an experience based on a skewed perception of risk or threat.

In essence, distinguishing between paranoia and intuition is not only about the kind of information you're receiving but also about how you process and act on that information. The workshop's ability to validate intuition through empirical evidence might serve as a touchstone for those struggling to differentiate between the two, confirming that what they sense energetically has a tangible, measurable impact.

One of my teachers insists that we are all empathic; another argues that we merely mirror emotions for each other, reflecting what we project into the world. Another teacher brings up the concept of mirror neurons, which "mirror" the behavior of others as though the observer were themselves acting. While these perspectives offer valuable insights, they may not capture the complexity of our energetic interactions. The distinction between paranoia and intuition serves as a case in point. Paranoia could lead us to project fears and anxieties onto others, potentially clouding our ability to genuinely mirror or empathize. On the other side, intuition, when honed and trusted, could heighten our empathic abilities, allowing us to sense and respond to the energies and emotions of others in a nuanced way.

It's also worth considering that mirror neurons and empathy might operate on a spectrum. While mirror neurons offer a biological explanation for how we may naturally reflect and understand each other's actions or emotions, empathy suggests a deeper, more conscious level of emotional resonance. Meanwhile, intuition, as explored in the workshop on heart-centered energetic changes, provides another layer to these interactions, challenging us to consider how we can influence and be influenced by the energies of those around us, often in ways that defy simple explanation.

Therefore, while some of what we sense may undoubtedly be our own narratives or fears reflected back at us, I believe there's often much more at play in these interactions. From the energetic shifts detectable through muscle testing to the subtle interplay of intuition and empathy, our connections with others are multidimensional, going far beyond mere person-to-person projections.

This brings me to a poignant observation: we are not just biological beings reacting to stimuli; we are intricate tapestries of experiences, beliefs, and energies that inform our relationships with others and with ourselves.

So, likewise, when we speak about making decisions based on what our "hearts" tell us, is it just poetic language or can these experiences be empirically validated? While many of us routinely state that we act or make decisions based on information from our hearts, the question remains: is this heart-governed thinking realistic or scientifically documentable? The complexities of our interpersonal dynamics suggest that we may be tapping into something deeper—something that science is only beginning to understand. While many of us routinely state that we act or make decisions based on information from our hearts, is this heart-governed thinking realistic or scientifically documentable?

Demonstrably it is.

TRUER HEARTS

The HeartMath Institute (HMI) has extensive studies and research documenting the heart-brain interactions between persons in close proximity to one another. Most people can sense this when watching friends or partners interact, seeing a parent relate with their child, or even individuals in contention with one another. We can feel the other person's energy; we act and react. We entrain with some people unwittingly and, in a sense, allow this entrainment to consume us or influence us to the extent that we can become drained or "filled up" and buoyed by our interactions.

According to HMI Director of Research Dr. Rollin McCraty: "Although more research in this area is still to be done, I do feel that we can affect our immediate environment. It appears that there is a type of communication occurring between people above and beyond body language or verbal communication. I believe we'll see in future research studies that we are affecting each other's moods and attitudes, both positively and negatively by the electromagnetic fields we radiate."

The institute has documented that a type of heart rhythm synchronization can occur in interactions between people and their pets. Many of us who love our pets can appreciate the results of an experiment Dr. McCraty conducted with his then fifteen-year-old son, Josh, and the boy's dog, Mabel. Dr. McCraty used electrocardiogram monitors to record heart rhythm data when the pair was together and apart.

The research shows that Mabel's heart rhythm shifted when Josh entered the room and consciously experienced feelings of love toward Mabel. When Josh consciously felt feelings of love and care toward his pet, his heart rhythms became more coherent, and this change appears to have influenced Mabel's heart rhythms, which then also became more coherent. There was no physical contact between the dog and the boy. Many of us who have pets understand this influence intrinsically, and research supports the idea that having a pet relieves many symptoms of illnesses.

Positive human-animal interaction is related to the changes in physiological variables both in humans and animals, including a reduction of subjective psychological stress (fear, anxiety) and an increase of oxytocin levels in the brain. Science demonstrates that these biological responses have measurable clinical effects.

Specifically, pets and therapy animals can help ease stress, anxiety, depression, feelings of loneliness, and social isolation. What's really beautiful about this is that loving interactions with animals can also help people manage their long-term mental health challenges. Major institutions in human medicine, including Johns Hopkins Medicine, Harvard Medical School, UCLA Health, and the Mayo Clinic, are also increasingly recognizing the benefits of pets to human health.

Pets offer a sense of security and routine that provides emotional and social support for many people. "My dog creates a sense of cohesiveness and rhythm in my everyday life. I'm needed, and I'm loved back without questions or drama or conflict," stated one of my group participants. I welcome dogs in many of our workshops, and even those participants who claim they are not "dog" people often find themselves stroking and nuzzling our fur-covered visitors.

Studies have also shown that pets are also great facilitators of getting to know other people. Further, they assist in friendship formation and are co-creators of social support networks. "Many of us pet parents get to know the dog first," remarked one of my clients. Dogs open the lines of communication between people where some of us often cannot comfortably do so.

Regarding these connections that can occur from person to person and between people and pets, McCraty later wrote:

"In our work with pets and their owners, we're seeing that a pet owner can create what we call a heart-filled environment when practicing heart-focused techniques (a cornerstone of HeartMath tools and technology). The pets respond by becoming more affectionate, more animated, and more connected with the pet owner." Those of us who have beloved pets understand this quite well.

Further, Dr. McCraty explains that "we have also found that the clear rhythmic patterns in beat-to-beat heart-rate variability are distinctly altered when different emotions are experienced. These changes in electromagnetic, sound pressure and blood pressure waves produced by cardiac rhythmic activity are 'felt' by every cell in the body, further supporting the heart's role as a global internal synchronizing signal."

Research indicates that the gentle action of stroking a dog is linked to the release of bonding and affection-related hormones like oxytocin, serotonin, and prolactin in the brain. Concurrently, this activity also contributes to a decrease in cortisol levels, a hormone connected with stress, leading to reduced heart rates, more regulated breathing, and muscle relaxation.

When those of us who have cherished pets say we love them, we really do.

And they, in turn, love us back and help us heal.

VITAL ROLES

Research likewise supports that we do have a brain within our heart and that there are cells in our heart that think and remember matters independently of the brain in our head.

The recent discovery of the "little brain" in the heart—a collection of sensory neurons that think, remember, and learn independently from the neurons in our brain—provides a different interpretation of heart-based meanings. Accordingly, the states we might access via our heart-brain coherence may provide a truer picture for us in any given situation. As the scientific author Gregg Braden says: "Our heart-intelligence knows instantly what's true and meaningful for us. [...] There are different kinds of challenges in life that are best solved through various ways of thinking: some with the brain and some with the heart. And while heart-based thinking may be less familiar in our fast world of technology and digital information, in a very real sense, it is perhaps the most sophisticated technology we'll ever know."

John and Beatrice Lacey made groundbreaking contributions to the field of psychophysiology by conducting extensive research throughout the 1960s and '70s. Their pioneering work focused on exploring the intricate interactions between the heart and the brain. During their two decades of investigative research, the Laceys made a remarkable discovery: the heart communicates with the brain in profound ways that have a substantial impact on our perception of the world and our responses to it. Their observations and documentation shed light on the intricate connection between our heart's activity and our cognitive and emotional experiences.

According to HeartMath, the connection between the heart and brain is a continuous, dynamic, two-way exchange, with each organ constantly influencing the other. The heart's rhythmic activity serves a crucial role in generating waves of blood, sound, and electromagnetism, all of which have the potential to synchronize or impact every cell in the body. Furthermore, the heart's energetic field has a notable entrainment effect on the brain, and directing focused attention to the heart enhances this heart-brain entrainment.

Research has revealed that the heart communicates with the brain through four major channels: neurologically, via the transmission of nerve impulses; biochemically, involving hormones and neurotransmitters; biophysically, through pressure waves; and energetically, via electromagnetic field interactions. This multidimensional communication is far more intricate than previously understood and has been shown to influence performance.

Additionally, the intrinsic cardiac nervous system possesses both short-term and long-term memory functions, operating independently of central neuronal commands. This intricate web of interactions highlights the remarkable and multifaceted connection between the heart and the brain.

Neurocardiologists have extensively explored the anatomy and functions of the cardiac nervous system and its connections with the brain. Regarding heart-brain communication, it's recognized that the efferent (descending) pathways in the autonomic nervous system play a crucial role in regulating the heart. What's less understood is that the majority of fibers in the vagus nerve are afferent (ascending) and are primarily related to the heart and cardiovascular system.

One intriguing aspect is the role of emotions in this communication. It's fascinating that the heart sends more information to the brain than the brain sends to the heart.

According to Dr. Rollin McCraty, Research Director at the HeartMath Institute, "Coherence is the state when the heart, mind, and emotions are in energetic alignment and cooperation." When this physiological coherence is driven by positive emotions, it's referred to as psychophysiological coherence. Positive emotions enhance coherence in all physical processes, including the heart's rhythm.

This shift in heart rhythm has significant implications. It facilitates higher cognitive functions, emotional stability, and states of calm, ultimately establishing a new inner-baseline reference. With this new coherence baseline, individuals are less susceptible to living their lives through the automatic filters of past traumatic or negative experiences.

Dr. McCraty highlights the contrast between harmony and trauma concerning baselines. Coherence represents harmonious synchronization and flow, while trauma often signifies disconnectedness and dysregulation. Therefore, shifting our perceptions through the heart and how we perceive things through the heart-brain connection becomes not just a suggestion but a vital measure for good health.

The heart's knowledge and its likeness to the Universe within our physical form are striking. As Paulo Coelho aptly puts it, "You will never be able to escape from your heart. So, it's better to listen to what it has to say."

The brain, with its divided right and left hemispheres, reflects the dual structure believed by mystics to be a fundamental characteristic of the Universe. This inherent duality of the brain is often exacerbated by brain lateralization, where the two hemispheres become unbalanced. As a result, our brains tend to interpret reality in a split-brained manner, perceiving things as separate and in opposition rather than interconnected.

Could this filtering of reality be the reason we all struggle when we know in our hearts what is good, right, and true for us alone? We reference our Heartfelt Desire in iRest® Yoga Nidra as our deepest, most precious reason for being alive. In Sanskrit, the word is dharma. Dharma is also known as cosmic law and order.

Even as each person is different, a distinct, separate individual physical entity, so are we a part of the vast collective realm of consciousness.

The profound interconnectedness of everything in the Universe is a fundamental reality. As the author Bill Harris beautifully expresses it, "You cannot be otherwise than at one with everything." The

Universe operates as a vast matrix of energy and matter, where every element is intricately connected.

This interconnectedness finds representation in sacred geometry, particularly in the sacred symbol known as the Flower of Life, as mentioned earlier.

It's important to note that being "at one with everything" doesn't necessarily imply a heightened state of awareness or what Bill Harris describes as being "spiritually awake." Harris offers his perspective on spiritual awakeness, emphasizing that a spiritually awake person doesn't find themselves in opposition to the world. Instead, they are an integral part of it, yet they remain unattached to specific outcomes. In essence, they embody the idea of being "in the world but not of it," a concept resonating with the teachings of figures like Jesus.

In meditation, the practitioner seeks to minimize and eventually eliminate the effects of brain lateralization through some form of focusing, and virtually any focusing will bring about a degree of brain synchronization.

As a person focuses during meditation, there is a shift from a beta brain wave state, typical of ordinary waking consciousness, into a slower and more relaxed alpha brain wave state. Those with a substantially more disciplined practice will gain enough mastery to foray into the deeper theta brain wave state.

CATEGORIES OF BRAIN WAVE PATTERNS

Bill Harris explains that the most rapid brain wave pattern is known as beta, ranging from approximately 14 Hz to over 100 Hz. This pattern characterizes the state of waking consciousness, closely linked to activities such as concentration, cognitive processing, and vigilance. When beta activity reaches higher levels, it becomes associated with feelings of anxiety.

While beta brainwave states serve essential functions like focusing on tasks and maintaining alertness, it's crucial to understand that staying in a high beta state for extended periods can be detrimental. Elevated levels of beta brainwave activity are linked to stress, anxiety, and even insomnia. Importantly, prolonged periods in a high beta state can dysregulate the autonomic nervous system, upsetting the balance between the "fight-or-flight" and "rest-and-digest" responses, thereby exacerbating stress and potentially impacting overall health. Essentially, when the brain is continually operating in high beta, it's like keeping a car engine revving at high RPMs without letting it rest. Over time, this can lead to emotional and cognitive exhaustion, making it less optimal for long-term well-being compared to more balanced brainwave states like alpha, which are associated with relaxation and creativity.

As one becomes calmer, brain wave activity slows into the alpha range, from 8-13.9 Hz. These are brain wave patterns of deep relaxation, similar to the twilight state between sleeping and wakefulness. The alpha state is generally considered beneficial for several reasons. It is associated with increased relaxation, heightened creativity, and reduced stress, making it advantageous for mental well-being and cognitive function.

Theta waves are slower than alpha, generally between 4 and 7.9 Hz. This state is associated with dreaming sleep, super learning, increased memory, and higher creativity. Theta waves are intriguing for several reasons. They are predominant during REM sleep, essential for emotional regulation and memory consolidation. The theta state is also linked to "super learning," where the brain absorbs and retains information more effectively, particularly important for studying and skill acquisition. Additionally, higher levels of creativity are often observed when the brain operates in the theta state, making it beneficial for problem-solving and artistic endeavors. Essentially, the theta state serves as a kind of "mental spa," providing the brain a break from higher frequencies, which can boost emotional well-being and cognitive function.

The slowest brain wave pattern is delta, at less than 4 Hz. Dreamless sleep occurs in this state, and it's in delta that our brains are triggered to release large quantities of human growth hormone.

Some believe that the yogic meditative sleep state of Yoga Nidra is also associated with the delta state.

Delta waves are significant for multiple reasons. Firstly, they are crucial for deep, restorative sleep, the kind that helps rejuvenate the body and mind. The release of human growth hormone during this phase aids in tissue repair and regeneration, making it indispensable for physical health. Additionally, some practitioners (me included) of Yoga Nidra, a form of yogic meditative sleep, believe that the practice helps induce a delta brainwave state, promoting deep relaxation and healing.

There is substantial evidence supporting the possibility of maintaining alertness in a trance-like, non-physical state. Those of us who have trained in clinical hypnotherapy or have experienced hypnosis in a controlled environment often aim to access this state during our sessions. It's worth noting that this may result in sensations and reactions that could be disconcerting to an outside, untrained observer.

The first time I entered this particular state in a clinical setting, I was fascinated and acutely aware of what was taking place while adrift in another place of conscious awareness. A long-time meditator, I was unconvinced of the validity of the hypnotic processes and doubtful that the clinicians would be able to work with me. Rapid induction techniques seemed too simplistic to be real or viable.

The general public has, unfortunately, been led to believe the outlandish claims made by stage magicians, movies, and errant journalistic reporting when it comes to understanding the vital elements of moving past the self-imposed limitations of our current conscious awareness and into the healing and growth realms of our subconscious. Hypnotism is not mind control from another; no one can make you do, say, or act a certain way under hypnosis. The same is true of Yoga Nidra. You, as the inductee, patient, or client, are in control. Is it an altered state of consciousness and a shifting of brainwave states? Yes.

Much like free writing or introspective journaling, we are moving past the intellect. We simply listen to our thoughts and let the flow of the story take place without judgment or intervention. We set aside our internal editor, and things will come forth—an image, then the memory, and then the flow of associations. Secrets may surface that you never knew you were consciously harboring; preoccupying dreams and recurrent thoughts are given expression. In deeper stages, such as Nidra, we go into the Void of timelessness, a delicious and healing place of nowhere, nothing, and detachment. In hypnotherapy, we can go into much deeper realms: space is held, we are facilitated, and we can detach a bit further. On our own, the subconscious is still on the ready—what if the phone rings, what if someone needs me, what if, what if, what if. In a session, however, those what-ifs can be set aside.

In clinical hypnosis sessions, the scenes are exquisitely real and very palpable. What was captivating for me from a detached state of the hypnotic trance was the incredible detail and accuracy of memories that I have accessed during sessions. Our subconscious catalogues every memory we have. In the hypnotic trance, a doorway is created to access those memories and process them from a very different perspective. With a trained and caring clinician, you will experience this yourself under your terms, at your right time.

My childhood was very traumatic; some of the memories I accessed were petrifying and consequently left me catatonic during the sessions. Emerging quite relieved, I was still somewhat dazed and physically spent afterward. I didn't expect to feel this way at all. I have relived and re-experienced many of the underlying traumas in present time. These issues shrouded by my subconscious were causing me to react to everyday circumstances in ways I hadn't comprehended. Some may argue that I was re-traumatized during some of these sessions, and in retrospect, that may be true as some of the practitioners were neither familiar nor trained in aspects of abuse and trauma such as I had endured.

During the session, I was observing what was taking place, yet I felt as if I was there physically reacting to what had happened. While I was terrified within the realm of the sessions, I was also well aware that I was safe with the therapist, could pull myself back to the place of being the observer, and most importantly, that I had survived.

One of the doctors I was working with had asked me to describe certain elements of what I remembered to him after a particularly challenging, physical, and lengthy session. He'd been in private practice for over three decades and noted that my session was quite fascinating to him from a professional standpoint. "Let's explore your, ahem, indignations in more depth from a traditional standpoint, shall we?" he had said.

The indignations he was referring to were the anger and terror that had surfaced and been expressed, in his words, as terrified hatred. The need to explore them further was gone for me at that point though; whatever fury my body had harbored had vanished, and the healthy bridge between my mind and heart had been built. What had been stored on a physical level, whatever had been grotesquely lodged, had been processed and had dissolved. Instead, I was observing what was taking place while I was involved in remembering and reacting to what had happened.

During that particular session, I relived a near-fatal accident that wasn't an accident at all. My body knew it wasn't an accident; the toddler child-me knew who was responsible and why, saw and relived the experience, and transcended the horrors. The child-me was mortified by the knowledge and the experience, and the memories had been stored away at a level under my conscious awareness since I was approximately two years old. Throughout my life, I had continually been triggered by people, sights, sounds, interpretations, and conclusions I had made as a helpless child and responded in ways that I could not decipher as an adult. Clinical hypnosis brought these memories to the surface, into the light of awareness, and broke them-and-me wide open for me to heal and to forgive.

Many people ask, "What if I discover things I don't want to know?" regarding hypnosis. To quote a dear friend, Miki Bryant, who is also a heart-centered hypnotherapist: "It is possible to discover past events that were consciously forgotten, and that may be painful; however, these events are not forgotten in the subconscious. They are often key to identifying patterns of behaviors and thoughts that are controlling present experiences. Hypnosis is a way to access those subconscious patterns so you can choose how you wish to change the patterns that control your current experience. You might think of this like checking for tooth decay. While no one wants to discover a cavity, only through discovery and treatment can you ensure strong, healthy teeth." I would like to note here that an infected tooth can kill a person if left unchecked. Memories that are too painful for a person to deal with can sometimes kill as well.

This type of trance state is entirely different from that of self-hypnosis or meditation, and the training that those of us who are classified as advanced clinical hypnotherapists require is extensive, sometimes arduous, and quite challenging. The work also requires a great deal of ongoing, personal healing. For me, though, the work is rewarding. Excavating the past events that may be causing corrosion in our present-day existence can be a lifesaver for some. I've been blessed to assist patients and clients as they pry loose the underpinnings of subconscious patterns and heal such challenges as morbid obesity, long-term heavy smoking, substance abuse, addictions, self-sabotage, financial hardships, and relationship blocks. It isn't always easy work for the therapist or the patient, and quite frankly, the work I do is sometimes physically exhausting in indescribable ways. Excavating the past events that may be causing corrosion in our present-day existence can, however, literally save lives.

CHAPTER 9
INSIDE INFORMATION

How often I found where I should be going only by setting out for somewhere else.

—R. Buckminster Fuller

Every aspect of the therapeutic hypnosis sessions I have experienced firsthand felt as if I were there, not here. I could see and feel the constriction of my attire, for instance. I could smell the environment; could feel the sensations of emotions, be it sheer joy or terror, and could feel the safety, happiness, or the pain of the situation. I could taste the metallic taste of sickness rising; I could feel the temperature of the surrounding environment.

My clients often report things in such vivid detail that it would appear they are reciting from a script.

As with much of the paranormal and metaphysical studies I have undertaken, I had been quite skeptical about past-life regression before the session I will share momentarily. I would question my instructors, the practice, the protocols, the procedures, and the reality of "the facts" I had witnessed with others while I was in training for my certifications. I was sure that the patients or clients were recounting a fantasy, something they had read somewhere, or something they had made up.

Cross-referencing of historical details would often substantiate clandestine information, much to my amazement and to the chagrin of the resolute naysayers. My clients would return from verifying details with their parents about traumatic childhood events that had been secreted; some exhumed deeply buried family secrets unintentionally. Others sourced hospital and adoption records for corroboration of what their hypnosis sessions brought forth. The facts became undeniable.

My first parlay into a past-life regression came about unexpectedly. Going into session, I had intended to work through the root causes of a free-floating anxiety that had appeared unexpectedly and without warning. What I could discern is that the episodes began approximately the same time I'd found a box of my mother's belongings that I'd stored away without opening several months after her passing. While I'd been able to identify an approximate beginning to the anxiety, I didn't know the underlying causes nor why my body was reacting as it was and found that the occurrences were really beginning to trouble me. The body does keep the score, as Bessel van der Kolk, MD says.

The anxiety manifested most predominantly when I was driving, which was another curious aspect for me. A therapist pointed out that I hadn't grieved my mother's passing (although I insisted I had) and, secondarily, suggested that I may still be harboring some anger and resentment toward her that I was now ready to process. I found myself agitated that Mom was, once again, creating chaos that I didn't fully understand.

The box had been stashed away six years earlier and contained various knickknacks and photos, some sheets of writing paper, a couple of old books, and nothing of any monetary value. I'd stored it away at a time when I was utterly exhausted from sorting out the details of her passing. I'd forgotten that I'd even kept the box.

Most of the contents were meaningless to me: pictures of people she'd known when she was younger, a sad, dark picture I'd scrawled as a youngster, and some odd handwritten notes. There were typed pages that were dated from the 1950s with teachings and references to numerology, which I found a bit surprising since she'd rarely spoken of the esoteric and routinely shamed me for practicing what she believed to be witchcraft.

Throughout several pages, she'd hand-calculated the name and birth year numbers for several other people and for me as well. From what I could determine, her pages were done sometime in the late 1980s. What startled me somewhat were the pictures she'd kept of my ex-husband and me. We were quite young when he and I had first gotten together; we were each other's teenage first love and had a tumultuous relationship replete with maladroit and unrealistic expectations, growing pains, and pseudo-adulting.

My father liked him, and they had been remarkably similar in retrospect. Within the context of patterns, we will subconsciously seek out those who are like our parents or initial caregivers for a multitude of reasons. We may ardently deny so initially and yet, in doing the honest, raw work of deep healing, candid exploration of the relationships we attract to subconsciously attempt to fix or heal within our Self can lead to remarkable insights.

The relationship I had with my first husband splintered on assumptions of youth and the shock that pervades boundaries when critically injured partners do not communicate as adults, are aware enough to seek out counseling, or truly grow together.

Both of our fathers mirrored each other, as did our mothers; neither of us had grown up with healthy parents or examples of happy marriages. Similarly, our grandparents were afflicted with alcoholism and toxic abuse, which was normalized in both our families. Such destructive behaviors were perceived as normal to us at that time.

Normal. All families were like ours, weren't they?

He and I subconsciously sought out the familiar, as we all do, a phenomenon that perpetuates itself through generations. We both knew how to navigate these illnesses.

His mother would take her depression and her despair to bed; mine would hide in her big tumbler of alcohol and romance novels. Both of our fathers were exquisitely angry in their own ways; both raged and externalized their emotions; both raised their children in a setting where love was conditional and had to be earned. No one ever discussed depression or mental illness or alcoholism or what a healthy negotiation of boundaries might have looked like because boundaries were nonexistent.

I had no recollection of the pictures, had previously disposed of the others I'd kept years earlier (burned them, in all transparency), and there had been no contact with him in over two decades. He'd hung up the phone that final day, telling me that the money he owed to me would, instead, be going to his new stepdaughter's college fund. I was destitute financially and in a place of transition out of the marriage and out of a business we'd had together. I hadn't landed, hadn't secured new employment, and was still somehow odd-jobbing my way through paying the bills. He wasn't paying support, nor had I requested any, and he had taken a well-paying job as a medic. The child was a toddler at the time, and he wasn't married to her mother. It was a course-correcting moment of awareness that came through for me: he'd promised to take care of his half of the debt we both owed, the debt that I was paying for both of us, so that we could divorce quickly and amicably. He had done so only briefly, and then he chose not to honor his word.

Why would I have believed he would? "There's nothing you can do," he'd mockingly said. His father was the Chief of Police, he had also reminded me.

We were "wounded children of deeply anguished people" is something I'd scrawled, freehanded, in my journals. His father was at the top of the totem pole in the police department then; so, no, I had supposed there was nothing left to do but move on and accept the final blow as fatal to whatever shred of a friendship we might have had. I moved away and began anew.

Not long before the box surfaced, he had begun tenaciously showing up in my dreams. Had he left or was he making plans to leave this physical plane? He said he had something to show me and to tell me about. The first few times I'd asked him why he was in my dreams he had refused to answer. "Evading; nothing new from you," I'd said to him. Also, each time he showed up initially, it became clearer to me that something in his lower back area or gastrointestinal area was problematic. When I mentioned the dreams to a friend who is an Empath and a Healer, she nodded and knit her brow together. She'd never met him, and I hadn't said much about him to her or anyone in my present circles. Before I could tell her where I'd sensed his disease was, she'd blurted, "Second chakra area, lower stomach. Cancer, perhaps?" She also added, "He may be seeking you out to provide you with an important message or to settle something karmic for himself."

As a child I would often get medical intuitive hits, and I learned early on that I knew, 100 percent of the time, the gender of unborn babies. Later, I was jarred by a number of real-time visions: a friend, living miles away, as he was committing suicide; a high school teacher having a heart attack that claimed his life while swimming; another friend that was on the verge of leaving the planet following a horrific motorcycle accident. Another friend as he was living through a single-engine plane crash. My grandmothers both understood when I shared these visions with them; there were no others I would share the information with. Oftentimes the scenes were too much for me to bear witness to, and eventually, it got to a point where I stopped tuning into those frequencies altogether.

Time knows no bounds; it is liminal. Why he was showing up for me so many years later with some obscure message and why I was encumbered with a medical intuitive diagnosis for him was baffling.

A quick internet scan showed he was still physically Earth-bound, and my network confirmed he was now living in California 2,600 miles away. I was due to fly out to Washington for clinical training the following month and toyed with the idea of taking a turnaround flight to drop in on him after my sessions ended. My schedule was packed; I had no real curiosity about how his life had evolved nor did I have a quantifiable reason to see him.

Are we obligated to help others? I believe we are; however, there is a point of contention as to where the obligations end and rescuing or advising without being asked begins. I've had patients and clients sit with me that I know are riddled with tumors and listen compassionately as they insist they cannot (read: won't) give up their poisons of choice.

"Are you okay if he dies?" my Empath friend asked. Considering the betrayal from years ago and the decades of silence that followed, I realized my feelings were indifferent. His presence in my dreams, persistent yet uninviting, didn't seem to plead for my help or advice. Each time he appeared, gesturing for me to follow and insisting on delivering vital information, he seemed amiable and harmless. Yet, despite his non-threatening demeanor, the trust he had broken long ago left a lasting wariness in me.

I let go of the idea of taking the extra day to stop by and see him in California. Instead, I asked for energetic healing assistance for him if he was open to receiving it. My hope was that we, he and I, could have that adult set of non-confrontational, current-day conversations, even on another level of frequencies, and be done with all the baggage and stories we'd created about each other so many years ago. Further, I was hopeful we might harmoniously complete our path work in this incarnation. Those people, our younger selves, were different versions of who we are today, and I hold no conscious resentment nor ill will toward him.

I'd done a great deal of therapeutic work around the relationship, around my tribe of origin, around the pervasive alcoholism and depression that ran rampant in our families during our time together, and while I might say I felt complete with him, I was questioning of the *samskaras*—the unconsciously held knots of stuck energy—that may still be lingering. It seemed there was a karmic subset of lessons that required elucidation.

There is no anger or sadness; there is no longing or tormenting curiosity. It, whatever "it" was, is done and dead. He is a stranger to me now.

Damaged Rudders

We cannot change our past. We can, however, change our response to how it shows up—and how we show up in response to our past—in our current reality. We can maintain our boundaries and our dignity. We can let those outdated iterations go and move on with grace. Yes, even if someone who used to be part of your life—perhaps for a long time—has resurfaced, wants back in, or otherwise intrudes on your present reality. You don't owe them anything. While your brain may believe you have made too much of an investment in time, energy, or money to stay away, cut your losses and move on. You do not have to let the abusive ex back in just because he or she had the realization that you were worth keeping. You do not have to hand your adult child who has failed to adult properly your keys or your credit cards any longer. You do not have to let that "best" friend from childhood say abusive things to you just because she always has.

Please pause for a moment when these lessons show up. The person you once were is no longer accessible to others in the way they might expect. As the adult you are now, you have the power to choose whether to stay or leave. See any encroachments or violations as signals, highlighting how much you've grown beyond your previous Self and, yes, hold your boundaries. Life's cycles, or samsaras, demand this level of commitment from us. You're being tested, and now you have the wisdom to make choices from your current state of growth.

When I found the box, I suspect its contents might have subconsciously stirred memories, emotions, or unresolved conflicts linked to my relationship with my mother, her passing, and elements of my own past that are connected to her. And it did. The inconsistency between my mother's teachings and what I found in her belongings also introduced cognitive dissonance that my mind might have been struggling to reconcile.

It's worth noting that trauma and emotional responses can often manifest in non-linear ways, sometimes triggered by seemingly innocuous objects, scents, or visual cues. The box, for me, served as a catalyst, awakening a host of feelings and reactions that I had not been consciously aware of. This phenomenon reflects the intricate workings of our brain, where sensory inputs can activate deeply embedded memories and emotions, a process underpinned by the brain's neuroplasticity.

When cogent dreams appear, I will typically go into some sort of retreat to do my own work through deep meditations, hypnotherapy, Nidra, and freewriting to better understand and connect with the messages from the Divine. This practice is grounded in the understanding that our thoughts and meditative states can physically alter our brain's structure and function, enhancing our mental resilience and capacity for emotional healing.

I always advise my clients to do the same. When we forget to step back and witness our own power, we can get swept away into places, energetically, that are less than healthy for us. Cognitive psychology suggests that maintaining an optimistic outlook and engaging with positive, life-affirming individuals can significantly influence our mental state, a testament to the power of emotional contagion.

You are more powerful than you know, and your thoughts do matter.

In my practice, I will often ask my groups to focus on controlling the speed of a fountain in my office during our mindfulness exercises. Once they move beyond the initial skepticism and embrace the process, they often find that they can conclusively influence the flow of the water. This exercise is a practical demonstration of the principle that everything is energy, and our thoughts and intentions can manifest in tangible ways, shaping our reality.

PRECOGNITIONS

Precognitive dreams are commonplace for many and used to be routine for me when I was young; quite a number of them, however, were foreboding, and I was ill-equipped to deal with the flood of emotions and feelings that came with them. My father understood but remained dismissive and aloof, since he, too, was riddled most of his life with precognitive dreams. My grandmothers were both well-versed in the esoteric yet were not always readily available. I always had pets, though, totems and guardians, which helped to offset much of my angst.

My father gave me a puppy when I was eleven. The gift was two-fold: I wanted a horse; he would absolutely not allow that (he'd been thrown as a child), and my beloved dog had died. He later told me that he had gifted me the puppy to appease "the horse thing" and alleviate his own anxieties regards to me being a preteen and a stubborn, introverted, empathic loner.

The dog, a miniature English bullterrier named Sam, was with me for seventeen years. He was my constant companion, my cohort, and my co-conspirator. He was the invisible playmate so many children can see and converse with. He was packaged into a dog body and gifted to me.

He went virtually everywhere with me during those years. I smuggled him into school, and we ended up in the principal's office more than once. He slept on my bed; we wandered together for miles in the desert, and we had our own unique language. I took him with me to the hospital where I volunteered, a half-mile from where he and I lived in my late teens, and he loved interacting with the patients as a therapy dog decades before there was such a title. He let me know when he preferred I not date someone, loved to snuggle, and got along well with all my other animals, with the exception of my giant rabbit. We moved many places together over the years, and even when dogs were not allowed to be residents, he was always welcomed. Well-mannered and quiet, he rarely barked and made friends with people and other animals quite easily. He was the consummate, clumsy, good-natured clown and was unique in many ways, from his egg-shaped head to his oversized ears. He was small enough to tuck neatly into small places, including my oversized duffle bag, and strong enough to easily snap a bovine femur or a 2x4 in half. He was a great dog.

Animals understand the world around us in ways and on levels so very far beyond our comprehension. Children seem to know this and allow them to communicate; adults, not so much until we are in a place of shifting paradigms. Sam was with me during some of the darkest times in my childhood and adolescent years, and looking back, I believe he was responsible for keeping me alive more times than I was consciously aware of then. He was hyperaware of multi-dimensional energies, would alert me to a phone or a doorbell that was about to ring, and always let me know of looming dangers, both seen and unseen.

When I was in my late teens, a friend brought a new boyfriend by to meet me one evening. We were all planning to go out together, and Sam, the love-everyone dog, wouldn't let them in or me out. This was a first for me. He had growled at potential dates, and when he did, I would decline going out; other times, he'd gone right up to strangers and insisted we meet. I knew to listen. Growling and barking like someone was hell-bent on attacking us, he blocked them from entering the house and planted himself squarely on my feet so I couldn't leave. My friend insisted Sam had "popped" and gone crazy as she had never seen him react that way over the years she had known him. I stayed home; Sam was fine as soon as they left.

The boyfriend was arrested for rape and attempted murder of another girl less than two weeks later.

On another occasion, I was having nightmares, and Sam went manic in the early hours of the morning. Only a few months out of high school, we were living alone in a small house in the middle of town. There was a four-way stoplight on the next block and an empty lot that separated the house from a busy thoroughfare that was a main artery through town. Sirens and street noises were commonplace, and I'd learned to shut them out.

Sam pounced on me to wake me and began dashing back and forth to the front door of the house, barking wildly and pawing at me to get my attention.

My chest and head were hurting terribly, things were blurry, and I felt sick. The more I attempted to calm Sam, the more he refused to mind. Peering through the peephole, I could see nothing, and as I started to open the door, Sam grew frenetic. He was insistent that I keep the door shut, growling at me (he never growled) and herding me away from the front room of the house.

Several minutes later, the squeals of tires, the sickening, unmistakable sound of vehicles colliding, car horns and alarms going off, and the screams of sirens filled the night as a multi-car versus motorcycle crash ensued at the intersection and to the front of the house. Part of the debris from the accident ended up in the lot next to my house, and the sirens and noises and cleanup lasted the rest of the night. One of my friends, the one on the motorcycle, perished in the crash. Thrown from his motorcycle, he had landed so forcefully that his chest had been crushed and his helmet had split open.

He had been the subject of my nightmares earlier that night.

THE PLUMMET

One of my Soul sisters, Miki Bryant, LPC-S, NCC, is someone who honors the work of unearthing our deepest memories and holding space for the matrix of what those memories might reveal and does so with empathy and compassion. We met while in training with the Wellness Institute and were instantly bonded as sisters. We both know that we've known each other across lifetimes, and we've helped each other achieve some extraordinary milestones in this one, from working through personal generational traumas to real-time, broad-scale healings for assemblages of people from all walks of life. Miki owns and operates the Soulflower Healing Arts Studio in Starkville, Mississippi.

The session Miki facilitated for me had begun calmly enough. While often resistant to hypnosis with various clinicians, I'm a curious patient and can drop into a deep meditative state quite easily when I feel safe. With Miki, I could freely go exploring during the initial parts of the session and provide her with intrinsic, traumatic, and sometimes maleficent details about scenes from my childhood. Since I had processed many of the passages repeatedly during earlier hypnosis work, I was no longer triggered nor bound by the reactions I'd experienced before and revisited them as they came up from a place of detachment. I trusted my clinician; I had survived those traumas; I had my adult Self within me, and I was safe.

During therapeutic hypnosis, we as clinicians will regress our patients to the beginning stages of the concern that may be triggering their current reactions. This may take place through various regressions within a single session or throughout multiple sessions.

In my case, I had begun experiencing anxiety that popped up inexplicably as near panic while I was driving. I love to drive, had not had anything like this happen before, and was not prone to having anxiety or panic attacks. A wave of lightheadedness would knock me out of balance, and I felt as if the breath was being choked out of me. Physically, I'm in great shape, and blood sugar imbalances, allergies, hormonal issues, etc. had all been ruled out. A colleague who is a physician was dismissive and noted that the episodes were intermittent and probably due to a severe lack of sleep or working through mealtimes and forgetting to feed myself. "You work long hours, always go-go-going. You'll get over it, it's no big deal," she'd blithely noted. The onset of these episodes coincided with the discovery of the long-forgotten box of my mother's belongings and the unwelcome intrusion of my ex into my dreams.

The feeling of being on the verge of blacking out while driving was a big deal for me, especially since I routinely drive the bridges here in Florida. I wanted to know what was triggering the episodes and knew there had to be deeper messages.

With this regression, everything gave way to darkness. Miki gently prodded me to breathe and work through the shock she noted I was exhibiting. I felt as if I was drowning and that something incredibly heavy was sitting squarely on my chest.

At the next moment, I was standing amidst a group of people in a dry, dusty area alongside a dirt road. Looking down at my dress, studying the potholes and rocks in the road, grimacing at my worn-out boots and the grime on my hands, I could feel the sweltering sun and the prickle of sweat on my skin. I sensed I was in my early twenties and that the people and I were moving across the country. There was a large, open-top, wooden wagon hitched to two draft horses about thirty feet from where I was standing; several other pack horses and mules were loaded with gear and grazing beyond the wagon. Miki asked me to look around and see if there was anything that could identify what year it was. A wooden crate on the ground near the wagon was lettered; the year was 1868.

The dress was long-sleeved, a mahogany-brown cotton print with small pink flowers. The air smelled of pine trees, dust, and acrid sweat. I wasn't feeling well, and the heat was causing me to want to vomit. The woman in front of me was angry; I recall watching over her shoulder.... There was a man that I felt intense love for adjusting the loads on the pack horses about a hundred feet away, and I sensed that he is my husband, Dan, in this incarnation. He was watching the scene unfold and was agitated by my sister's actions. I could not make out what he was saying, but I could see him very clearly and could feel his energy as if he were in the room, next to me, during the induction I was undergoing.

There was another man leaning against the clapboard wagon speaking with a woman. I could not identify the woman; the man at the wagon was clearly my ex-husband (energetically) from this lifetime. He casually glanced over, shaking his head disdainfully; he was chewing on something akin to wheat or a stalk of straw and had his hands tucked into the pockets of his jeans. I felt sadness and confusion toward the couple. The woman was rolling her eyes in my direction and stroking the man's arm.

The man with the horses was the father of a child I was carrying, and I felt a crushing wave of feelings come over me when I saw him during the induction.

The woman directly in front of me, whom I realized was my sister in that lifetime and whom I sensed energetically to be my mother in this incarnation, then shoved me quite hard because I wasn't listening to her, and she was furious.

We were near a ravine that led down to a river; the overgrowth of the brush had concealed how close we were actually standing. We'd been moving closer to the edge as I had backed away from her verbal assaults. She finally pushed me so forcefully that I stumbled backward; the loose ground and rocks gave way, and I went tumbling over the embankment. As I struggled to catch myself with my left arm, my shoulder dislocated, and my arm went limp. The fabric on my dress tangled briefly in the bushes; I realized my fall had been stopped briefly, and as the material and shrubbery gave way, I plummeted over the edge of the cliff. I knew I was four months pregnant; the folds of my dress had hidden the pregnancy and only the father of the baby knew I was pregnant.

The fall was surreal, in slow motion, and disturbing for me to watch and experience under induction. I knew I could swim; I didn't know this river. I knew the fall was a long way down, and there were areas of outcroppings, loose rocks, and brush. I also knew that the river was swollen with melting snow. I feared for the baby's life. I recalled seeing the woman, my then-sister, screaming down from the cliffs above and watching in astonishment as the man, my ex in this lifetime, stood there holding her back from the ledge. "There is nothing we can do. She's dead," he was saying as he led her away.

I was not physically dead at that point; she knew it, he did too, and he also knew that he could have attempted to somehow save me and willingly chose not to. There seemed to be no sense of remorse from either one of them.

As I hit the icy water, I had the momentary realization that I was still alive before getting caught up in the rush of the water washing over me. I glimpsed the man that I had felt the intense love for as he came to the edge of the ravine. Gasping for air, I surfaced briefly before the turbulence plunged my body under and plowed me into the rocks. I surfaced again much further downriver, and the back of my head and neck were in excruciating pain. The man was running alongside the cliffs as fast as he could and had tracked me downriver. At this point, I recognized that I was still alive in that incarnation but had taken a life-ending blow to the back of the head. My body was shivering almost uncontrollably during the induction.

Watching him was tragic for me. I could feel his panic, the depth of his anguish, and his sense of desperate urgency. He could not find a place to descend the cliffs and kept calling out to me, even after he knew I had died. The last memory I have of him in that lifetime was watching him fall to his knees at the top of the ravine, pounding the ground with his fists as my body disappeared within the rapids of the river. He watched me, and his unborn child, die in that lifetime and was devastated. I also knew he would not survive the rest of the trip we had been making with the others, though I do not know how he perished in that lifetime.

The event from 1868, although recalled under clinical hypnosis, produced real-time physical manifestations for me. My left arm was numb with little use of my hand for several hours afterward. Aggravated purple and crimson streaks spread from my elbow up and under my left arm and extended partway down and around the ribcage on my left side. There were what appeared to be deep scratch marks within the area, along with large, raised areas of welts. This rash, while blood-free and painless, appeared during the session and lasted for nearly a day afterward. Miki noted that she'd initially thought it was an adverse reaction, perhaps to soap or deodorant, which was being triggered by my fluctuating metabolic responses. Another clinician had joined us as I began recounting the fall, and both witnessed the colors appearing. I shared the disclosures with a group of therapists later that afternoon. The vocal skeptic of the group, a medical doctor, was absolutely confident that it was "simply an allergic reaction to something." Several of us know otherwise.

CHAPTER 10
ATTACHMENTS AND PINNACLES

Before we can make the shift to a more enriching life, we have to tame the ego or that part of us whose primary concern is the physical world.

—Wayne Dyer

In hypnotherapy, the hypnotic state allows for a bypass of the conscious mind and its defenses, including the ego and its constructed personas. This state leads to a less-defended ego, one not as tightly bound to a self-image crafted for external presentation. Characterized by heightened suggestibility and a form of thinking that's more primary and instinctive, this state facilitates a unique balance between receptivity and activity of the ego. Emotional learning is enhanced during phases of receptivity as well, while insights are often gained during active ego phases. This dynamic enables a deeper exploration and understanding of the Self, distinct from our usual conscious processing.

When someone is in a state of hypnosis, there is the potential of accessing the other 90 percent of the mind to discover, explore, and treat an underlying pattern, or to effectuate changes. Nevertheless, just being in the state of hypnosis and receiving suggestions does not resolve the deeper issues, nor does it address the activities or reasons behind the patterns. We're effectively running on "autopilot," and until we find out what program we're running on and do the necessary work to regulate the glitches, changes won't occur.

Ego activity involves decision-making, goal orientation, logical reasoning, and the maintenance of defenses, independent of external and internal pressures. Ego receptivity, on the other hand, is a state where control over internal experiences and critical judgment is relaxed, allowing unconscious and preconscious thoughts to surface. Additionally, there's a third mode, ego passivity, characterized by a sense of overwhelm or helplessness, where an individual may feel overpowered by their circumstances or internal states.

Many of us are quite conversant with the retreat into overwhelm and helplessness whether the withdrawal is voluntary or involuntary in nature.

I believe some of this overwhelm stems from a karmic place, one that can be explored through meditation, hypnosis, yoga such as iRest®, and the study of our personal history. Being cognate of this panic, or willing to take responsibility or ownership of it, is another matter. "Not my circus, not my monkeys" is a witticism often used by a friend—who is also on a potholed toll road of personal spiritual growth—in response to undue stressors.

She and I are trail mates: the same books appear for us at the same time, we have had paralleling life experiences, and we are both dealing with karmic compost heaps. Wherein I was demoted to the odd child out (and labeled '"morose, defiant, and difficult") place in the family constellation, my friend was relegated to the "pretty daughter" position ("marry well since you ain't so smart") in the family dynamic in her tribe of origin. She is, in fact, one of the potentially wiser women I have the privilege of knowing, albeit still comfortably stuck in her own compost heap of toxic behavioral patterns. My paternal grandmother used to quip that I, being openly connected to Source as I was as a child, "terrified my mother." How better to assail a child's sense of place in the world than to question their God-given gifts? This is another parallel. This friend has been a teacher and a mentor for me, and I do not believe our meeting in this lifetime was by chance.

In contrast, an attendee I worked with at Kripalu one summer, a professional woman with an advanced set of degrees, panicked during an open group therapy session and blurted, "My brain is broken! My horrible mother stresses me out with her chaos and unreasonable demands. All she does is demand things of me. She has broken my brain! I don't understand why I instantly react the way I do. Is it all my fault?" Of note, this participant has adult children of her own and is not her mother's daily caretaker. Clearly in overwhelm, it was unfathomable for this woman to accept that her mother's drama wasn't her daughter's circus.

After the group work, I asked her to explain the why of her "broken brain" statement, and she was at a loss. "I have an expensive education, a good job, a long-term therapist... and my mother still reduces me to a quivering mass of nothing... a scared little girl. She terrifies me."

MESSAGES AND LEARNING TO LISTEN

"Miss Laura, you be a witch?" one of the neighborhood boys asked as he stood outside the fence, fingering the leaves of a plumeria I'd propagated some years back.

Why, yes, I remember thinking. My mother often said I was. If seeing the glitter surrounding the growing and living things, having a ridiculously full yard of plants and trees and flowers in the middle of a city block, and feeding stray black cats makes me a witch, so be it. I love green, growing things. I have always had an affinity for animals.

"Ain't no other house here like you yard. I likes you yard," the little boy further stated. "You must be a witch to get it to grow like that. My momma say she scared of you cause you grows things so fast, and all the animals be happy to live in you yard."

The yard was definitely out of place in the neighborhood. People there have risen to the level of their training and do not hold higher expectations for themselves or their offspring. Patterns and ways of being beget continued ways of being.

Creator landed me there for some hard, hard lessons.

I believe it is our birthright to grow and evolve and to allow others and our world around us to do likewise. I maintain that it is our God-given directive to learn, to live, to be happy, to love, and to be a more evolved person when we leave this planet. Growth is distressing for many people though; watching others grow when you have no real desire or understanding of change can be worse. Why do people seek to thwart growth in others? Why do they block themselves? "I fully support your growth!" a loved one or a friend or a neighbor may say, and when you place a benchmark you are aiming for in front of them, they rebel, disrupt, or outright sabotage your attempts at growth.

What's really stopping you from embracing your own growth or celebrating the growth of others? The obstacles are often not external but deeply rooted in our own fears, insecurities, and limiting beliefs. Our subconscious may invent countless reasons to remain static, but these are mere illusions that mask a deeper truth: change, though unsettling, is the path to true fulfillment. Whether it's through traveling to distant lands to gain new perspectives or by taking local steps toward personal development, the journey toward growth is one we're all capable of embarking upon. You don't have to go far; sometimes, the most extraordinary transformations occur within the four walls of your home or the hidden corners of your mind. And yet, when you or someone else sets out on this transformative journey, resistance can manifest from those closest to you. This resistance is often not about you, but a reflection of their own struggles with change. Understanding this can be the key to compassionately navigating interpersonal dynamics as you evolve. So, again, what's really stopping you? The answer, more often than not, is an internal barrier waiting to be acknowledged, confronted, and ultimately, transcended.

I, for one, find that I am called to unusual parts of the planet when Big Lessons are waiting for me. The work I do abroad finds me, even when I'm without tangible financial resources at hand. When I left as a teen, I worked in Europe to pay my way, and I didn't know any better than to lie about my age to support myself. When I traveled to Peru, I did so as part of an archaeological team that traded room and board for work and a minor amount of pay. I funded several months in Italy and a nearly year-long stint in Korea the same way.

GOING ANYWAY

My father used to petrify me when I was a child. I would hide in my toybox as a small child to escape his wrath, and later, hide in my schoolwork. Many years would pass, and after the epiphany that only standing toe to toe with God can provide, he would embrace his Higher Power, and we would finish his incarnation as great friends.

As a child, I was sure he would kill me when he raged. Literally, not figuratively. He'd been in WWII, and I knew he'd been responsible for his duties as a ground pounder—a foot soldier—and returned stateside alive when most of his friends had not. It haunted him and us and made me wonder as a child if he, at some point, would go to that Someplace Else of shock or unconsciousness that he used to go and think me the enemy as well.

My mother used to control us with the scare tactic of giving my father The Great Big Heart Attack: if he were unsuccessful in killing me, I, in turn, would be the reason for the heart attack he would surely die from, as his father had done at the age of fifty-five. I'd made the connections in my teens prior to leaving for Europe, and one night, coming home from school much too late while waiting on another person to drive me home (coupled with miscommunications I had no intended hand in), my father exploded in anger and raised his hand to hit me. He had been drinking, and I could tell he was seeing-red angry and had gone into that Someplace Else. I blocked his arm and dodged him as he tried to grab me. My mother appeared as I hurriedly gathered a backpack full of clothes as my father stormed off somewhere. I'd blocked the scene from my conscious memory, and while colors and smells would sometimes bring bits of the scene back for me, I could not string together a narrative of what had happened. Years later, the entire memory in all its terror erupted for me while I was under hypnosis during a therapeutic session. The implicit became explicit for me.

It is said that lessons repeat themselves in cycles until we learn them. In yoga, we understand the cyclical nature of Life to be a series of learning and refinement. How do we know when we've completed a lesson satisfactorily?

When someone I believed I loved raged at me twenty years later in a way that I had suspected he might be capable of and had hoped never to witness firsthand, it was under very similar circumstances. He had been drinking. He decided something was my fault. While he didn't raise his hand to hit me, the words and the energies were more than I could handle. Emotional and verbal abuses are so much more damaging than many people understand.

When I removed myself from the environment, it was in much the same way emotionally as I did as a teen. This time, however, I left for Korea to work at a university there.

Moving to Korea was not my preferred choice. Asian women and I would often clash when it came to opinions and our place as females in the patriarchal schematic of family constellations. I do not believe, for example, that women should ever be or consider themselves subservient to men; many of the Asian women in my life at that time did. Further, I do not believe little boys are more special or important than little girls. Some Korean elders assured me that girls were often discarded.

Soul insisted I go, and it seemed nothing I could do would allow me to do otherwise. The constant stream of déjà vu moments and all-too-familiar people I met bewildered me. I was frustrated by the push from invisible forces and deeply saddened by my partner's refusal to go to counseling with me. The work took me across the planet, away from the toxicities that life in California had held. The miles to such a foreign place created a divide I needed at the time.

Alas, we all have our own pace on the path of life. I learned a great deal about myself living in Korea for most of that year. It was a laborious year of holding personal boundaries in the throes of pollution, overcrowded conditions, and unfamiliar customs. I learned many things I would also have preferred not to know. I learned that dogs are raised to be eaten in Korea and witnessed the carcasses being hung alongside other four-legged once-alive stock in the open air of the marketplaces. I learned that men are still considered superior, are to be treated as such, and are not to be touched, ever, not even casually in public. I learned that hitting a girl child in the face is acceptable as was allowing little boys to run amuck like wild, feral, animals. I learned that cigarettes are encouraged during meals. I learned that people burned trash that included plastic and bone on city sidewalks. Niceties? Elbowing someone to get through a crowd is also considered customary. Cleanliness? Rinsing hands, laundry, or dishes in icy water without soap is also commonplace.

Hangul, the language of Korea, still sounds angry to me and sounded hostile, demeaning, and filled with animosity when I heard it spoken then.

I also learned to trust my inner knowing and my own internal compass. I learned to navigate an exceptionally foreign land in a language I could not read or speak when there were no cellphones, and I went six weeks without seeing another English-speaking foreigner outside of the university. I learned about calmly holding my ground with a bipolar, narcissistic female supervisor and with those who insisted I eat meat to be accepted or polite. I learned that I could take care of myself in a hostile, pollution-filled environment even with a severe case of pneumonia. Most importantly, I learned that I could communicate through artwork, merriment, and creative play with the children when the supervisors were not around. I learned that being safe is a matter of perspective. I also learned that self-protection was more important than the money they were willing to pay me to continue to live and teach there. I learned to trust my inner compass when contamination and skyscrapers hid the sun. I learned to sit in silence safely and calmly with a bubble of protection around myself on crowded subways and buses.

PINNACLES

In leafing through the tattered pages of my mother's numerology notes all these years later, I'd found that she'd scribbled that year as the beginning of a pinnacle cycle on the back of the only page with my name on it.

In numerology, the pinnacles are said to be four long-term cycles on a person's life path, with each pinnacle representing a particular lesson a person is working on at any given time. The first pinnacle lasts from birth to between the ages of twenty-seven and thirty-five (calculated in numerology based upon a person's date of birth), the middle two pinnacles each last nine years, and the last pinnacle will stay with a person for the rest of their life.

These pinnacle cycles are thought to be especially important. Pinnacles reveal the general conditions and events you will experience during the period, describing the atmosphere or essential challenge you will be faced with. My mother had calculated that year, 1997, based on the date of my birth and had done so in the early 1980s. She and I had been estranged for some months before I left for Korea. "You're just like your father," she would quip. "And you hate him, right?" was always my rebuttal. She did; we both understood what she meant.

Our relationship was strained and tumultuous under most circumstances, and she believed I was wild and impetuous, discordant, asked too many questions, and belonged to another planet, parent, or time. Among other things, she considered me a tenacious, morose, albeit much-to-inquisitive little being that, in her words, had fallen off the turnip truck.

She also considered my forays into the esoteric to be reckless and bizarre, so it surprised me to find the pages she'd done on numerology.

CHAPTER 11
COMPULSORY LESSONS

There are no mistakes. The events we bring upon ourselves, no matter how unpleasant, are necessary in order to learn what we need to learn; whatever steps we take, they're necessary to reach the places we've chosen to go.

—Richard Bach

It has taken years of work to understand and unravel my connections to addictions. In retrospect, I realize that I had an abundance of unfinished work to do with my partner on the path of spiritual growth. While a multitude of promises were made, and I returned, the underpinnings of the relationship had not permanently changed as promised. Trauma bonds were present. We were both too stubborn, fear-based, headstrong, and entrenched in old pathways to do anything but stay with one another at the time. It was my house, too, I countered. The dogs were not only his; they were mine also. We could occupy the same space without real intimacy and did so for years—far longer than I consciously wanted. He never agreed with the wildness that is me, and I, in turn, wasn't comforted by his constant and consistent procrastinations nor his expertise in defensive tactics such as stonewalling.

I'm the first one in a group to take ownership of my mistakes, and no one here in Earth School is perfect. And yes, as the saying goes "if you spot it, you got it," whatever the "it" may be, from stubbornness to complacency. The difference is I am choosing to work on my growth, however agonizing, ugly, messy, disturbing, and treacherous that may be, and slog through the mud. As the saying goes "no mud, no lotus." We consider the lotus in some mythology to be a symbol of rebirth; personal growth is certainly that in many ways. Mud gets messy, nonetheless.

SIGNPOSTS

On good days, my husband was bright and cheerful and easy to talk with, and I considered him to be a friend. People love him; he's extraordinarily talented and always willing to help others at work. On the less-than-better days, we were platonic, quasi-amiable roommates. The elephant in the room, otherwise known as our marriage, continued to be avoided, and when it was nudged, I was the one with the issues. I honestly felt like I only got the leftovers or crumbs of his affection, energy, or attention. It seems that was all he had left for me at the end of most days, and that wasn't enough.

Friends would note that all marriages have rough patches, and people who had been married for more than a few years would offer unsolicited opinions ranging from separate vacations to leaving for good. One even insisted that if I felt that the crumbs—of affection, attention, and of understanding—were no longer acceptable, then I was to blame. In essence, I was more guilty than my husband was for allowing his behaviors to determine my responses.

Triggers vary from person to person. Most of us understand the reflex reactions we have to an unexpected sound or to something that otherwise startles us. Him opening yet another beer would surface old traumas for me. The sound of the tab popping was enough to trigger me physically, and frequently, it was as if I were being smacked in the chest. Sometimes my body would flinch as if someone had slammed a nearby door; other times, I would catch my breath sharply. He contested that I didn't have the same issue with other people; the fact was that I wasn't married to those other people, nor did I know their stories. He wasn't ready to understand this, however. I felt he had sat down on a rock on the side of his path and was steadfastly refusing to move.

Damaged Rudders

A woman I thought was a friend from childhood said I was weak. Another pointed out that my husband was a great guy who liked to drink "a few beers" to relax. "So what?" she'd said. "He helps to provide for the household, right?"

Providing for the household was not taking care of the marriage. Perhaps you, too, can relate to this.

Some people insist that everyone has an addiction, and he honestly didn't feel that he had a problem. That likewise panicked me. My mother had said the same thing to a nurse who was drawing blood in preparation for a major surgery. The nurse had eyed my mother knowingly, asked her if she had been drinking that morning, questioned what her daily alcohol consumption was, and went on to explain that, from a medical standpoint, they could not operate that day if she had been drinking. The nurse asked my mother if drinking had, maybe, just maybe, become a problem in her life. My mother emphatically stated that she didn't drink that much, drank "maybe occasionally" (mocking the nurse), and repeated several times that she felt fine. Her appearance was quite the contrary; her skin was sallow and jaundiced, her eyes were sunken, and her hands were shaking. I had taken a large mixed drink out of her hands that morning as I had arrived to take my mother to the hospital; she was livid and insisted there was "mostly only juice" in the quart-sized tumbler and refused to get into the car until she'd finished what was left. I interjected and told the nurse that we'd be rescheduling surgery and bit my lip to hold back the tears. My mother was enraged at me for the interference. "Well, I guess I'll just go back to work today since you've interfered again and made them cancel my surgery!" My mother spat the words at me and demanded I drop her off at work. She was employed part-time at a craft store; her friend worked there also and she, too, was in the habit of rescuing my mother.

A counselor at an Al-Anon meeting explained many things to me, including the more accurate definition of a functioning alcoholic, and things finally began making sense. Another asked if there were narcissists or covert narcissists in my family of origin. That question was the missing puzzle piece for me.

Further, I was trying to save the people I loved, and I was failing in my attempts at rescuing them . . . all while I was allowing myself to drown. I was, instead, enabling their behaviors. "Doing things for them because they are sick or tired or angry or unwilling is not helping them. In reality, it is giving them your permission to do more of the same, and it is hurting you," the counselor told me. While I had heard and read this before, her words finally hit home for me because I was ready. It dawned on me at that point that there is an exceptionally fine line between enabling and assisting, and between self-protection and self-sacrifice.

People will only hear you when they are ready; you cannot force them. Neither can we force anyone to heal.

People will only hear you when they are ready. This is where many of us, as caring, empathetic individuals, stumble when it comes to those we love, yet it is not our job to rescue others. To be there to support them through their journeys, yes, but not do their work for them. Our truer job is to respect the other person's journey.

People will only change their behaviors when and if they are ready to change and when they are in too much pain to do anything else. There is no "should change" that will work; it becomes a "must do," and it is their decision, not ours. We can never force another to be ready if they are not ready or willing. It is not our job, nor is it our right, to interfere with the journey they choose. We may feel that we know this; we, instead, reflexively respond to the contrary and wonder how we manage to keep repeating the same old, toxic patterns.

We will only change when *we* are ready. They will only change when and if *they* are ready.

We have to meet others where they are at, and we have to hold ourselves accountable for our own personal well-being.

My mother died from alcohol abuse, as did her younger brother and her mother. My mother would say, "It's [alcohol] that makes me happy; it's a treat for me. Your dad eats chocolate, you do whatever you do, and some of your siblings smoke. Why are you always F-ing hassling me?" I admit that I *was* always hassling her; I shed so many tears of frustration and sadness in my attempts to rescue her when her life wasn't mine to rescue. And no, I hadn't learned my lesson trying to save my younger brother through countless interventions and rounds of rehab a couple of years earlier.

You may have experienced this yourself with someone you love or something you feel you should change about them or yourself. Maybe it's body weight, smoking, drinking, spending, or eating habits.

Perhaps you feel deprived on some level, and when your special something is threatened or removed, you find that you become resentful and possibly even quite angry. Is there truth in that for you?

Circumstances will only change when the pain of your current "should" becomes unbearable; you can view the discomfort as pain or as necessary growth to a healthier you.

You are the only one that can make changes for you. You are responsible for you. No one can do it for you.

A therapist once told me to "get outside" more often with my bare feet against the Earth as much as possible—to go earthing—and to spend as much quiet, contemplative time alone as possible (some of the best advice when it comes to healing an overstimulated nervous system). She said I was in a state of shock, which at that time, I did not comprehend. The therapist I'd seen prior had insisted that I go on medication—yes, drugs, she'd noted, prescription medicines which truly scared me when I researched them—to control my complex post-traumatic stress disorder. She'd also noted that C-PTSD is a disorder that she was certain I'd have to live with for the rest of my life.

That advice had left me bewildered. Medication for the rest of my life? How could C-PTSD be a life-long sentence, and why would taking drugs possibly for that life sentence be a good idea? She also pointed out that I was extraordinarily broken, and simply unable—and perhaps would never be able—to gather the necessary strength to heal.

I was glad I rejected her well-intentioned bad advice and went looking for the person who prescribed the earthing.

You may also be at that same place of bewilderment, and that's okay. It's okay if you don't want to take drugs or don't understand what shock is, or if you still feel that your world is spinning out of control. The fact is that you are now becoming aware. The good news is that with awareness, change is imminent. This may also be a time of retreat for you as well, a time where you rest and gather your strength.

Please understand that it takes energy to heal.

Please know, also, that we are all a little broken.

I have always done what I can to avoid prescription medications. Going barefoot is something I still do as much as possible though, and it is the universal prescriptive advice all my students, clients, and patients get from me. Connecting with Pachamama, our Mother Earth, works wonders.

The same therapist who insisted on me "earthing" did provide some other solid advice. She patiently explained that marriage is the third entity: "you, your spouse, and the marriage." She helped me begin to see through the fog, and I finally acknowledged that the third entity was headed for hospice, and I was as much to blame as he was.

There was complicity within the complacency.

Those of us in committed relationships may know intrinsically that this third entity exists, yet how many of us forget or ignore that the third entity requires attention and nurturing beyond the day-to-day existence? "I didn't get married to have to put up with the constant yakety-yak-yakking from my wife about date nights and taking care of each other and leaving the kids with a sitter so we can be together," said one of my colleagues. "All she does is nag about things. Marriage, for me, was the last stop. When we agree on everything, things are great. She stopped agreeing." When I queried if he had stopped growing and was perhaps treating her with less enthusiasm than he showed to his other friends, he shrugged and said, "She agreed to get married." They divorced not long afterward.

Some claim that we teach others how to treat us. My contention is this: while we may teach them how we expect to be treated, I believe it is inevitable that those expectations will alter as we grow. We all grow at different rates into different versions of who we were before.

And as we grow, those who honestly love us will either grow, attempt to stay in a place of tenuous neutrality, or regress. There is no simple stasis; a relationship is a living entity that requires nurturing in order to survive.

From my perspective, I was living with a talented, handsome man who was in the process of a slow, ugly suicide. Further, we were enmeshed in a furtive sort of relational regression. How could we be otherwise? When he was angry, the alcohol was like kerosene on embers. He took my shocked, frozen silence as a confession of whatever stories he'd created; I was too stunned by his behaviors to explain my version of the stories I'd created in my mind about him, and I was completely immobilized with shock. I was on subconscious autopilot, fully in the place of survival based on what I knew.

Alcohol is a surreptitious, covert monster, and it was consuming him much like it had my mother and so many others I knew and had known. He was defensive when I told him I sadly believed beer to be his mistress. Why wouldn't he be? He staunchly defended the mistress, even as I explained that I felt my heart was breaking. My response was definitely my responsibility.

As Einstein said, "We cannot solve our problems with the same level of thinking that created them."

Accordingly, during that time, I became evermore hypervigilant and subconsciously engaged in blatantly codependent behaviors in a failing effort to keep the mistress at bay and keep the peace between the three of us. So I withdrew and began shutting down; I had reached a place where I was detached about so much, and still, I hated the mistress. Still more work to do, so back into counseling I went.

Hatred is among the lowest places, vibrationally and energetically, that we can be. I hated the mistress.

Like many others in my place, I often found myself with the refrigerator swung wide open, counting the beers: what was there, what was missing, looking behind things to find the ones I knew had been carefully stashed. I stopped drinking with him so he wouldn't have the additional permission or excuse of "you drink too" even though I sometimes enjoy a glass of wine in the evening hours. Caught up in a vicious cycle of work and school and attempting to rebound physically and financially also included doing everything I could not to upset the status quo. Within every habituated cycle, there is a reward or a payoff. The payoff for me at the time was a roof over my head, time with my pets, a routine that I was familiar with, and tidbits of attention when he was in that space of not hung-over and not quite drunk.

This, understandably, meant stuffing my feelings, which, in turn, caused a war within me. I wanted to maintain enough harmony to avoid confrontation during such a grim time. I was exhausted on every level.

Perhaps you have experienced this as well. I'm not talking about stonewalling here. I'm referring to how many of us squash intense feelings because we honestly don't have the tools, understanding, self-awareness, or wherewithal to appropriately handle them.

Stuffed feelings show up in many forms, and we often seek to numb the pain with too much of something else, such as work, sex, shopping, television, social media, food, or alcohol. My pain-numbing-too-much of choice became work and doing for others. I was always working, felt as if I were always cleaning up after someone else (because I was better at it or it was easier for me to do—yes, enabling), and then working some more. It hurt.

As Rumi said, "The cure for the pain is in the pain."

Damaged Rudders

Two of our dogs, with the combined weight and manners equivalent to that of a large, unruly teenager, conveniently began sleeping on the bed between us. I was frustrated with insomnia, and yet he was steadfast in allowing them to sleep on the bed. There was another wall of defense. The dogs provided a constant stream of distractions from the disappointments we both harbored. He was constantly and consistently tired and rarely, if ever, asked about my days, my work, or what project I was fleshing out. I grew weary of the myriad of excuses that hinged on his fatigue and found I was fretting incessantly about the state of his liver. Admittedly, I also felt shame about how angry the atmosphere seemed much more of the time. My mother's liver and heart had failed her at the age of sixty-eight; my brother went from owning a successful restaurant to divorced, destitute, and living on the streets before the age of forty. He didn't want to hear about those concerns either.

The collateral damage that alcohol abuse can inflict on those within a family constellation can be brutal, and as one of my clients has noted, the alcohol-fueled behaviors of those we care about can be a "daily battering ram" for our personal boundaries and well-being. It was for me.

John Gottman writes that there are four apocalyptic horsemen that kill a marriage: criticism, contempt, defensiveness, and stonewalling. All couples engage in versions of these types of behaviors at some point in their marriage, but for us, the four horsemen had taken up an earnest residence. Gottman's forty-plus years of research shows that the prolonged presence of these four factors in a relationship can be used to predict, with over 80 percent accuracy, which couples will eventually divorce. When attempts to repair the damage done by these horsemen are met with repeated rejection, Gottman says there is over a 90 percent chance the relationship will end in divorce. The handwriting seemed to be on the axiomatic wall. I wasn't sure why we were married at all.

In the past, I realized I would sometimes drink with him to have the comfort of his kinder side emerge, to feel something connecting us, and to feel less alone when I was with him. How can someone feel so alone in a marriage? I would wonder. And by alone, I mean lonely when with the other person.

Being alone and being lonely are two different states. As an introvert, albeit admittedly also a type-A personality, I require time away from the noise and chaos of television and traffic and the news and the trivial get-togethers to recharge. Most introverts wither if they do not have a healthy modicum of quiet, unstressed, alone time. In my perfect mornings, I am outdoors, in meditation, in the quiet time prior to sunrise, welcoming the beauty of life and another day.

GENERATIONAL MEMORIES

One therapist pointedly asked me if I liked my husband better when he was drinking. I didn't reply with words; my body gave away my real response, and the therapist patted my arm knowingly. "Think about how your body responded, and please give some thought as to why you are allowing this to continue," he said.

That was an epiphany of sorts and my first real introduction to somatic work, which has been a vital component of the work I do as a therapist.

For me, there were (and still are) generationally embedded memories and post-traumatic stresses associated with alcohol. To be clear, I don't take issue when people are enjoying alcohol responsibly, and many of my friends and colleagues are wine enthusiasts. I'm also vegan and have been since childhood; I would no sooner eat animal flesh than butcher one of my dogs. Do I sit down for meals with people who are carnivores? Yes, I do, and I can do so with detachment. One of my colleagues summed up my challenge with alcoholics and alcoholism this way: "Watching an alcoholic drink and being able to do nothing is like watching someone with lung cancer smoke, isn't it?"

People who don't have ancestral challenges around abuse and addictions don't always understand how these issues can seep through the generations or why certain behaviors elicit certain triggered responses.

The alcoholic gene, per se, wasn't mine to bear personally, and while I enjoy a bit occasionally, I can go months without even thinking about buying alcohol. It is simply not an issue. The same goes for various foods as well. I like fine dark chocolate; I know people who eat pounds of the stuff in secret. There have been times in the past when I have worked until I fell asleep at my desk, so yes, I have been labeled a recovering workaholic. Alcohol, however, has never been my poison of choice.

My siblings are another story. I had very troublesome alcohol-centric memories rooted in severe abuse associated with many people I considered family: my mother, my maternal grandmother, my grandfather, my step-grandfather, my father (who did get sober), and several of my younger siblings. An uncle died in his mid-forties from alcohol abuse; another relative committed suicide while intoxicated. I admitted a younger brother into rehab after driving all night to retrieve him only to have him transported by ambulance back into an emergency medical detox thirty-three days later. The last time I saw him in person, he was black-out drunk, hiding under a vehicle in my parent's garage. My mother had allowed him to stay with them "temporarily"; my father had called me out of desperation and asked for my help in having my brother re-admitted "far, far away" for treatment. "He's killing me by being here," my father had said. My father died less than six months later. My father's condition had worsened dramatically with my brother living there. My father's physical body was in its final days, and his depression had returned full force.

I nearly—quite literally—drove my car off a mountain road at twice the speed limit one afternoon, not long afterward. Unchecked depression can be a guileful, ruthless co-pilot, and it seemed the most straightforward solution at that time. From the outside, it looked to others like I was getting everything back together and really had nothing to worry about. Depression is terrifying in that regard. My thinking that afternoon wasn't muddled by a lack of sleep or alcohol or drugs. The Something snapped the wheel of my car out of my hands, and the car whipped back into the lane of traffic a hair's breadth from the guardrail. I told no one about that incident at that time—not my friends, not my family, not my therapist.

Most of my days leading up to my mother's passing were a blur of complete physical exhaustion and being in a hyper-vigilant state of autopilot, shock-related responses. The Something, the same Higher Power or Higher Self or other-worldly awareness that made its way through that afternoon a split-second before I went through the guardrail on a mountain road, suddenly began showing up more frequently in my quiet times. It showed up as coincidences: the hairs rising on my forearms, the sense of my shoulder being gently bumped so I would turn and face in a direction I hadn't been looking. Tingles and glitters of light and an absolute feeling of "do this, not that" started showing up. I began seeing the dances of lights around the plants again, took the shimmers as a sign from The Above, and dutifully planted clippings and seeds and propagated the yard until I had a veritable rainforest. Verdant and lush, it was a sure sign of abundance and magic, growth, and most importantly, Creation itself. I shared the bounty with as many neighbors as I could and felt my heart swell when the neighbors directly across the street asked for more so they, too, could share the wealth with their Church.

HOLDING BOUNDARIES

It is sometimes so much easier to go along to get along with others in your life for a multitude of safety-related reasons. Sometimes. Some may even claim it is easier to let them have their way, to think they are right, or to nod and smile even though you are furious. Avoiding confrontation may be the right thing to do in the moment; a matter of taking the high road. But is it? From the perspective of the autonomic nervous system and safety, this "intentional fawning," or taking a few deep breaths before replying, may also be the best course of action in response to danger.

Damaged Rudders

Acquiescing nonstop doesn't necessarily equal the best course of action for you in the long run, especially if those you are accommodating aren't at the same place in their journey as you are. It may likely cause you to wage a war borne of bitterness and resentment within yourself for not saying what you feel you must, and that will, I assure you, drain the very life force right out of almost anyone.

You have to hold your personal boundaries with love and compassion for yourself. Please don't allow someone to tell you who you are and what is best for you; you know what's best for you and where your heart is telling you that you must go. I also acknowledge that this is sometimes much easier to consider than to actually follow through with doing.

Do know this: there will always be a plethora of reasons why not, and they will be the first to levy that advice in your direction for (their interpretation of) your safety or betterment. Always. And there will likely be the brilliance of the opponent's argument that leads to a stalemate of who will pull the trigger first.

Please don't allow anyone or any circumstance to shame, cajole, or threaten you into submission as I did with so many at that dark time in my life. Allowing that to take place is a trauma-based response; I didn't know that at the time and mentions of the possibility of depression were dismissed as "you're stronger than all that; it's all in your head." Right. Instead, I withdrew into internal warfare, and my world fragmented into a place of "why bother anymore?" None of those in my immediate circle understood how dark my interior world had become, and I smothered my feelings, my emotions, my voice, and ultimately my life force until I nearly, quite literally, drove my car off a mountain road at twice the speed limit one afternoon. I never considered myself suicidal before that day. Depression became my present-tense place because it was repeated again and again and became a chemically based, naturally activated response for me.

DISPARITY

"It's not fair," they might counter as many did when I was blessed with some absolute Yes or an aspect of growth that would require travel or disruption of the situation at home. The discord at home, when I was a child and a young teen, was often staggering for me; some days were bristling with tension so thick that my body would react with hives and allergies. I blotted out the memories as many of us do, only to have them surface with full ferocity later. Thus, as an adult, I experienced a bigger bout of the same type of disparity: I wanted to grow, travel, learn, and experience. That wasn't happening. My body grew weak and sick; depression took hold and grew talons and was often staggering for me; some days were bristling with tension so thick it was palpable.

Why does anyone in any sort of definitely not-so-healthy relationship stay? There are layers and layers of memories and old patterns, creating automatic ways of responding. For many, there are valid, real-time reasons that are most assuredly not excuses, such as finances, contractual obligations, children, or even utter physical exhaustion, which precludes forward momentum.

Things may superficially appear to improve—and there may even be a modicum of peaceful coexistence—as those involved in the relationship make almost-promises and steadfastly avoid dealing with the elephant, also known as the relationship, which is rotting in the living room. We act and react the way we do because we survived by subconsciously employing those behaviors before.

Many had vilified me when I had admitted my brother that final time to in-patient medical detox and refused to allow him to come home with me afterward. "He has no place to stay; he is your brother; he is sick; you have room in your house." The arguments went on and on, and still, I held my ground; he was a toxic, belligerent, grown man who was consistently choosing not to heal. I was done rescuing him at my expense—emotionally, financially, and physically. He had hidden a small arsenal of guns within reach in every space he occupied; he openly threatened me and others with a gun he kept on his person. I could no longer force my will upon him to survive, and I couldn't save his life if he was intent on taking it. While I had the room in my house, I had no more room in my heart.

Some of us have weighty restraints that don't belong to us, so why do we haul them along with us for so long? "We're all born to be rescuers," one of my friends insists.

That doesn't leave much room for taking care of ourselves, though, does it? Nor does it allow another to have their own journey in this incarnation. I maintain that it is also not our right to interfere. Enabling and assisting are two different journeys.

Facilitating growth and merely sustaining existing conditions are distinct pathways in the therapeutic journey. While enabling might provide immediate relief or comfort, it often reinforces existing behavioral patterns that may be detrimental in the long run. It's akin to applying a bandage without ever treating the underlying wound; the symptoms might temporarily fade, yet the root cause remains unaddressed.

And sometimes debriding becomes absolutely, terrifyingly necessary.

On the other hand, assisting is about providing the tools, resources, and emotional space that empower an individual to confront, navigate, and ultimately transcend their challenges. This is not a short-term fix; it is a transformative process. It's like educating someone about the how of healing their own wounds—equipping them with the techniques and an understanding that will serve them in a more complete, holistic, and substantial way. This requires a much deeper level of engagement—and a multi-faceted willingness—to delve into complex emotions and thoughts and, most importantly, the breathtaking courage to make sustainable and truly meaningful changes.

In my work, the goal is always to assist rather than enable. Through a blend of experiential psychotherapy, trauma resolution, and yoga practices, the focus is on providing a holistic healing experience that fosters lasting transformation. We're not just aiming for surface-level improvement; we're nurturing an extraordinary internal shift that can ripple outward, positively affecting every facet of one's life. Whether you're a Gen Xer grappling with life transitions or someone seeking deep-rooted change, my absolute commitment—if you are doing your authentic, honest work—is to walk alongside you in this journey, equipping you with the skills and insights needed for long-lasting empowerment.

We each choose to stay in certain situations or in less-than-supportive environments at various crossroads in our lives for our own specific reasons and purposes. There is no shame in that; we're all doing what we can in order to survive under our unique set of circumstances, and I ask that you be gentle with yourself if you are in this place of liminal time. One of my clients noted that she had no savings or credit when she made the decision to leave her abusive marriage and stayed on long enough to procure both before leaving. Another patient said that she spent almost a year undoing things such as joint accounts, taxes, and property titles so she would not be without her own things when it came time for a divorce. "He is wicked and mean when he is mad—wants revenge for tiny infractions. Those things were mine before we married," she said. Her in-laws feel otherwise.

Those who have intimate knowledge might share in the suffering of the disturbing insights you already know to be true and may offer some tenuous degree of solace or advice. They, however, do not live in your life, in your skin, in your heart, in your house, in your bed next to the other parent of your children, or in your head.

Those peripheral to our unique situations simply have no true comprehension of what we, personally, are going through; there is no way for them to authentically know. How can they? They have their own dramas, either real or created, and they, in the end, may only hear every other word through a screen of their own preformed opinion, of what you are attempting to convey. And I don't believe, in the end, that our inside, personal business is really any of their business unless we choose to share.

Please understand that some of them are—and will continue to be—harshly opinionated, nonetheless.

There are those who will always be someone on the ready to salvo some compelling disagreement that may or may not include any combination of your selfishness, your lack of concern for the family, the kids, your parents, your responsibilities, the dogs, the work, the bills, the house, the routine, the length of time you may be away, or the money. The yard, the cats, neighbors, your Church, or any number of others who may require attention may also be included. Are you flattered when someone reprimands you for going away with friends or by yourself or on retreat for learning or growth purposes?

Ah yes, the great divide: What if something goes wrong / happens / transpires / erupts / fails / breaks down / needs to be paid while you are away? You know, the One Big Thing that only you can handle? Only you. Truly, only you.

They, from their perspective, will always be right. "What do you mean? You are leaving your cell phone at the front desk of the hotel? I have no idea where you are, where you'll be, or how to find you, even if I had a GPS tracker on you," a partner once said to me as I was going into a specialized training that presented quite a learning curve for me. As participants, we agreed to the necessary immersion that the training involved, and I went, with the understanding, that the trivialities and constant tick-tick-tick of the day-to-day life outside of the training would be handled by a responsible, supportive adult. "Even the president doesn't get to take a week out of life; people can always find him," he stated flatly. The same adult then launched into a diatribe of how errant the idea of a retreat was in the first place and buttoned up the conversation with how unfair my thinking was to continue to take classes that demanded so much of my time and attention when I teach classes myself.

Was that supportive? I didn't think so nor do I now. In retrospect, it was the proverbial last hole that sprung in the dam of the wall around that iteration of the relationship.

And lest we forget, some of those other responsible adults in your life, also sometimes known as family or friends, may claim you are the "lazy partner" for not demanding different behaviors from your significant other. "You have trained them to be that way; you made your own bed, and you are committed," they may say.

You know you never would have consciously chosen this path or this partner and certainly would have never condoned that sort of behavior for—or from—someone else. You know all of this madness you are currently in the midst of started as a tiny drip too. There was a snide remark justified as a joke or an unwelcome transgression into your personal business. Maybe he was out too late that one particular, pivotal, night and swearing he only had one drink when the credit card bills you continue to pay clearly indicate otherwise. Maybe you found that bag of pills or pornography or drugs or maybe you intercepted a call or some questionable mail inadvertently. Maybe you found bottles or cans hidden behind the recycle bin when your significant other claimed to have stopped drinking.

Within this miasma, you know in your heart that the situation you find yourself in currently is a pathetic degeneracy of sorts. Please understand that you are not the only responsible party for this corruption, and you are not, by any stretch, lazy.

Also, please know that you cannot demand another change their ways or their behaviors any more than someone can force you to change yours if you are not willing. The fact is that they may not even remember, consciously, that they spent all the money on drugs or drinking, remember what they said to you, or even recall getting home sometimes. Addicts literally go blank on those things because their own autopilot has taken over.

There will be those who openly accuse you of putting yourself first. So be it; own and embrace that, please. Being selfish, that of putting yourself above another when the other is in sincere need and taking care of yourself—self-care—are two entirely different paradigms. Being selfish is using others and succeeding at the expense of others in a calculatedly hurtful manner. Protecting yourself from an abuser or an abusive situation is self-love and self-protection.

You are the only one who knows what you need to do for yourself to take real, authentic, and compassionate care of You. That is self-care, not toxic selfishness.

I believe that personal growth, like self-care, is mandatory and non-negotiable. We are living, growing, evolving entities; we are not complete here as we are, and you are a different version of yourself now than you were ten years ago. You'll also be a different version of the *"You"* you will be ten years from now. I was, and am, taking care of myself in my quest to live my life, even when those around me launched situations into really uncomfortable straits, and I implore you to do the same for the sake of your own sanity. In the words of Mary Oliver, "This is your one precious life." For me, this passage is to be read *your* precious life. Yours.

And I ask you this: Why are you choosing not to live your life, to heal, and to get on with your growth? I challenge you to honestly explore your myriad of procrastinations for what they honestly are: fear.

At some point, we each reach that Descanso, the landing or break or trail marker that is the definitive point of no turning back, on the path of our Way Home. My hope for you is that you find it sooner rather than later.

CHAPTER 12
WALKING HOME

Never forget that every time we move onward, the whole of Humanity does so with us. Let us walk on into the life that is real, the one that is not limited to our own, nor to the time that we have in this incarnation; let us walk on into that infinite space where everything becomes possible. In the life that is "real," we have unlimited access to a great universal power. Once we become aware of what this "real" life is, we are holding the key that gives access to all the answers we are looking for, as well as to happiness.

—Christian Bernard

A favorite dictum—*"Solvitur ambulando"*—it is solved by walking (attributed to St. Augustine) reappeared for me, and I sought new, safe, quiet places to walk, most always barefoot so that I could connect with my Something without interference. I went back to Al-Anon as I had done as a teenager. Boundaries became stronger and I began to flourish; my will to survive and thrive was returning.

I once trusted the Universe implicitly as I was blissfully free-falling into incredible new adventures. I always believed that the net would appear, or I would sprout wings, or there would be a big fat down-filled mattress placed exactly where I'd splat. I trusted. I had faith.

Then the final blows: it was openly declared that that sort of thinking and those days are illusory. I was reminded that I was failed miserably by Source and several of those in the sphere of influence began snarking, "All that education and travel and experience ... and for what? Your world exploded and here you are in a really fucked up place in life." My faith had shattered along with so many other things. People were vocal; I allowed caustic words to undermine my purpose. I began to doubt.

UPRISINGS AND ERUPTIONS

This time was, and on some levels, still is, the phoenix of me, the person of all those years ago, the sum of my youth that went without emotional nourishment. The wild mustang, the child of the people of the horse, I am the great-granddaughter of the Princess, she who was a daughter of Cherokee Chief White Horse. They are part of Me.

The lineage: the shamanic liminal time-walkers, peacekeepers, and healers. The witches and medicine people who were burned at the stake. They, too, are part of Me. And I am part of you; we are all connected, and we are all one.

Relationships of any sort require participation. A healthy relationship is one where co-creation takes place, where lives intertwine, and each person is part of the other's growth in a way that is supportive and genuine, caring, and gentle. We can be friendly with someone without being friends; there is a difference. Perhaps this is where some of us fail to comprehend healthy boundaries: just because someone is being friendly doesn't mean they have your best interest at heart. A true friend does; you matter, you are important, and you are cherished for the incredible, unique and wonderful person you are.

When nothing more than the mundane or pedestrian may be discussed without melodramatic eruptions or when verbal daggers, obliquely abusive behaviors, or outright stonewalling from someone else is all one gets, change must occur. That is not friendship or love, it is manipulation. Slowly the fog begins lifting, and we realize that going along to get along is no longer an option. We are healing; our resilience is better. "How did this happen?" we muse. "This isn't what I wanted!" we insist. The world around us is reflecting the fight-fight-fight that saved our very lives as children. We're repeating old patterns because that is all we know... until we begin waking up and doing the work of healing. The crazy-making and gaslighting may ensue; we've changed, they insist. Things around us begin to erode.

They don't like it—the way we're standing up for ourselves, questioning old standards, asking new questions, and expecting loving treatment and solid answers. Instead, they hastily let us know. They don't like the fact that they no longer get to treat us as they once did. We've outgrown that response, we've outgrown the disingenuous shadow side that was once a protective cape, and we've outgrown those who seek to hold us down or back or under.

Change is no longer an option; it is a necessity on the path of our development, and change must begin within us.

In the words of Matt Kahn, we deserve more love, not less. We all do. People do. Animals do. The planet, sum total, does. Why do we feel that we do not or feel that we are not worthy?

Maybe you've been hiding from yourself out of fear. I was. Fear had calcified around my heart and showed up as depression and severe breath-stealing illnesses, such as pneumonia. I was hiding toxic, virulent tribe-of-origin truths from myself that needed to be brought into the light to heal so that the real me could flourish and grow. There were things I needed to be done with and move on from and family secrets I'd kept buried deep within my subconscious that manifested as self-sabotaging behaviors.

Toxic relationships can manifest for us this way. The covert passive-aggressive narcissism demonstrated by those who profess to do things because they "love" us can wound us in ways that others cannot see—and yes, our bodies rebel and will remind us otherwise. Further, those around us may diminish or seek to invalidate our feelings or emotions regarding the abuse and the abuser, which, in turn, wreaks more havoc for us internally.

Just because someone cannot see your wounds does not mean that they do not exist. You do not deserve to be diminished, belittled, talked down to, or mistreated. That is not love; that is abuse.

I took a devastating and life-altering fall financially for things that had happened that I did not consciously nor intentionally cause. From there, I fell gravely ill physically. Likewise, I was still firmly wedged on the triangle of victim, rescuer, and persecutor. I willingly set about rescuing people who refused to care for themselves, and I internalized my role of the victim in doing so. There were people I trusted who betrayed me as a colleague, and I wanted them persecuted but failed to follow through with having them arrested. There were greedy, addicted family members that were getting away with heinous acts because, somewhere in my programming, I was trained to "take care of them" because they "needed it" more than I did. So I continued to do so until I literally had nothing left to give. There were so many, many lessons and the more "done" I became with taking responsibility for the actions of others, the more I became the accused. People rebelled; relationships fragmented. There were many days I felt the Universe was genuinely spiteful. I had to let go, and maybe you will find that it is best if you do that for your sanity as well.

Sometimes we feel we must be right or we think we cannot be happy. Sometimes we do have to prove—to ourselves—that we are happy and right with that alone.

Sometimes we do truly have to maintain grueling boundaries to save ourselves. This is an absolute requirement if we have been the target of an abuser.

Here's what we must remember: We can do everything someone thinks they want us to do, satisfy their every whim, answer every question, and address every desire. And in the end, they can, and may likely, change their mind.

It is our job to take care of ourselves. While another person may be a part of your life, they are just that—a *part*. You and the other person are separate individuals. This can be difficult to discern if we're entrenched in a codependent or abusive relationship. We each are separate people with separate lives who choose continually—not just once—to share parts of our lives with each other. Whether this other person is a spouse or a partner or a child or a friend or a family member, this person is still a separate being from you. It is your life; they have theirs. They are in charge of their life and theirs alone; they are not in charge of yours, nor do they have an absolute say over what you want out of life. They do not have the right to tell you what to think, how to act, how to feel, or how to behave. They do not have the right to keep you from your friends, from your family, or from your growth. They do not have the right to extinguish your light.

But what do we allow those who abuse us to do when things aren't so healthy? Deeper still, I ask you to ponder the why. The why does go so much deeper than simple ties of marriage or partnership or the family unit.

We have met, the Great Creator and me, toe to toe. The breath and the consciousness knocked out of me each time. That Something that appeared at the split second before the final Earth-bound checkout that snapped me right back had no longer been the stranger it once was.

I got the message, and the message became a warning. As author Gregg Braden counsels, "The world is a powerful (and often literal) mirror, one that isn't always easy to face. With complete honesty, life gives us a direct window into the ultimate reality of our beliefs."

A petite, discarded dog was a window for me. I share this story to illuminate the metaphorical significance of the interaction of the Divine in our lives when and where we sometimes least expect to find the answers.

THE LITTLEST MONKEY

It was a government holiday Monday, and I'd just gotten home from running errands and training at the gym. Dan, my husband, was outside of the front fence, squatting down, patting the sidewalk with one hand and gesturing at something across the street. A wiry little dog, approximately a third of the size of our other two dogs, was barking furiously and darting back and forth across the asphalt. She was dragging a leash behind her as I approached the house and skittered past me into the neighbor's yard, barking wildly, growling intermittently, and showing her teeth. Dan noted that she'd been doing this for most of the time I had been gone, and even though he had attempted to ply her with treats, he was unable to get close enough to take hold of her lead. She was curious about me and zoomed up to sniff my running shoes. The tone of her barking changed slightly, and she tiptoed just close enough for me to step on the leash. A short tug and she promptly backed herself out of the collar.

Off she darted again across the street, scrabbling through trash someone had left on the ground, while keeping a wary eye on us. We left the driveway gate open, continued to offer her treats, and patiently waited. She slunk in a few minutes later, a quivering, starving, dirty, bony, little barking beast.

Once in the yard, she gingerly ate out of our hands and allowed her back to be petted a tiny moment at a time. Oddly, her two lower ribs protruded and turned up and out in a strange way, as if someone had broken them or as if she had been tied so tightly around her midsection as a puppy that the ribs had grown into a sort of malformed hook on each side of her diminutive body. I surmised she might have been originally destined to be a bait dog given her stature, and a round of unexpected tears welled up for me. The leash looked as if it had been used as a tie-out; the collar was two inches too big and had been crudely lashed together. There were license tags on the collar, which seemed contradictory. In calling the number on her tags, the staff informed me that she was currently licensed, microchipped, and was someone's dog. While the pet tracking entity gave me her name, Chica, and told me she was two years old, they refused further information because of privacy laws. They promised to contact the owners with my information and call me back. The licensing entity, the Humane Society, was closed for the holidays.

Chica, whose name means girl in Spanish, calmed down after she was in the yard for an hour or so. She was famished and ate more than any dog I'd known that day; I was astounded that her tiny little body could hold as much as she was eating. She let me pick her up, and I found that she understood some basic commands in Spanish. She seemed friendly enough; her appearance indicated neglect while several of her behaviors, such as sitting before being fed and jumping right up onto the sofa, suggested she had been an indoor dog. We managed to keep the dogs separated via baby gates, a rather monumental task given the curiosity, intelligence, and play-seeking co-conspiratorship of our other two pittie rescues whom we referred to as Velociraptors. She was quiet after she ate, was already crate-trained, and was good while camping overnight in the extra dog crate in the front room.

The next day I made the same round of calls again. This time the Humane Society explained that "Lady Chica" was two years old, had been adopted there a year prior, and gave me the owner's information and backup contact numbers since their records were public information. The Humane Society workers were incredibly kind and provided references for a new veterinarian and counseling regarding how to integrate her best if she were to become a permanent family member. They said they would also call the owners, send a round of emails, and mail the owners a letter.

We drove to the address on her license after not getting any return calls. The house had no fenced yard and was located adjacent to a busy, four-way intersection. Chica had covered at least five miles and crossed several busy intersections dragging that leash to end up in front of our house. Why? The boyfriend of the owner, who was the alternate number listed, answered the third time I called. Apparently, I had roused him from a sound sleep in the early afternoon. He told me they now lived four hours away, that the girlfriend/owner "had her a new doggy," that the roommate was an asshole and had turned Chica loose. He also told me to take Chica to the shelter if I "ain't got no place or use for her."

He said he could not even afford a carburetor for his car. "Besides," he drawled, "we be havin' way too many dogs now anyways," he said. I felt my skin reacting as I overheard children crying and screaming in the background.

Chica had, evidently, been abandoned and turned out to fend for herself. The weave of the connecting threads, parallelisms, and what the world was doing its best to show me (and a multitude of others) through her presence continues to surprise me.

Chica is a pocket-sized pit bull, and pitties don't last long in the shelters here. They don't last in shelters anywhere, really. Only one in six hundred pitties nationwide stands a chance of finding a forever home as it is.

It is estimated that there are 3-5 million pit bulls in the US. The term "Pit Bull" is nebulous and primarily encompasses three breeds of dog: the American Pit Bull Terrier, the American Staffordshire Terrier, and the Staffordshire Bull Terrier. Considered a "bully breed" and subject to breed-specific legislation (BSL), they are by far the most euthanized breed. Studies estimate that 2,800 pits are euthanized each day; that's a staggering 1 million dogs that are put down each year.

Debates rage over the validity of accusations made against these dogs. Did you know that pit bulls were the original Nanny Dogs? Petey from the Our Gang series, and Sergeant Stubby, a World War 1 super-dog who served eighteen months and took part in seventeen battles, are classic examples of how great the breed is.

They are misunderstood, mistreated, and often cruelly maimed, mishandled, and horribly misguided by those who are supposed to be their caretakers ... just as some children of abuse are.

People who treat dogs this way also procreate. Thus, I pose this question: why would these types of miscreants treat a baby human any differently than a puppy? I've seen countless toddlers, some still in diapers, wandering the streets of the Southside in Saint Petersburg without an adult in sight. I've heard children wailing late into the night as adults shouted obscenities at them. I've witnessed children and adults physically hitting and kicking "their" dogs. A few days ago, a young teenager was dragging a puppy who was tethered by the neck to a fifty-pound weight plate down the middle of the street. When I asked him to remove the weight and change the knotting on the lead, he shot back that he was teaching her to be tough, like his daddy told him to. The rope had a cinch knot at the dog's neck, and the animal was clearly suffocating as the weight plate outweighed the puppy by well over half the dog's weight. I was able to calmly explain why what he was doing was wrong and hurtful; thankfully, he listened, understood, and complied.

Pit bulls and pit bull mixes average about 33 percent of shelter intakes nationally, and in large cities, the numbers are estimated to be as high as 40-65 percent. About 75 percent of municipal shelters euthanize pit bulls immediately upon intake, without giving them any real chance at adoption. And those that are available for adoption are usually the first chosen for euthanasia when overcrowding forces decisions: a study by the organization Animal People reports a 93 percent euthanasia rate for pit bulls.

People also breed pitties to fight; it's big business in some places where I have lived. People haphazardly crop their ears; they starve them; they beat them. They use the smaller, weaker dogs as bait dogs to entice them to fight.

These same people live, vote, drive, and produce offspring among us.

My beloved friend Neely Bryan, the consummate "Dog Mom" and founder of the nonprofit Neely's Ark, has made it her mission to save as many of these dogs as possible, and she does so passionately and from her heart. She can often be found walking several of the chained pitties in the area where she lives and has indeed found her calling with dogs and children. "Dogs are my life," she says.

She has used her love of animals to reach out and teach children. "As we care for animals together, the children and I are constantly discussing personal growth and evolution. We talk about breaking cycles, being the change, becoming leaders rather than followers, the importance of good grades, kindness, making eye contact, being in the present moment instead of being glued to a phone, gratitude, and everything under the sun that will help us grow into the most loving, compassionate, light-shining beings possible," says Neely.

Neely, her husband, Cole, and her beloved rescue pittie, Bronx, moved to her husband's hometown, West Point, Mississippi, from New York in 2017. Neely found Bronx, whom she refers to as her "child in dog's clothing," tied to a fence and abandoned before she and Cole left New York.

Within a week of moving to Mississippi, she had found two pit bulls chained in a yard and, being the compassionate soul and dog mom that she is, asked the family if she could walk them. Walking these dogs became an avenue for Neely to meet many children who have since become family.

The children are also learning about animal love and compassion. "Not only do we care for animals together, we also discuss how the treatment of animals is a reflection of how we treat humans," Neely says.

"The greatness of a nation and its moral progress can be judged by the way its animals are treated," taught Gandhi; it's a mantra Neely uses daily. Neely is now the director of a no-kill shelter and had a part in saving and rehoming over seven hundred dogs this past year.

THE PLIGHT OF THE PITTIES

What makes pitties such excellent family pets can also make them quite fierce as fighting dogs: their determination, their stamina, their devotion, their loyalty, and their sense of duty.

Children also inherently have these traits.

In her autobiography, *The Story of My Life* (1903), Helen Keller wrote: "Whenever it is possible, my dog accompanies me on a walk or ride or sail. I have had many dog friends—huge mastiffs, soft-eyed spaniels, wood-wise setters, and honest, homely bull terriers. At present, the lord of my affections is one of these bull terriers. He has a long pedigree, a crooked tail, and the drollest "Phiz" in dogdom. My dog friends seem to understand my limitations, and always keep close beside me when I am alone. I love their affectionate ways and the eloquent wag of their tails."

During World Wars I and II, pit bulls were so loved that they were used in advertising as a national mascot. They represented protection and fearlessness and, in some early ads, neutrality as well.

It wasn't until the 1980s that things began to change for the pitties. Hollywood, Florida, was the first city on record to pass a breed-specific law (BSL), and in 1987, *Time Magazine* ran a hostile, disparaging cover story entitled "The Pit Bull Friend and Killer," which further fueled the public fears. Unfortunately, the negative stereotype for pitties has been maintained by sordid characters, such as football player Michael Vick, who have inbred and overbred them for use as fighting dogs. Another problem is that they are the most reported on of any breed involved in domestic disputes. This is not surprising to those of us who have lived in drug-infested and/or poverty-ridden areas where dog fighting is a wagered sport.

What many people do not understand is that pitties also consistently outrank most other breeds in positive traits. According to the American Temperament Test Society, pitties are among the most tolerant and least aggressive of all dog breeds, outranking Golden Retrievers, Boxers, and Collies. Thankfully, pitties are now gaining more positive recognition as search and rescue dogs, therapy dogs, and K9 police dogs.

Dan, though an amazing Dog Dad, was initially resistant as he felt we didn't have room for another dog. The other two dogs were three times her size, had been siblings and rowdy playmates for several years, and had well-established territories and routines. He wagered that our small house was already too full; that she was more feral, more needy, required more of this or more of that, he'd said. While I wasn't sure about how to keep her, I did know that she showed up in front of our house on that day at that time for a reason.

Chica spent the first month with us doing her level best to escape. I could easily and comfortably pick her up; she was wary of open hands coming at her from strangers as if she was afraid of being hit. I would sometimes tear up as I watched her react because she reminded me of so many of the traumatized people I had come to know and love over the years who were dysregulated and constantly on high alert. She nipped at having her head stroked by those she didn't know and gave a defensive growl (with her ears firmly pinned back) about having her paws touched. She wanted affection and was also dodgy, elusive, and independent—again, so much like so many of the people were when they first came to see me in my private practice. A remarkable storm barometer more accurate than the local weather channel, she would begin making monkey-like noises and shaking almost uncontrollably when the sky clouded over in certain ways.

Other times, we would find her tucked into places impossible for us to access, such as under the dresser or behind the washing machine, as if she were looking for a secret escape. She knew her name and would come when called. She responded to basic commands in Spanish, which was apparently her primary language.

She had to be kept separate from the other two dogs as she gave signs of bristling fur, diverted eyes, and low-voiced grumbles that they were troubling her. They wanted to play; she refused. How often do we do that as traumatized people? Play is no longer a safe place for us, and play is a necessity.

She dug under the fences; she moved objects that were virtually immovable to find a way out, and she seemed to levitate to scale areas and things, including tall baby gates that neither of the other dogs could. While she was initially happy about being crated in her own den at night, she abruptly changed her mind one thunderous morning and broke the metal bars of the big dog crate (and snapped the solid plastic crate bottom) in her efforts to escape.

At a tad over twenty pounds, she was also able to break a solid wood, half-inch fence board from the bottom, against the grain, just minutes before a heavy rainstorm. The fence had been dog-fortified around the entire perimeter, and the tiniest of crawl spaces small enough for her to wiggle through were blocked. She'd been able to see a tiny sliver of a world—beyond and outside—between those fence boards. It still astonishes me that she was able to break a solid board against the grain at that angle. I couldn't do it under normal circumstances, and I'm quite strong.

The area around the house is densely populated and brimming with drug abusers; people drive fast and recklessly, ignore the stop signs and, as I have gravely witnessed, intentionally aim their vehicles at animals. I thought she was gone for good.

Gregg Braden's words echoed in my head: "The world is a mirror," as I realized she had escaped through the hole she had made, and I wondered how badly she had injured herself in her efforts at escape. The world was not safe in any way for her, even with someone doing all they could to provide a haven. People who have been abused and who have been traumatized live in that very same place of unsafe: their body, the world, everyone and everything else, people who want to help—all are considered a threat. I have heard those who have no real understanding of the impact of trauma say that the subconscious death urge is taking over.

What would most other people do? "If she goes, she's not meant to stay," a neighbor had said. The message had gotten through to me; I'd heard it said to me at various times in my life in a way that had threatened my already-tenuous safety. "If you want to go, go."

What we all want is a safe haven, a place in a protective pack, and a loving family.

It was in the middle of a busy workday for me, and important deadlines were looming; I had appointments to keep, and hours of computer work to complete. Instead, I got into the car and drove several blocks to find her. In doing so, I felt the wash of awareness come over me. I, too, wanted to keep going; to go and go and go away from where I was in my head at the time. I wanted to be done with the frustrations of feeling blocked at every turn, of having less freedom and more entities to answer to than I preferred. Of having large entities in the form of city governing bodies and officials come at me and being caged by the neighborhood that wasn't feeling like a safe and predictable homebase. I winced at the weight of worry that had tied itself into knots of pain in my shoulders and neck, recoiled from the feelings of wanting to play with abandon but not wanting to play with those who were currently in my world. Every attempt at personal freedom seemed thwarted, and while I primarily worked my preferred schedule, the feelings of being fenced in and having my schedule questioned, examined, or critiqued were grossly oppressive on some days. Where was this stemming from? Ah, yes, I knew in my heart. Have you experienced this and perhaps had the retaliatory remarks flare from yourself or from others of "Oh, you just want to run away?" And maybe you do feel that way. We all do from time to time. A dear friend who obtained her Compostela after her five-hundred-mile Camino de Santiago quipped, "I'd give anything just to run away right now.... There is too much noise, and I don't have the tolerance anymore." My tolerance was shot at that point as well.

A Compostela is a certificate of completion given to pilgrims who have walked the Camino de Santiago and have covered at least the last 100 kilometers on foot or horseback, or the last 200 kilometers by bicycle. This document, issued by the Pilgrim's Office in Santiago de Compostela, Spain, serves as proof of the pilgrimage and is traditionally given to those who state a religious or spiritual motivation for undertaking the journey.

The journey of the Camino, though, is ultimately about self-discovery, spiritual awakening, and the transformative power of resilience. Many individuals embark on this pilgrimage at major turning points in their lives, seeking not only physical travel but also a phenomenal inner journey of understanding and growth. It is a journey where resilience in the face of chaos, both internal and external, becomes a guiding force, reminding us of our inner strength as we navigate the unpredictable twists and turns of the Camino and life itself. It was time for a Camino for me.

What I yearned for was to discover the joy and serene clarity of effortlessly flowing through time, being both productive and contributive while experiencing personal growth. This aspiration came with its challenges then, especially as I balanced my work alongside Western medical practitioners, clients seeking quick-fix solutions, and the complexities of navigating different facets of my professional life.

In the past, amidst chaos, I found my own peace. I yearned for this serenity to become a constant in my life, not just an occasional retreat. The challenge was to discover the steps necessary to integrate this continual calm into my everyday existence again.

While one person may claim that it's easy enough to "not take that shit personally," another who is empathic and has let their guard down knows exactly what I mean. We Empaths are individuals who possess an extraordinary capacity for deep emotional understanding and connection with others. It's not just about feeling sympathy or empathy; it's about absorbing the emotions of those around us like a sponge.

Empaths often find themselves caught in a delicate balancing act between the desire to help and the need to protect their own emotional well-being. When we let our guard down and fully embrace our empathic nature, we become like emotional conduits, open to the joys and pains of the world. We feel the highs and lows of others as if they were our own.

This heightened sensitivity can be both a blessing and a burden. It allows us to offer tremendous support and compassion to those in need, but it can also leave us emotionally drained and completely vulnerable. We become acutely attuned to the energies and emotions in our environment, making it challenging to maintain healthy boundaries and preserve our own emotional equilibrium.

For Empaths, the act of "not taking things personally" is more than just a saying; it's an ongoing daily practice. We must navigate the intricate web of emotions that surround us, discerning which emotions are truly our own and which belong to others. It's a journey of self-discovery and self-care, where we learn to protect our own emotional well-being while still extending our empathic hand to those in need.

As Empaths, our constant emotional engagement can sometimes leave us feeling overspent, like a battery that has given all its energy to power the world's emotions. In these moments of emotional exhaustion, our overstimulated nervous systems can sometimes interfere with the messages our bodies are trying to convey, including the origins of pain, reflexes, and reactions.

Signs from our Higher Self, our body, and from the Universe manifest in various shapes and forms, akin to golden breadcrumbs along our life's path. However, the challenge arises when we become so inundated by the constant noise within our minds and the distractions in our external world that we often overlook or fail to acknowledge these messages.

Chica entered my life during a phase when my own journey had turned "awkwardly disruptive." It was a period marked by an intuitive nudge, a figurative smack on the back of the head, prompting me to seriously start planning my first Camino. This planning, undertaken quietly amidst the chaos, signified a pivotal shift in my own journey, with Chica's arrival marking a key moment in this transition. A few days later, a mysterious notecard with a quote by Brene Brown appeared in the mail that read: "I think midlife is when the Universe gently places her hands upon your shoulders, pulls you close, and whispers in your ear: I'm not screwing around. It's time. Time is growing short. There are unexplored adventures ahead of you. You can't live the rest of your life worried about what other people think."

During that time, my world appeared to be filled with individuals who thrived on drama, unrest, and yes, utter mayhem—this was true both in my practice and within my primary social circles. I often found myself questioning why I seemed to attract these specific life lessons and why I tolerated people who, despite claiming to be friends, frequently criticized my work, my living situation, and my choices regarding how and with whom I spent my time.

While we resided in a modest house within a neighborhood marred by corruption, the immediate neighbors proved to be more authentic, caring, supportive, and genuine than those we had encountered in supposedly better neighborhoods. I still have two linebacker-sized neighbors, both former-felons-turned-law-abiding citizens, on speed-dial who will show up for me faster than the police department would if needed.

What I truly desired, though, was a homebase that could serve as a sanctuary, especially in a neighborhood plagued by the turmoil of drugs, shootings, and other hardships. It was in this challenging environment that I sought to create a haven where tranquility and peace could prevail, despite the anarchy that often raged just beyond our doorstep.

The world was undeniably holding up a mirror for my introspection, signaling the deep need for change. So that very morning, I took a decisive step and booked air tickets for my long-awaited Camino de Santiago journey, a pilgrimage I had postponed for various reasons for over two decades. It was something I had yearned to experience on my own, solely for my personal growth and evolution. Opting for a solo adventure, though, was a hard choice that generated significant dissent from a myriad of sources.

In essence, I yearned for a life that celebrated each moment, where each day was marked by the authenticity of "I've got you" hugs instead of energetic turmoil. Life wasn't that at the time, and I needed a massive reset.

Walking more than five hundred miles solo across the Iberian Peninsula, I was assured by those who had already completed the pilgrimage, would solve this for me.

TRAFFIC

A neighbor's son, Eddie, stopped me and said, "She gone, she done run that way." That way was into heavy two-way traffic. The traffic in the area was the kind that disregarded stop signs, signals, crosswalks, animals, children, other drivers, and speed limits.

Was I running into the traffic in my life at the time? Yes, admittedly I was. Everything was moving too fast, life was too loud, I couldn't shut off the commotion and the confusion and I was going headfirst into all of it.

There was just too much noise.

Constantly dodging the oncoming traffic, questioning the norms and failing to go along just to get along....

"She be ya'lls dog?" he'd asked.

"I thought so. I'm doing everything I can to save her life," I'd replied. And I was.

"Why she still be a runner?" he said.

Why indeed. Many ask that of those of us who work with people who have endured the unthinkable. Why do they willingly still run, go back to the abusive partner, dangerous lifestyle, or horror-filled environment? Why do they leave treatment when they have been making such great progress?

Maybe what some perceive as dangerous or wrong or detrimental is what others of us have learned is our own personal solution.

Chica was getting nightly baths (all of five minutes in the shower when it took twenty to wash the eighty-pound boy dog), lots of treats, all kinds of affection and praise, and stayed with me during the day when I worked from home. She showed me she was super smart and keenly aware of every detail of the environment. I'd taken her to the veterinarian's office the day before and updated her shots, her permanent tags and health records, and gotten her a new last name. We had a wonderful visit with the new vet, another gift the Humane Society had bestowed via referral. Chica had been on her very best good-dog behavior, and everyone had given her too many treats and gleefully patted her on the head and played with her feet when I'd mentioned she'd been reluctant to allow that sort of touch before. She'd loved the attention, and she'd shown up as the playful puppy I knew she was. I thought we'd turned a significant corner.

Yet, she had bolted.

Twenty minutes later, Eddie showed up at my door and said he thought Chica was in the park behind the house. He'd gone out of his way to help me and offered to drive around the backside of the park. I was speechless. I'd been told that he was one of the neighborhood drug dealers; we'd never exchanged more than an obligatory nod or wave in passing before that day. I know his dad, a retired veteran, who lives a block away, and know and adore his younger brother, Leo, the "first human daddy" to one of my dogs, who is currently competing in bicycle races across the US. Leo lost a leg just below his hip in a freak motorcycle accident some years ago, and he was in contention for placement in the next Paralympics.

I thanked Eddie profusely as he motioned to a man waiting in the car for him.

"Everybody know you, Miss Laura. We cool. No worries," he'd said. He smiled a huge smile, and I saw his beautiful humanity, that spark I see in people that no one else really wants to work with and with people who are broken and working so hard to find their light. I am certain he would have hugged me if I was standing any closer.

Five minutes later, there she was as they followed her in the car. Chica ran full speed toward me in the middle of the street before speeding right past me as fast as her tiny, incredibly muscular legs would go. She seemed punch-drunk giddy and 100 percent consumed in the freedom of running in the pouring rain, oblivious to everyone and everything in her path. Eddie offered to drive me around to collect her; I said it would be easier if I followed her on foot.

And I followed her calmly for more than ten city blocks through some of the seediest parts of town—parts I'd never seen even though I lived within easy walking distance. She wound her way through yards and bushes, under cars, and over short fences. We went through 'The Projects" where two teenagers were exchanging goods and money with guns sloppily tucked into the waistlines of their low-hanging pants (why the local boys and men wear their pants down past their buttocks exposing their underwear still eludes me).

"Everybody know you, Miss Laura. We cool. No worries," Eddie had told me.

The teens just nodded at me as I passed them. No threats, no flares, no worries.

We crisscrossed neighborhood streets and the park in Midtown where mobs of teenagers routinely erupt and deadly sets of shootings had claimed numerous lives over the years. She stopped long enough to bark at cats on doorsteps and at one of the very few Caucasians within the radius of what is known as the "South Side." She finally sat down and allowed me to pick her up just short of crossing a busy four-lane, two-way thoroughfare in an area where I hadn't dared to even drive through before.

The mantra echoed: "Everybody know you, Miss Laura. We cool. No worries." It was if Eddie was walking with us.

I carried her back nearly a mile in the rain; I swear she was smiling as she burrowed into the crook of my elbow. Neighbors I'd never met before waved and said, "Hey there!" Several I'd never seen before addressed me by name.

That night she sat squarely on my foot with her eyes on me while I was working at my desk, and from then on, she made it her duty to guard me when I worked from home. The baby gates came down, the dogs all shared the communal water bowl, various parts of "their" sofa, and parts of each other as pillows.

She had found her pack, and she was home. She finally understood she was safe.

The pack played hard, and Chica could easily outmaneuver either one of the other dogs. It occurred to me as I watched her that while she was still engaged, she simply didn't let the others scare her or tackle her or even provoke her anymore.

Nothing seemed to bother her.

What changed?

She felt safe. She *knew* she was safe.

She would joyfully wiggle her way under the furniture, eluding the Velociraptors in furtive games of hide and seek without the obstacle or protection of the baby gates. They all sat together and gave me a paw in exchange for treats during designated Family Time. She also slept outside of the crate, curled up under my arm and snugged against my ribcage that night. She has since become one of the best dogs I've been a pet-parent to.

She found her way home that day. I think I did too.

CHAPTER 13
FINDING HOME

I cannot think of any need in childhood as strong as the need for a father's protection.

—Sigmund Freud

My father and I had a date every Tuesday for several years after I finally confronted him on Father's Day fully ten years after he'd dismissed me from the family pack. I'd reached the tipping point, that place of complete detachment to the outcome, and ambushed him in forgiveness after nearly a decade of stilted, hostile silence between us.

What I did, as I was later told, resembled ripping off a sticky, pus-soaked bandage from a festering wound. I'd learned a great deal about anger management and complex post-traumatic stress syndrome (C-PTSD).

After learning about complex post-traumatic stress syndrome, I began to understand the layers of my emotional responses and behaviors in a new light. This knowledge revealed how the consistent strain and stress from my father's actions had not just left isolated wounds but a deeper, more intricate pattern of psychological injury that shaped my reactions and interactions throughout my life. I learned about the enormous avalanches of traumas that those of us in a narcissist's path endure and fall prey to. I learned that we often repeatedly bring in those people until we learn what we need to learn in order to heal. I also learned much about patterns: where we learn them; how we adopt, adapt, or reject them; and how and why they determine our behaviors. And importantly, how we fall back into our patterns when we are depleted or emotionally spent.

Here's what I told him: that while he was entitled to his opinions, I was not his property and furthermore, that I had been out of his home much, much longer than I had ever lived under his roof. He glared; I didn't cringe. He did his level best to stare me down, and I stood my ground because I no longer was attached to what the outcome might be. I told him I forgave him for me, not for him, and that I did this for me to move on past the paradigm that had become the both of us.

I told him I forgave him so I could be at peace. Not him, me. I wanted peace and closure for myself.

He was at first quite livid that I'd dared to show up unannounced—a major disobedience, especially since I walked right into his home as if I still were welcomed there. Secondarily, he was angry that I asked my mother to stay out of the discussion as I told him, no matter what he thought, I still loved him in spite of all the transgressions, misunderstandings, and unresolved karmic debts that we may have been hauling around on the barge we both were dragging. I also told him I was no longer concerned that he may kill me, nor was I remotely concerned that he may give himself a heart attack from the unnecessary anger he may be experiencing. It was time for both of us to move on in order to truly heal.

Thanks to my personal growth journey, I not only meant it but I also felt emotionally and physically comfortable expressing what I needed to say. Consider for a moment that this was the same man I used to hide from in my toy box as a child, fully convinced that he had the capacity and intention to end my life. Reflecting on that fear from my childhood, I now see the vast journey I've made, from a terrified child to someone who could stand unflinching before the source of that fear. This work is hard, and it doesn't get easier. We do, however, get stronger.

It was one of the two times I recall seeing tears well up in his eyes. The first was when his enormous Boxer dog, Toro, my first "pony" (he was that big and I did ride him around), died. Toro had been with him for nearly two decades, he was my Faud's totem and one of my best friends. I, too, was devastated when Toro died, and his death had introduced me to big, fat, fast-growing tumors and something known as "untreatable cancer." The second was when I'd gone to kindergarten and absolutely did not want to be left there, at that place, as I was certain it was a jail.

It had taken nearly forty years of my life to reach this stage of forgiveness and acceptance between us. Paradoxically, he'd been doing his own deep spiritual work since he'd cut me from the family pack.

For several years after my father left the planet, I still picked up the phone to call him on Tuesdays for our prescribed Tuesday at 10:00 a.m. telephone call. We would spend an hour chatting affably as friends, solving the current crisis of whatever the world offered at the time, discussing metaphysics, and musing about world travel. He'd admitted fears I'd never known about, and he conveyed that he was proud that I had taken myself through college. He'd found his way to Source, and he was no longer angry or scared.

He wanted to come to visit Dan and me so that he could go fishing in the Pacific Ocean again, something he had so loved to do before he'd fallen ill. We'd set a date for nine months forward; he'd conquered a bacterial infection that had resulted in a six-week stint in ICU; he'd healed and felt good. When I'd asked him, "Why not right now, this week?" he'd sidestep the subject with banalities and observances about the best times of the year to fish or tide tables or the weather or interrupting my work schedule. "You've always been so go-go-go," he had said.

"There is plenty of time," he insisted. I remember staunchly disagreeing.

Less than three months after that initial conversation, I was collecting his cremains and making the necessary arrangements to take the ashes out to sea.

My father didn't believe college was a necessity for those of us born as females in this incarnation. I did and was accepted early. My father would have none of it then, refused to sign release paperwork of any sort, and was steadfast in blocking any attempt I made at independence.

So I moved out of my parent's home at a very young age, at a time when my peers were discovering makeup and clothes and the opposite sex and set about the arduous task of working full time and going to school at night. Later, I would commute three hours for college classes, three to four nights each week. There was no college education fund, nor financial or emotional support from my parents. The state where I lived did not have all-inclusive college grants in place either. I took on a second part-time job to offset the peripheral college-specific expenses and save for a trip, an archaeological dig in Peru that also offered credits toward my degree. The days stretched into sixteen hours most of the time. I was on my own and thriving despite the dire predictions to the contrary that my parents had made. I bought a car worthy of commuting and was funding my education myself through grants and scholarships.

Soon after I decided to go to Peru, my car was totaled by a drunk driver who ran a stoplight—a bizarre and parenthetically odd karmic segue that I remember watching in the rear-view mirror in slow motion as I braced myself for the impact.

People who survive horrific accidents often report having a slow-motion experience. For me, it was twofold: First, as I braced myself for the impact, and then as I watched from outside of the vehicle as the metal squealed and twisted and was crushed all around my body. Harvey, my play-pal pig from next door as a child, must have squealed that way when Mrs. J slaughtered him, I remember thinking. A huge human betrayal and a defining moment that immediately gifted me with veganism. I loved that pig so much. He was smarter than most dogs I've known. He was super curious, clown-like in so many ways, and charged to greet me every day after school, snorting in his funny Harvey way, gleefully trotting back and forth along the fence line with his "fetch ball" in his mouth. We would play catch, go on long trot-walks around the desert, and root around in the garden together. Mrs. J would scratch his head and call him a "good piggy." He'd grunt and rub his enormous snout against her weathered hands and wag his piggy tail. She cooed at him, and I swore he would smile. He was an enormous, huggable, loving creature I'd been with since he was the size of a baking potato. He was the coolest best friend ever.

I came home from school one day, and much to my dismay, Harvey didn't come to greet me at the bus as he did every single day rain, wind, or sunshine. Racing around in a panic, I finally found Mrs. J, who was calmly plucking the feathers off a chicken carcass on her back porch. When I tearfully asked where my Harvey was, she dryly and casually stated he was in the freezer.

I was eight years old and learned about pure, unadulterated hatred that day. I hated her. I hated the world. I hated being human. I hated the loneliness and isolation of the desert. I hated my parents. I hated my siblings for laughing at me, calling me "weird" and "stupid," and for the "family" siding with Mrs. J. Most of all, I hated God.

My father would angrily chastise me when I would counter his spouting of must-eat-meat Bible passages with those of my own that supported veganism. My parents would send me to bed countless nights without dinner when I refused to eat anything animal. My mother would insist that chicken and fish and eggs and ducks and geese didn't count as "animal" and plop another round of cheese or butter or lard into whatever she was preparing. My parents gave my pet goose, Gus, whom I had rescued as a gosling, to Mrs. J.

Gus vanished the next day.

I especially hated Mrs. J and was certain that she ate the puppies that were disappearing from the house across the street too. I often wondered if she was cannibalistic. Why wouldn't she be, I would ponder. What truly is the difference between dogs or pigs or people? My Faud had spoken of pig parts being used in humans as replacement parts in hearts and such, so why would a person be any less edible?

The thoughts knocked me back into the vehicle several times.

LIMINAL TIME

The plasticity of time is fascinating to me.

The time between "No Longer" and "Not Yet" is a liminal time. It is a threshold. It is a space, an edge, a ledge, a moment in time when something changes from one state to another. And within that space and time is where we are "Becoming" and where the development of our soul's truest strengths is occurring.

Threshold moments occur ... and what do we do? Sometimes we hesitate, and we are shoved through, ending up beaten and bloody, and yes, outraged at our Creator for the impudence. "How could you? You F-ing pushed me!" we shout, and Creator has a great big belly laugh as we struggle to regain our footing. "Why, yes, yes! Of course, I did! Because I can. You were dawdling about, and it is high time you get on with things! Go on now, run, be free; I'm sending you to someplace new. It is time, and you must go."

The fringe dwellers, with the blatancy of their own darkest fears being reflected back to them, will posit that we ran away. In our hearts, though, we know we are following a calling.

A.S. King wrote: "We have this judgmental way of looking at the idea of leaving a home or a family, and our society has reinforced this idea that if we 'run away,' we are 'running away from our problems.' In some cases, though, to face certain problems ... the family members who are capable of facing reality must realize that leaving is a viable option. Some environments are harmful. As fellow humans, it is our job to judge less and encourage more when others choose to remove themselves from harmful environments."

Laura Weber Garrison, PhD

The environment I was raised in was unquestionably harmful, and sometimes I find myself wondering how I even managed to survive it. As adults, my siblings have tragically normalized their own dysfunctions, and that simply isn't safe for me. The emotional and psychological toll of constantly navigating their toxic patterns and venomous hostility was unbearable. A pivotal turning point: I faced harsh judgment for my steadfast refusal to rescue my alcoholic brother once again and for my conscious choice to distance myself from the painfully dysfunctional dynamics of our so-called family who were further enabling, and denying culpability for, his deplorable behaviors. The undeniable truth remains that more than one of my siblings should have faced legal consequences for their actions. And yes, I chose to walk away, fully aware that it was a matter of self-preservation. I refused to further subject myself to a toxic environment that had already nearly claimed my life.

As I reflect on those turbulent times, I'm reminded of the importance of making tough decisions. In the midst of such challenges, we must pause and reflect and remember this is our one precious life in this incarnation. Can we embrace these moments for what they are, with the philosophical perspective of allowing the grace of our God-Self, our Higher Power, to lead us?

The accident happened shortly after midnight, directly across the street from the police station at a larger four-way intersection with multiple traffic lights. I was in the through lane, waiting for the light to change.

My days were filled with two jobs and a commute to and from college, and that day had begun for me well before 5 a.m. I remember being so happy to be a few blocks from home and looking forward to seeing my cherished dog, Sam. He was getting older and slept most of the day, and I had to wake him before I'd left for school just to love on him. I'd aced a colossal exam, had a confrontation with an instructor who hadn't done her homework that resulted in a terrific learning experience for the entire class, had a new job offer, and was making plans to go on a big trip to Peru.

Moments later, I was hit from behind by a truck going more than 50 mph. The driver never even hit the brakes.

Watching the scene unfold was surreal in a multi-dimensional way for me: realizing the truck coming at me wasn't going to stop. Noting I had nowhere to go. Pulling my legs up into a leg press position against the dash and thinking that perhaps the fact I could leg press more than five hundred pounds might help save my life. Bracing my arms against the steering wheel, making sure my head was against the headrest. I was remembering to breathe. And breathing. Thinking about Harvey and hatred and humanity and wondering if I wanted to stay Earth-bound.

I realized I really did not. I watched every moment from so many different angles and was acutely aware of Something outside of me informing me it wasn't my time to go. The calm of all things being right, at that moment, and that within that very moment, there was a fulcrum point. I was staying, and I had bigger work to do.

When the door was finally pried off my car and they extricated me, I fought with them, tumbled out, and lost consciousness for a moment. I recall standing outside of the vehicle, looking at the crumpled body of me. The officers were checking for injuries and chattering at each other. The memory is crystal-clear. I listened to the officers talk about how I should have been "road pizza" given the severity of the impact and wondered about their amusement. They were laughing that the other driver was so drunk that he was a "fucking rag doll" and commenting on how being so inebriated may have allowed him to survive the wreck unscathed. Maybe she's drunk too, they were speculating about me. The bigger one was complaining about being off duty and having to deal with this "crap." They weren't gentle with my lifeless, crumpled body.

The officers did not insist on admitting me to the hospital, which was less than a block from the accident. I had no one to help take care of my work or my dog at that point. I had finals. My boss wasn't always kind; it was likely he would be dismissive and mean. "Look, she's fine; she's standing; she wants to walk home. Let her; she lives right around the corner," they were saying. My head was throbbing; I wasn't bleeding.

There was no offer of driving me home. They radioed for tow trucks, had another officer take the other driver across the street to jail, and watched me walk away. It would be weeks before I remembered what had happened and years before I could discuss what I remembered.

CHAPTER 14
PARALLEL PROCESSING

The cave you fear to enter holds the treasure you seek.
—Joseph Campbell

What I do know is that we all operate—and manage information—from different perspectives and from various parts of our brains. Some information is learned; some is karmic. Receptivity to meditation and pathways of communications within often leads many of us to an interest in the philosophy, spiritual practices, and science surrounding meditation and prayer, and many of us seek to understand how our bio-computers transmit information.

Our brains are cell matter, and brains can be artificially kept alive after the host body has expired.

According to the American Medical Association and the American Bar Association, death is legally defined as the "irreversible cessation of all functions of the entire brain, including the brain stem." Research supports, however, that approximately 20 percent of those who die and then are resuscitated report that they retained consciousness even during the near-death experience.

Is consciousness merely a brain function, or does it extend beyond this physical realm? This question leads us to explore the brain's complex cognitive processes. The brain operates with two distinct cognitive processes, each linked to a different cerebral hemisphere.

Primary process thinking, stemming from the id, the unconscious segment of our psyche fueled by primal urges and instinctual desires, manifests as illogical and preverbal, driven by the need for immediate gratification. This form of thinking is prevalent in early childhood and in our dream states. In contrast, secondary process thinking, which is logical and grounded in external reality, symbolizes a more mature and conscious form of thought. Our consciousness toggles between these two modes, depending on our state of awareness, with primary process thinking allowing us to delve into the deeper, often unconscious layers of our psyche. Understanding the id's influence on primary process thinking sheds light on these instinctual, subconscious aspects.

Intriguingly, research, such as Gruzelier's work from 1984, indicates noticeable shifts in hemispheric dominance during hypnosis. My extensive experience in advanced heart-centric clinical hypnosis and hypnotherapy, along with thousands of hours working with clients in Nidra and hypnotherapy sessions, confirms these impressive shifts. These experiences reinforce the notion that consciousness and cognitive processes are intricately woven and are subject to remarkable changes under different states of awareness.

Many years ago, one of my clients regressed, unexpectedly, to a childlike place and tried to explain, while in the hypnotic state, that he was busy "doing things." His words captivated me; in the initial sessions, he was speaking in broken, elementary Spanish and working diligently to help us understand him. As the sessions progressed, so did his command of the language. Post-session, the patient insisted that he did not speak Spanish nor ever had any recollection of learning Spanish in this lifetime. He was perplexed as to why I asked "again and again," and when I noted he had responded during sessions primarily in Spanish, he was both dismayed and disbelieving.

Many such instances have occurred over the years.

While this may seem disconcerting to some, I understood a layered meaning: "Learning seems to take place in this state in a way that is reminiscent of childhood learning. There appear to be striking similarities between the absorption of young children intensely involved in the discovery and of adult patients in hypnotic psychotherapy. Adults in hypnosis seem to make use of atrophied areas of perception and communication that may only be operative in young children and the specially gifted" (Ballen, 1997). Making use of these "atrophied areas of perception" is another vital component of growth. I believe that many of us teeter on the very periphery of these atrophied edges and are utterly terrified to take the necessary steps into the realization of our higher ways of being.

BRAIN SYNCHRONIZATION

When we slow our brain wave patterns from beta through to alpha, theta, and finally to delta, there's a notable increase in the balance between the brain's hemispheres. This shift in brain activity is often linked to creative insights, a sense of tranquility, and even moments of euphoria. Additionally, people experience improved learning abilities and heightened focus during these states. This seems to echo the creative stance many of us seek as artists—a state that is not only healing but also deeply cathartic, aiding in the exploration and expression of our artistic selves. In the realm of self-hypnosis, the objective often includes positively re-educating the subconscious to shed negative personality traits, focusing on enhancing the outer, environmentally interactive Self.

As artists, we are always looking for ways to decorate and improve not only ourselves but our environment, and it's an ongoing job. We lovingly embrace change; it's our friend, not our foe. As one of my "co-Madres," Ann "Delight" Cash, notes, "You and me, Laura G., we're artists. We are contrarians. It's a constant, ongoing, every day, every way, inside job of change. We tear things apart—us included—to make them better." My artwork has been a gateway to connecting with my Higher Self, a journey for which I am deeply thankful, even though it sometimes leaves me perplexed. Just as meditation and hypnotic states act as unique pathways to different realms of experience, art offers a similar transcendence. For many artists, me included, the act of creating art is like a surreal meditation, where time seems to stand still, and we become mere channels for the artwork that emerges. In my most challenging times, art has been a sanctuary, providing healing and deep self-reflection. "Prayer moves through my hands and shows up as art," notes one of my clients.

HIGHER FORMS OF PRAYER

The objective of meditation is to contact the "Higher Self" and go beyond the limits of the personality on a conscious level. Many believe that meditation is a higher form of prayer. The late Dr. Wayne Dyer often said that "meditation is our way of making conscious contact with God." I often say that I am in constant communication with the Greater Creator; I know for a fact that I was never taught how to create some of the artwork that I produce.

Meditation, as an Eastern modality, is also summed up as simply as being in union with the Absolute or God. Our point of contact is the unconscious mind.

The practice of hypnotism, conversely, is that of communicating with the subconscious and unconscious—the "underlying 90 percent"—and eliciting changes that are supposed to influence daily behavior and attitudes. Attitudes generate emotional undercurrents or "background noises" that often become ingrained or automatic, and often these undercurrents can affect the way we feel, how we respond to situations, and how we act and react in the world.

Hypnosis is essentially a process that persuades the subconscious to accept certain beliefs as true. In our daily lives, we often experience shifts in and out of hypnotic-like states. However, hypnosis doesn't lead one to transcend beyond their inherent personality traits.

According to Diane Zimberoff, the hypnotic trance is the simple shifting back and forth between the conscious and subconscious mind, which happens to most people approximately 80 percent of any day.

The levels of the mind as defined by Zimberoff for The Wellness Institute:

Conscious mind: 10 percent
- Analyzes
- Thinks and plans
- Short-term memory

Subconscious Mind: 90 percent
- Long-term memory
- Emotions and feelings
- Habit patterns, relationship patterns, addictions
- Involuntary bodily functions
- Creativity
- Developmental stages
- Spiritual connection
- Intuition

Unconscious Mind
- Archaic memory
- Instinct
- Karmic patterns
- Dreams
- Collective development

Meditation, unlike hypnosis, emphasizes resolving issues directly. It's the unique methodologies of these practices that define their distinct "doorways" and the insights or transformations they facilitate. During hypnosis, the theta brainwave state is especially effective for rapid changes in beliefs and behaviors. This state acts as a bridge between wakefulness and sleep, allowing unfiltered absorption of new information. Techniques like Yogic Alternate Nostril Breathing, or Nadi Shodana, are instrumental in achieving brain balance and synchronization, key for accessing the brainwave states central to meditation and hypnosis, effectively harmonizing brain activity for deeper mental exploration.

Laura Weber Garrison, PhD

FINDING BALANCE

Raja Yoga, often seen as the science of meditation, involves engaging with the unconscious mind in a state of meditation. It's a path that is particularly appealing to the Western mindset, which values order and logical explanations. The Chopra Center highlights that Raja Yoga, favoring no specific belief system, encourages individuals to base their beliefs on their own direct experiences.

This form of yoga is largely attributed to the ancient sage Patanjali, who documented his teachings in a treatise consisting of four volumes of sutras or short aphorisms. These sutras delve into various aspects of human existence, including the nature of suffering and delusion, as well as psychic and magical powers. Central to Patanjali's teachings, and by extension to Raja Yoga, is the concept that personal experience is the most authentic basis for belief and understanding. The Yoga Sutras outline the eightfold path of yoga, known as the eight limbs—*Yama, Niyama, Asana, Pranayama, Pratyahara, Dharana, Dhyana, Samadhi*—offering a holistic guide to achieving spiritual enlightenment and self-realization.

This system of yoga is also known as eight-limbed yoga or Ashtanga yoga and has been translated as:

1. Yama: Universal morality (societal codes of conduct)
2. Niyama: Personal observances (personal codes of conduct)
3. Asana: Body postures (yoga poses)
4. Pranayama: Breathing exercises and control of Prana (breath)
5. Pratyahara: Control of the senses (*Savasana*)
6. Dharana: Concentration and cultivating inner perceptual awareness (present-moment awareness)
7. Dhyana: Devotion and meditation on the Divine
8. Samadhi: Union with the Divine

Several centuries after Patanjali, Adi Shankara, a renowned Indian philosopher and theologian, furthered the doctrine of Advaita Vedanta, emphasizing the concept of non-duality or oneness. Shankara played a pivotal role in unifying and shaping the main currents of Hindu thought. He built upon ideas from the *Upanishads*, ancient Indian spiritual texts, and his work, the *Crest-Jewel of Discrimination*, became a seminal text in Vedantic philosophy. Shankara is known for his elaboration on ten verses or Shlokas that encapsulate the omnipresence of Spirit, offering philosophical insights into the interconnectedness of all existence.

Shankara elaborated ten *shlokas* or verses that describe the omnipresence of Spirit paraphrased as follows:
1. The true Self is changeless and persists forever.
2. The true Self is above castes and creeds.
3. The true Self is the eternal witness.
4. All teachings of various religions and philosophies are shallow in comparison to the true Self.
5. The true Self pervades the whole Universe.
6. The true Self is colorless and formless.
7. The true Self is the absolute knower.
8. The true Self is above consciousness.
9. The true Self pervades everything.
10. The true Self is neither connected nor separate. The "true Self," it seems, is very much in alignment with Source or God.

Hatha yoga is often considered part of Raja Yoga due to shared elements like asana (physical postures) and pranayama (breath control). However, many see it as a distinct, comprehensive system that emerged centuries after Raja Yoga. Originally, Hatha Yoga aimed to facilitate a union with the Divine through physical practices, combining postures, breath work, and stretching to enhance bodily awareness and sensation, thereby enriching the practitioner's spiritual journey.

Union with the Divine or God terrifies many. Why else do we self-medicate or drown out our senses with food or alcohol or too much noise?

Is everyone addicted to something? I do not believe so. What I do believe is that we have addictive tendencies.

Laura Weber Garrison, PhD

AWAKENING

Yoga Nidra, or "deep sleep of yoga," is a state of deep relaxation coupled with inner awareness guided by meditation. It's not just about relaxation; it's about internal exploration. The body enters a regenerative sleep state, but the mind stays active. In a 1980 study in Cologne, Germany, EEGs showed consistent alpha wave activity across the brain during Yoga Nidra, unlike other relaxation practices. This indicates better communication between brain hemispheres. This finding, reconfirmed in 1997, underscores Yoga Nidra's unique impact on brain activity, contrasting with the common misconception that yoga is primarily physical.

Our physical state intricately reflects the mind-body connection. When the brain's chemistry changes, it impacts the body's chemistry, and this influence is bidirectional. This interaction is central to the self-regulation in physical yoga practice. By engaging in yoga, we can enact measurable changes in the sympathetic nervous system, the driver of our "fight-or-flight" response. This highlights yoga's significant role in managing stress and regulating our body's response to stressful stimuli.

Stress happens when the body is chemically jolted out of balance; the stress response is the body's innate response and reactions in regaining equilibrium. Unlike animals, we can turn on the flight-or-fight response by our thoughts alone: we can anticipate or recollect experiences and still elicit this response. Going into emergency mode is one thing; staying there is quite another. Yet some people have trained themselves—their body and their mind—to remain in this hyper-driven state, and they have become addicted to the feelings and the emotions of that state.

From a psychological perspective, many people are said to spend the majority of their time mired in negative thoughts and feelings. Overproduction of stress hormones creates the human emotions of anger, aggression, anxiety, fear, and insecurity. We suffer, and we perpetuate the vicious cycle of negativity. Why? It's where we place our focus. Repetitive stress is not only maladaptive; it is quite harmful to us physically and emotionally. Further, this mindset misdirects a vast amount of creative energy.

Scientists have explored how mindfulness practices like yoga can transform our responses to stimuli and how sustained involvement in these practices can reshape the brain's structure. Research shows that attentional training and mindfulness offer substantial benefits in managing conditions ranging from stress and depression to severe addictions. Yoga, in particular, works similarly, harnessing these mindfulness principles to effect positive changes in both mental and physical health.

Some studies have juxtaposed mindfulness training with cognitive behavior therapy (CBT), often seen as the "gold standard" in treating substance abuse disorders. CBT, blending cognitive and behavioral therapy, aims to identify and modify problematic thought processes and behaviors, teaching healthier ways to cope with stressors. In contrast, mindfulness training focuses on altering one's relationship with their thoughts. Cognitive therapy within CBT seeks to challenge and change cognitive distortions by examining and altering the assumptions behind these thoughts. This highlights our metacognitive ability: the awareness and capacity to understand and modify our thought processes. We have the ability to self-correct and self-direct.

If our thoughts can sicken us, our thoughts can also heal us. Certain things cannot coexist. If we are to thrive and circumvent what may be our genetically dictated destiny, becoming mindful of where we place our attention becomes paramount. We may indeed need to relinquish attachments, change our former habits and ways, and step into the unknown with faith.

MINDFULNESS

Over three decades ago, Dr. Jon Kabat-Zinn founded the Mindfulness-Based Stress Reduction (MBSR) program at the University of Massachusetts Medical School. This program, integrating mindfulness practices similar to those in yoga, emphasizes being "present in the present moment." MBSR aims to make individuals more aware of their situations, teaching them to consciously approach life's stressors. Kabat-Zinn describes mindfulness as awareness through intentional, non-judgmental attention to the present. The program, renowned for reducing stress, anxiety, and depression, is now a staple in many hospitals' stress-reduction protocols.

Becoming self-aware is also about detachment: allowing thoughts or actions to pass without direct interaction and response, as with vipassana training. With practice and over time, new neural networks are formed, and one's ability to inhibit unwanted experiences will stop the "wiring and firing" of the old pathways that previously created ongoing suffering.

Yogic philosophy is prescriptive in that we must endeavor to summon the opposite thoughts when adverse notions, or *vikalpa*, crowd our mind. Instead of thinking harmful thoughts, we seek to cultivate thoughts and feelings of love, kindness, and compassion. The actual meaning of *pratipaksha bhavana* is "cultivating positive thought every time a negative thought enters the mind." Pratipaksha means "opposite", and bhavana means "emotion/ sentiment."

Meditation addresses the same issue from a unique perspective. "You become more like the sky than the storm," says Kabat-Zinn. MBSR is described as "a psychoeducational experiential learning program based on the core principle of mindfulness." Is it analytical by nature? "While 'control' is not the goal of MBSR, it is a systematic [...] educational approach which uses relatively intensive training in mindfulness meditation as the core of a program to teach people how to take better care of themselves and live healthier and more adaptive lives." I see this mindfulness meditation approach as a way of connecting with our Higher Source.

Science has also shown how matter and energy are part of a single spectrum. The two, like waves and particles, are, in actuality, one—what modern physicists refer to as a "field." All of life can be seen as a dance of the universal energetic fields.

We are part of the quantum field. The Every When. All physical reality is primarily energy interconnected across all space, all time— us included. We coexist in a vast sea of awareness that holds all possible probabilities. Our bodies are forms of energy, made up of the very same things as the rest of the Universe; the same 99.9 percent "no-thing." $E=mc^2$, remember? Energy and matter are one.

CONNECTING

Hatha yoga, the yoga of balancing the polarities of the moon and the sun, has its foundation in this quantum dance. The mythological source of the yoga of transformation (Hatha) is the god Siva. Siva is symbolized as a great dancer, often depicted as dancing within a ring of fire.

Anything exposed to fire is altered, and this image of Siva implies the cosmic dance of energies of birth, of death, and of transformation. Learning about the flow of energies is one of the core principles of Hatha yoga.

The purpose of meditation, on various levels, and according to many sources, is to "create a free-flowing energy within us."

"By meditating, we come to know God rather than know about God," stated the late Wayne Dyer. "Our ultimate reason for meditating is to [...] enter the sacred space and know the unlimited power of our Source. Psalm 46:10 says: 'Be still and know that I am God.' To know is to banish all doubt. Being still in meditation can take us to that awareness."

Countless people argue that prayer is the answer when they experience imbalances within themselves and often confuse prayer with meditation. While prayer may be considered a type of meditation, prayer is a one-way communication with a high plane of Self, a sort of conversation with God. Meditation is likened "more to having a rapport," with prayer not fulfilling an actual means to an end.

Wouldn't the argument then hold that various orators and "people of the Cloth" may be hypnotists? Some ministers either quietly teach self-hypnosis or practice a form of hetero-hypnosis as part of their pastoral counseling. What they preach is galvanized and gospel to their constituents. Unfortunately, we are well aware as counselors that the "lay public has been given a great deal of misinformation regarding hypnosis." Clinical hypnosis and the therapy that is parcel to it can work absolute wonders for people in distress, and I have witnessed people make tremendous strides toward life-affirming changes on virtually every level from health to wealth through addressing the subconscious and involuntary systems within them.

Again, someone must have the desire to change. Merely saying one might want to explore a new modality doesn't work; it requires an actual desire for a change.

Ah, the great "what if?" I hear you. "What if what I'm asking for is worse than what I have, what I'm enduring or what I'm facing?" you ask.

And what if it is so much better, so much more?

What if it is the relief from all the pain you have in your heart and mind right now? What if, just what if it is that last really challenging set of high tide waves you must plow through before you can tread easily on the other side in calm and lovely waters?

What I will say is that it—the *it* you fear—cannot be in the Greater Good of what our Creator has in mind for us if it is harmful or hurtful.

It is our birthright to be happy, to grow, and to learn in this incarnation. Some of our lessons are harsh, I agree; yet in the bigger picture, they may lead to a new and more brilliant trajectory of our Soul's growth if we allow it.

My mother used to say, as I've heard so many others say, that we are "only given what we can handle." Ever the pessimist, I would generally respond with something akin to, "Are you saying that my growth is parsed, fundamentally deconstructed, and incrementally dispensed by a malevolent, mean-spirited God that may have suffered from a case of arrested adolescence?" She would shake her head and wave me off.

My God didn't assume the role of a hostile, immature man besotted with a higher hierarchal order and world dominance. Instead, the Radiant One—my Greater Creator—and I have two-way communication. I'm ignorant and will be, in human form, until my crossing to the next grade of Earth School. My Source knows this, and we work on things. It isn't always easy, and lessons abound. Taking ownership of the lessons is another matter.

FAIRIES AND STREET ANGELS UNAWARE

A gift from the Universe showed up for me recently and what a sweet and unexpected surprise it was.

"Look what is in my path today! It's sparkly and weird," I thought to myself, and, "Oh, and she smells kinda funny, like mothballs and Old Spice cologne. She is wonderful and crinkly, and I like her smile. And she's sharing such great stories with me! How did you know I wanted to learn all about her homeland in Germany? Oh yes, that's right, I have lineage there. Well, of course, I do! "Thank you for the gift!" I say aloud.

She was so pleased as I held her hand. We laughed, and we cried. She was in great physical pain, and I helped her that day, albeit just a tiny bit. "Some days it is all I can handle just to leave the house," the woman had told me. "It is just so hard for me to get around but get around I must."

She brightened my day.

That supposition of "all that we can handle" is borne of choice points. Some of us are given so much that we expire; the lesson kills us. We pray with conviction, and we pray hard.

Would people who pray for something with fervent conviction be practicing self-hypnosis without realizing it?

Everyday hypnosis is quite commonplace. If we don't do it to ourselves, through prayer or other means, then our subconscious seems quite capable of collecting data on its own—things that can become habitual beliefs that, in turn, will manifest as thoughts and, likewise, behaviors. It isn't necessarily, as some believe, that of one mind dominating another person's mind and of being influenced against one's wishes. When our attention is focused on one thing, and our awareness follows another, we are said to be "hypnotized." Driving a car while traveling a habitual route or becoming so absorbed in reading or a television program—to the point where all outside distractions, including the passage of time, go virtually unnoticed are two readily identifiable forms of everyday hypnosis. Who or what takes over?

Remember when you learned to drive a car? Play a musical instrument? Do yoga asanas or ballet? Everything was awkward, confusing, and sometimes maddening. And then your body learned the sequences and wired and fired everything together. You learned. Once we've mastered the learning of something, we let our body do the work.

We go into an autopilot mode, and our body-mind takes over. We've learned something so well—a task, an emotion, a reaction, a function in life—that our body takes over. How is this possible? Our fingers know the sequence of someone's phone number, reach for something in our desk or briefcase, we "absent-mindedly" finish a mundane task.

DAMAGED SOFTWARE

But what about those of us who have suffered trauma?

As long as the trauma remains unresolved, the stress hormones that we produce to protect ourselves will keep circulating, and the responses will continue to be replayed. The neural pathways are well-worn; our body knows how to respond. If the elements of the trauma are continually repeated, the stress hormones will acutely etch those memories in the mind. Our autopilot is impaired.

Children are innately programmed to be loyal to their caretakers, even if those people brutalize or terrify them. The memories of the abuse or trauma may not even be cognate or in immediate awareness, yet the reflexive patterns of survival will manifest.

Therapists rely strongly, however, on conversation and talk therapy to extract and resolve issues surrounding trauma. Invaluable in many ways, we must remember that words carry different weights of meanings dependent upon our perspectives. We all see things through different lenses.

One "guru," for example, insisted I tell the group that I was "sorry" for leaving during his hell and brimstone sermon, one that had my skin crawling and had other members of the group in tears. I shot back over my shoulder that the word "sorry" was demeaning, as in wretched or worthless (per the original meaning of the word) and I am 100 percent not a sorry being as a child of my particular God. I will apologize when it is appropriate, and I apologize openly, freely and with ownership; I will never, however, say I am sorry.

Freud, in his seminal work with Breuer in "Studies on Hysteria," observed that trauma could be effectively addressed by thoroughly revisiting and verbalizing the triggering event and its associated emotions. This process of detailed recollection and emotional expression, he noted, could lead to the immediate and permanent resolution of the traumatic symptoms.

Traumatic events are often impossible to put into words and instead, manifest as images and sensations that are replayed again and again. We also store these events as implicit or explicit memories.

Sometimes many of us can remember what seems like the tiniest, most insignificant details: our first phone number, a locker combination from middle school, all the words to an obscure song from long ago. These memories—full of facts, words, and events—are explicit memories. We also have diverse kinds of memories—ones that are evoked by sights, sounds, and smells. For example, the smell of baking cookies can, for some of us, bring back a flood of delicious, happy memories. Your mouth might even water, and a smile might cross your face. Conversely, being repelled by the scent of a particular odor, for instance, could elicit feelings of fear, panic, or even terror. Your skin crawls, your heart beats a little faster... you cannot catch your breath.

A person who was traumatized as a child might physically re-experience the all-too-familiar sensations of shaking with fear or experiencing anxiety and the physical reaction may have very little to do with the verbal thought process of "Oh, this reminds me of the time when my father threw me against the wall and broke my tooth." Or "Mom threw a wine glass at me in a drunken rage and said horrible, nasty things about me."

Here's why: Traumatic memory is formed and stored very differently than everyday memory.

According to Dr. Van der Kolk the brain can become wired to believe "I'm a person to whom terrible things happen, and I better be on the alert for who's going to hurt me now." This has particular significance for many of us who were traumatized as children and those conscious thoughts of being on alert get stored in a very elementary part of the brain.

Adults process differently. The thalamus shuts down and the entire picture of what happened during a traumatic event cannot even be stored in the brain. Simply put, the brain becomes overwhelmed.

Thus, instead of forming specific memories of the full event, people who have been traumatized remember images, sights, sounds, and physical sensations without much context. Certain sensations can just become triggers of the past. We, as people who have been traumatized, may not even be consciously aware of those sensations.

Our brains continually form maps of our world, maps of what is safe and what is dangerous. This is one of the reasons I say to my clients that I am a cartographer. I both map and chart our work together. I teach them to map and chart what is happening within them, what they are feeling, to notice what sensations are present or not present, and we work together to create a foundational map.

All of us carry an internal map of who we are in relationship to the world, and this becomes our personal memory system. It is, however, not a known memory system like that of verbal memories. It's an implicit memory system. What that means is that a particularly traumatic incident may not be remembered as a story of something that happened a long time ago. Instead, it gets triggered by sensations that people are experiencing in the present that can activate their emotional states. It's a much more primal level of a single sensation triggering the very real state of fear.

A person might keep thinking about the sensation and say, "Oh, this must be because it reminds me of the time that my father hit me." That's not the connection that the mind makes at that particular time.

So what difference will it make in our work knowing that a traumatic memory was encoded without context? "It's important to recognize that PTSD is not about the past. It's about a body that continues to behave and organize itself as if the experience is happening right now," according to van der Kolk.

When we're working with people who have been traumatized, it's crucial to help them learn how to navigate the present as it is and to tolerate whatever goes on. The past is only relevant insofar as it triggers current sensations, feelings, emotions, and thoughts. Hence, this is the reason that many practitioners of Holistic Health choose not to spend copious amounts of time with our patients and clients dwelling on "what happened." We want to know what conclusions and decisions our clients have made about how to remain safe regarding a traumatic incident so those decisions can be changed from a somatic/reactionary standpoint. While we cannot alter our past experiences, we have the power to change our reactions to them as we move forward. This shift in perspective is crucial for healing and personal growth. By reframing our response to past events, we can transform our emotional landscape and influence our future experiences. This process involves understanding, processing, and finding new meanings in our past, empowering us to create a more positive and proactive approach to life's challenges.

The story about the past is just a story that people tell to explain how difficult the trauma was or why they have certain behaviors. The real issue, though, is that trauma changes people. People who have experienced trauma feel and experience certain sensations differently. That's why the main focus of therapy is that of helping people shift their internal experience or, in other words, how the trauma is stuck or wired within them.

THE DISTRACTION OF TALKING

Feelings are the language of the body—messengers—and can indeed be allies for us. Talking, for some people, though, can convey a defense against feeling. They will seek to mitigate or deny or defend what they perceive, and, for some, this will shut down components of the healing process. Through the use of brain imagery, we've learned that when people are feeling something very deeply, one particular area of the brain lights up. And, likewise, when people are beginning to talk about their trauma, another part of the brain lights up.

Talking is undeniably important in the therapeutic process. We must have clarity and be on the same page in the same book in the same library with our patients and clients. Talking about some "things," though, can be a distraction from helping people notice what is going on within themselves. We, as trauma-informed people, have to feel our way through to the healing. And that's why some of the best therapy is very largely exploring the non-verbal aspects, where the main task of the therapist is to help people to feel what they feel—to notice what they notice, to see how things flow within themselves, and to reestablish their sense of time inside. We also seek to reconnect to sensations and move from sensations to awareness.

As I always tell the people I work with, "If we are feeling, we are healing."

All too often, when people have been or currently feel traumatized, their bodies can feel like they're under imminent threat, even if all the conditions around them are calm and supportive. The work of therapy accordingly becomes helping people to feel those feelings of threat, to notice what is taking place in the body, and to observe how the feelings disappear as time goes on. I help the people I work with to learn to feel, to observe, to note, and to notice what is going on in their physical body, rather than get caught up in the "I" of "I am my body." The important thing to note here is that the body never stays the same because the body is always in a state of flux. I seek to teach my clients to detach and just "be" with those feelings from a place of noticing, allowing, and accepting—without attempting to change, manipulate, or alter the experience of the feeling. I help my clients to learn that when a sensation comes up, it's okay, allowable, or acceptable to have it because something that they are noticing will pass and something else will come next.

This is one way we help people re-establish this sense of time, which gets destroyed by the trauma. Sensations and emotions become intolerable for many of us because we think, "This will never come to an end." According to van der Kolk, "Once a patient knows that something will come to an end, their whole attitude changes." I do not necessarily agree with this stance as "knowing something will come to an end" may be a perception that equals "I don't trust that this will really end even though someone else says it will." There are those of us who have been promised relief from pain, assistance from another when we're stranded or hurt, or some sort of support only to find that we have been betrayed or abandoned. We do not trust that something will end just because we're told it will. We have to experience the sensation *through* the sensation for us to believe there is a change. It is a scaffolding process for many of us to learn our way through.

What I also believe is that with awareness change is possible. Thus, once we are aware of the sensations and the feelings and can observe them with curiosity and compassion rather than attaching specific meanings to them, we can move into a place of detachment or non-identification from our bodies.

We are not our bodies, and yet we refer to the body as "I": I am sick, I am fat, I am this emotion, I am Indian, I am sunburnt, I am hungry, I am tired. Are those feelings or emotions? Are we describing the body or describing a state of being or are we describing Who we believe the "I" to be? It is important to remember that we are greater than our body and that we, through some event, traumatic or otherwise, have taught our body to respond in a certain way.

With awareness, we come to understand that we have choices, and within those choices, we learn that change is possible.

BURIED MEMORIES

"There are no words for the horrors my eyes have seen," my father said when questioned about the war and of his time on duty on hospital rotations. His face would tense and flush when queried. He would show all the physical manifestations of high stress, and I would notice that it took earnest effort for him to repress what he was feeling. There were many memories he noted that he completely "buried" and either would not or could not talk about. Others manifested as anger.

Freud, in his work on hysteria, observed that memories causing such phenomena are often deeply buried in the subconscious, remaining vivid and emotionally intense. These memories usually elude the patient's everyday memory, emerging only partially or not at all. However, when patients are questioned under clinical hypnosis, these memories resurface with the clarity of recent events, revealing the complex interplay between memory, trauma, and the subconscious.

Trauma is an everyday reality, affecting a significant portion of the population, from those growing up in challenging environments to veterans, first responders, and medical personnel who face extraordinary situations. This widespread impact underscores the importance of understanding and addressing trauma.

Transcendence, in the context of overcoming trauma, involves a sense of merging with something greater, leading to a loss of Self.

Deepak Chopra describes this as not only going beyond but also as a form of maturation. Remarkably, a study in the 1980s found that 40 percent of Americans reported having at least one transcendental spiritual experience, with 20 percent experiencing it more than once and 5 percent frequently. This prevalence highlights the potential for transcendental experiences to play a role in coping with and understanding the impact of trauma.

Transcendental Meditation, or TM, is a specialized meditation practice embraced by millions globally. Distinguished from other forms of meditation, TM's main focus is transcendence, and it uniquely incorporates the use of mantras. Maharishi Mahesh Yogi, who introduced TM to the world, emphasized that a mantra is a specific thought or sound received from a trained teacher, which aids in experiencing progressively finer states of thought, leading to the source of thought and achieving a transcendental state of being.

In learning TM, one typically undergoes an introductory course spanning about four days, often with a cost that can exceed a thousand dollars. This investment is for learning specific techniques and receiving a personal mantra. I learned from a conversation with a TM instructor that, while practitioners are usually advised to meditate for twenty minutes twice daily for optimal effects, some, including the instructor, choose to meditate for as long as three hours each day. This dedication reflects the deep engagement and commitment to the practice. The ease of practicing TM after initial training contrasts with its intricate, finely-tuned nature based on ancient traditions, underscoring the rationale behind learning it from a qualified TM teacher.

For self-improvement and addressing personal annoyances, self-hypnosis offers a practical approach for Westerners. It involves making clear suggestions to the subconscious, which then acts on them. Almost anyone can engage in this self-help method. Suggestion is guiding someone's thoughts, feelings, or behavior. However, working with the subconscious can be complex; it doesn't intentionally work against us but may hold onto previous directives given by us, sometimes creating opposition to new changes. This is where meditation or guided hypnosis can be particularly beneficial, helping to align the subconscious with our current intentions.

MEDICAL ANALYSIS OF MEDITATION

In 1963, Dr. Akira Kasamatsu and Dr. Tomio Hirai from Tokyo University's Department of Neuropsychiatry reported intriguing findings from a decade-long study. They investigated the brain wave patterns, through electroencephalographic (EEG) tracings, of Zen masters. This comprehensive study contributed significantly to the understanding of meditation's impact on brain activity.

The EEG tracings revealed that about ninety seconds after an accomplished Zen practitioner begins meditation, a rhythmic slowing in the brain wave pattern known as alpha waves occur. This slowing occurs with eyes open and progresses with meditation, and after thirty minutes, one finds rhythmic alpha waves of seven or eight per second. This effect persists for some minutes after meditation. What is most significant is that this EEG pattern is notably different from those of sleep, normal waking consciousness, and hypnotic trance and is unusual in persons who have not made considerable progress in meditation. In other words, it suggests an unusual mental state; though from the subjective reports of the practitioners, it does not appear to be a unique or highly unusual conscious experience. It was also found that a Zen master's evaluation of the amount of progress another practitioner had made correlated directly with the latter's EEG changes.

Another finding of the same study concerned what is called alpha-blocking and habituation. To understand these phenomena let us imagine that a person who is reading quietly is suddenly interrupted by a loud noise. For a few seconds, his attention is diverted from the reading to the noise. If the same sound is then repeated a few seconds later, his attention will again be diverted, only not as strongly nor for as long a time. If the sound is then repeated at regular intervals, the person will continue reading and become oblivious to the sound. A normal subject with closed eyes produces alpha waves on an EEG tracing. An auditory stimulation, such as a loud noise, normally obliterates alpha waves for seven seconds or more; this is termed alpha blocking. In a Zen master, the alpha-blocking produced by the first noise lasts only two seconds. If the noise is repeated at fifteen-second intervals, we find that in the normal subject, there is virtually no alpha blocking remaining by the fifth successive noise. This diminution of alpha-blocking is termed habituation and persists in normal subjects for as long as the noise continues at regular and frequent intervals. In the Zen master, however, no habituation is seen. His alpha-blocking lasts two seconds with the first sound, two seconds with the fifth sound, and two seconds with the twentieth sound. This implies that the Zen master has a greater awareness of his environment as the paradoxical result of meditative concentration. One master described such a state of mind as that of "noticing every person he sees on the street but not looking back with emotional lingering."

Meditation transcends specific groups or occult associations. Willard Johnson observed that it's often seen as exclusive to certain spiritual groups, perceived as irrelevant to most people. However, I believe meditation is a natural way to connect with our inner consciousness. In the West, practitioners may hide their practice due to social or religious stigma. This issue is compounded by certain groups promising mystical powers or exaggerated benefits, which often attract vulnerable individuals. These organizations may misuse "esoteric" meditation techniques. There's a trend where ritual supersedes self-discipline, faith replaces insight, and prayer takes over understanding. Meditation should be viewed as a natural, approachable practice, not one shrouded in fear or mystery.

Meditation, traditionally rooted in religious practices, is predominantly used for spiritual development across the world. Its techniques were particularly refined within Hinduism and Buddhism and also among Sufi communities within Islam. This historical and cultural evolution of meditation underscores its deep spiritual significance and varied practices across different religious traditions.

Meditation is not exclusively a Buddhist or Hindu tradition, however. The two religions utilize similar dogmas and systems;

hence, they are often confused and clustered into "Eastern" teachings. Both schools do advocate preparatory moral disciplines, moderations (such as eating), calming the mind and body, and denial of self-serving desires. The props and postures employed by both are similar, and the breathing meditations are comparable and practiced by many yogis. Here is where the similarities cease. Buddhism focuses on the empirical aspects of conscious experience, making its meditation practices psychologically oriented. In contrast, Hinduism's approach to meditation is more mystical, with a strong emphasis on religious and metaphysical elements. This distinction reflects the diverse spiritual underpinnings and objectives of meditation practices in different religious traditions.

Yogic meditation does have religious overtones and aspects which often include a form of prayer of unity with Source or the Infinite. It is also customary to say "Namaste" at the end of a yoga session or while sitting or studying in *Satsang* ("sitting in truth" or as part of a spiritual gathering of truth-seekers), which, of its very nature, implies Oneness. "Namaste is usually spoken with a slight bow and with the hands pressed together, palms touching and fingers pointing upwards, thumbs close to the chest. This gesture is called *Añjali Mudrā* or *Pranamasana*" and is considered an active opening of the heart chakra from one person's heart to another. The mudra looks very much like hands are being held in prayer position, and I have witnessed students new to yoga balking at the ostensibly religious overtones of "praying to one another" at the end of a class.

One of my Christian co-workers once smashed the flowers growing in a large vase outside of an adjacent yoga studio with the statement that "yogis pray to other gods and should be punished." When I disagreed with her and tried to explain, she hastily rushed off muttering that I must have "heathen tendencies."

Namaste is used both for salutation and valediction and is often taught and explained through yogic oral traditions as "The Divine Light in Me Honors the Divine Light in You."

The word Namaste is derived from two Sanskrit words: *Namas*: "bowing" and *Te*: "to you." In Hinduism, the word Namaste means "I bow to the Divine in you."

Buddhism in its meditation practices places a strong emphasis on motivation and gaining insight, whereas Hinduism focuses on concepts like Infinite Consciousness and Cosmic Reality, emphasizing unity with the Divine. This contrast highlights the diverse spiritual goals within these traditions. In the realm of authentic yoga, there's an emphasis on a gradual journey of healing and balance, as described by one of my teachers who often remarks on the slow but steady progress of authentic yoga practice to repair whatever is broken.

We are all part of Earth School, a journey of learning and healing. As we seek truth, we can significantly change our minds, spirits, and bodies. Neville's teaching, that believing in the fulfillment of our desires shapes our reality, suggests persistence can move metaphorical mountains. And it does. This aligns with Ephesians 5:13, where the manifestation of all things in light symbolizes conscious awareness materializing into reality. This process often manifests itself in unexpected ways, guiding us back onto our path, sometimes when we least expect it.

CHAPTER 15
THE OPPORTUNITY OF ABILITIES

Initiations are opportunities for us to grow larger. They are death channels. And they are birth channels. They require everything we've got.

They destroy us to recreate us.

—Stephen Cope, *The Great Work of Your Life*

As Byron Katie teaches, "It's not reality that makes us suffer; it's our thoughts about reality." Perspectives, of course, and suffering. And suffering is something many of us do quite well. Emotions are energy in motion; negative emotions carry a tremendous charge. Even our language is predominately negative.

Are we, as a societal norm, addicted to negativity? I contend that many of us are. That negativity is, according to many sources, what we dwell on, most of the time. This becomes especially poignant when the world is focusing on something that creates an enormous amount of money borne on the fear-based response of the masses, such as with the pandemic. People are promised they will not become sick if they get vaccinated so long as they make certain to get their boosters. However, as of this writing, more than two million vaccinated, double-boosted people have been diagnosed with the Covid virus or some variant of it. Our governing officials claim that the virus cannot penetrate a simple paper mask and insist that these masks be worn . . . yet we're allowed to remove the masks to eat while seated next to a stranger on an airplane.

Has this absurdity not created more of a chasm of separation and fear?

With an average of fifty thousand to seventy thousand thoughts each day, equating to about thirty-five to forty-eight thoughts per minute, our minds are constantly active. This incessant flow of thoughts acts as a dense filter, separating our thoughts and feelings, our head and heart. This relentless mental activity clouds our clarity, hinders deep listening, and obstructs our connection to our inner well-being.

What are thoughts, really? Are they actual things or entities? It certainly would seem so.

Our brains work through repetition and association, and it doesn't take a major event to produce somatic reactions.

Cognitive-behavioral therapists advocate for alleviating emotional distress by modifying thought patterns. This approach seems practical, particularly for those experiencing chronic pain, highlighting the need for a nuanced understanding of the mind-body connection. Achieving this understanding and compliance necessitates exploring various states of awareness, emphasizing the complex interplay between mental and physical health.

Our emotions and moods and the chemical states they create in our bodies control who we are and who we can become. Habitual behaviors can and do become personality traits. What do we see with the driver who always flares and curses at other drivers, the co-worker who always complains, or the sister who is constantly making herself sick? He's an angry person. She's bitter. My sister is disabled. To change these traits, we have to want to move out of our conditioned thinking and out of the emotions that are keeping us anchored there.

The challenge is that our emotions are the sum of our past experiences, and we're emotionally addicted to our familiar chemical states of being. And some people really like those parts of who they believe they are.

DICTATES

A client recently asked, "Are we permanently anchored to our tortured past?" I told her that many people believe we are. I, however, do not.

Psychologically, our personality is said to be fully formed by the time we're in our mid-thirties. What this means is that we've memorized a specific set of responses, reactions, skills, behaviors, perceptions, beliefs, and attitudes that are now programmed and running on subconscious autopilot. Thus, we'll each continue throughout our adult life to think the same thoughts, behave in the same ways, maintain the same attitudes, and perceive reality to be a certain way.

Studies have shown that, by midlife, 90-95 percent of what we do and who we are is a subconscious, automatic series of programs. The body becomes the subconscious mind, our autopilot, and the conscious mind has little to do with our behaviors. Our bodies have memorized the routines, and they are dutifully running the show for us.

When that 5-10 percent that is essentially conscious attempts to seek control, the body naturally and spontaneously counters. Why wouldn't it? After doing something the same way for what may have been decades, it knows that change may be imminent. Our internal roommates, the ones that live in our heads, come up with a myriad of defenses of why we should not attempt to realign our habituated ways of being, and those roommates can be duplicitous and are adept at sabotage.

Change is scary; change means something has to go, to vacate or to die to make room for the new. We co-create worst-case scenarios, and our bodies rebel because they already know how to. The subconscious mind, our body, in this case, is only doing what we have programmed it to do. It complies by doing what it does best, often in spite of our conscious desire to the contrary.

By quantum law, we're compelled to create more of what we have had in the past.

And thus, we addict the body. We get so accustomed to the chemical expressions that it requires more of that particular stimulus to maintain homeostasis and harmony. We are desensitized. We become addicted to the stronger emotions and feelings and their accompanying chemical responses, and this becomes our new normal. We like our normal; it's what we know. Our body craves this condition, and we take our conscious mind out of the loop.

If we consciously no longer agree with that normal and desire to make substantial changes, we must access the body-mind to effectuate positive changes and, further, be untroubled with the knowledge that the work of change doesn't always come easy. The moment we begin to believe the signals the body, in its highly habituated way, is sending us, an odd stupor sets in for many of us, and we fail to recall our original intentions. "I suddenly found myself with a cigarette in my hand after two weeks of not smoking," said one of my clients. "I absolutely could not remember picking up the damn thing and putting it in my mouth. I even lit it without remembering. Does that make me crazy?"

Her body took over. It loves cigarettes and remembered exactly what to do to get them.

Many of us can relate, whether the addiction has been to another person, chocolate, cigarettes or alcohol, sex, or work. The moment we sense that our something is being taken away, our body and mind begin to erupt. As long as we stay mired in the familiar feelings and ways of being, change is not possible. Saying we *want* change or want to change our behaviors isn't enough. We must find our own comprehensive tools, become greater than our current internal environment, and somehow learn how to have the mind and body function together in cohesion rather than in opposition.

Yoga became my comprehensive tool, which, in turn, shifted my consciousness.

The three key states of consciousness of interest are the human state, self-realization, and God-consciousness. Achieving self-recognition in these states allows for deep self-knowledge and the ability to recognize the Divine essence within. This understanding marks a significant milestone in spiritual and personal development.

Sometimes it isn't just about finding God; it is about coming home to our God even after we feel someone has kicked us out of the heavenly and once-safe dwelling we thought we had with our God.

We question, and still, we doubt. Do we leap? And if we do take that leap, will there be a safe landing?

CHAPTER 16
THE ENERGY OF AFFLICTIONS

Extraordinary afflictions are not always the punishment of extraordinary sins, but sometimes the trial of extraordinary graces.

—Matthew Henry

Neuroanatomy, the study of the nervous system's structure, offers insights into the body's defensive mechanisms and postures. However, from a yogic perspective, there is a deeper exploration beyond what Western science currently understands. This viewpoint suggests layers of understanding about the human body and consciousness that extend beyond the physical and anatomical.

In the yogic view, the energy of contraction, resistance to life or trauma—or in yogic terms the energy of afflictions—is understood to permeate far deeper than the neuromuscular systems.

In yogic philosophy, *Pranamayakosha* is the second of the five bodily layers or sheaths, known collectively as *pancha kosha*. It's recognized as the energy sheath, composed of prana, the vital life force. Pranamayakosha is crucial as it embodies life, distinguishing the living from the dead. This concept underscores the significance of energy and life force in yogic understanding of the human body.

This energy of afflictions is recognized to penetrate the subtle energy body, the pranamayakosha, and remain held there. These unconsciously held knots of energy are called samskaras. Vipassana teachers implore students not to create new samskaras.

Some of us are quite adept at creating new knots, however.

Yogic belief holds that until energetic knots are addressed, they will continue to affect the body's structure and function. Yogic philosophy suggests we inherit mental and emotional patterns, known as samskaras, that we repeatedly cycle through in life. Combining yoga and psychology can be effective in combatting these negative samskaras, with yoga offering physical insight and psychology exploring the emotional realm. Joseph Campbell describes *sankalpa*, or intention, as a "call to awakening," uniting our conscious mind with deeper aspects of ourselves. This conscious intention is a powerful tool for communicating desires to our emotional and spiritual bodies.

Sankalpa, meaning "resolution" in Sanskrit, is about setting focused, sincere intentions, crucial in spiritual practices. In iRest® Yoga Nidra, which I teach, sankalpa is used to reach deep unconscious states, similar to clinical hypnotherapy, making the mind more receptive to suggestions. The principle "energy follows intention" highlights the power of focused thought in yoga. As Dr. Masters notes, our thoughts connect us to corresponding energies in nature, drawing physical manifestations of these energy levels, leading to a transformative awakening and heightened awareness.

Ancient spiritual traditions remind us that we make choices that honor or dishonor ourselves, each other, or our world. Each moment of every day, we can make conscious choices, and through the nonlocal holographic consciousness, each of our choices creates consequences.

What so many of us do not acknowledge is that our individual choices become the collective reality for us all.

What we think about, then, we bring about, whether for our betterment or detriment. To quote Joseph Goldstein, one of the first American vipassana teachers and co-founder of the Insight Meditation Society, "The possibility for our happiness and indeed our entire spiritual journey, rests on the clarification that what most completely determines the result of any action is the motivation behind it."The Tibetans have a saying that expresses this idea succinctly: "Everything rests on the tip of motivation."

What about all the horrors? Did some of us inadvertently take a wrong turn somewhere as children? Or were some of my later teachers correct in counseling that some of what we perceive to be negative is always a spiritual lesson and a blessing in disguise?

We want something more for ourselves; we yearn for the greater and work so diligently ... then something seemingly horrific sweeps through.

We may, then, be faced with a choice of doing things differently when something negative happens, which, in retrospect, may remind us that had those challenges not been present, we would not have been led to better things. Moreover, how can we, as mere mortals, hope to continuously make real spiritual progress, become more self-realized, and equitably develop our God Itself realization amid terror or pandemonium?

Learning to look deeply, in my case, meant delving into questionable methods of communication and exploring extreme tests of faith. Yes, I willingly put myself in precarious, dangerous places and conditions as a challenge to my Creator.

Would you willingly go through a lesson that, in hindsight, had leveled your world as you knew it? Many, including the me of today, would. It is the classic paradigm of "if/then": if that had not happened, I would not be where I am today. A note that I keep on my desk reads, "There are far better things ahead than any we may leave behind." Part of my belief system encompasses the upward movement of our learning and growth; this saying embodies that for me.

BRIDGING GAPS

Spiritual growth, for many, is a gradual transition from identifying with the ego-self into a realization and recognition of what is ego-driven and what is an awakening or awareness on a conscious level. We seek to become our own guru, and our creations teach us to become our own personal guru. Guru, in Sanskrit, means "from darkness to light."

As Jung said: "I cannot define for you what God is. I can only say that my work has proved empirically that the pattern of God exists in every man and that this pattern has at its disposal the greatest of all his energies for transformation and transfiguration of his natural being. Not only has the meaning of his life but his renewal and his institutions depended on his conscious relationship with this pattern of his collective unconscious" (Barry). Bridging the gap between the conscious and the unconscious becomes the directive, yet how?

All major scriptures echo a common theme: the revelation of fundamental truths through mystical encounters with higher spiritual realities. While such encounters may seem sporadic for many in the Western world—including regular practitioners of prayer—shamans, wisdom keepers, and yogis anticipate and regularly experience guidance from a higher plane, viewing spiritual experiences as normal and routine. As my grandmother used to say, "The Great Creator always shows us things. So pay attention! Creator shows all of us. Most of us choose not to see." This raises the question: does expecting a connection make it more likely to occur?

In reexamining the cartography of my younger years, receptivity surfaced as a theme. Meditation was always a practice in my youth, although teachers would often say I was "checking out." I would scribble and sketch while prayers were being recited, and I could easily recite the prayers back to the annoyed, often baffled, teachers. I, like most children, had my own form of prayers.

Though not as adept at instant recall these days, I still have my own way of communicating with the Divine and have a hugely different interpretation of the Bible than many people. The verses and parables often seem terse, fear-based, and controlling to me. Several of my personal mentors have conveyed that they believe that the Churches at large have edited the great works to suit their standards and have intentionally distorted the interpretations to create a mind-numbing control of their followers.

Thus, when someone insists I believe something "because the Bible says so," I doubt. I once mentioned to a church Elder, for example, that there are glyphs in the buildings in Egypt that predate the Bible and foretell of many things, including helicopters and devastations. I also explained the reasons why I believed Jesus spent time in solitude, meditation, and initiation inside the Great Pyramid. He countered with, "That's not possible... not at all possible." He made no efforts to mask his disdain either.

The same Elder conclusively put his hand on the Bible he was holding and said, "This is the absolute Word of God!" When I explained that the copy he was holding was not, in my opinion, the unabridged word of God, I thought for a moment he would throw the book at me.

I also believe that specific passages of the Bible may have been rewritten, misinterpreted, or intentionally removed and may, therefore, influence some of what many consider to be true.

When I asked the Elder if he prayed, he nodded. When I asked him if he meditated, he snickered. When I asked him if his prayers were ever answered, he nodded again and said that "God speaks to him."

I told him bluntly that meditation also was a doorway to the Divine. He informed me that yogis are pagans and heretics in his opinion.

When I asked him why he thought it was acceptable to practice polygamy, because he is, he slammed the Bible down on the table in front of me. "Women! Simple, stupid creatures! You are supposed to obey men; women are servants to our Lord God and to men! We are to go forth and multiply!" He began spewing citations to substantiate his position.

I saw this as a lesson in patience and tolerance, being handed directly to me, via this misogynist. I wondered aloud, though, why he thought he was suffering so terribly with a failing heart.

The Hebrew word translated as "helper" is *ezer*, which denotes one who surrounds, protects, or aids. "It is this same word that Jacob used of God when he said, 'May the God of your father help you'" (Genesis 49:25). Moses used it when he said, "The God of my ancestors was my helper" (Exodus 18:4).

God is primarily portrayed by the Old Testament writers as the Ezer—the one who surrounds us and helps us. This is definitely not that of a lowly servant role. Instead, it is a lofty role to bring help to one who needs it. And many men today will admit they need the aid and assistance of not only God but the expert aid and support of a woman.

When God created a female as a Godlike equal to help the male, it was a highly esteemed role, not one of inferiority or servitude. God considered the man to need a woman. This didn't mean he, as a man, was inferior. Women are not inferior for being a counterpart or companion to men, and men are not weak for needing women.

Perspectives, yet again.

CHAPTER 17
AT ONE

Have the courage to follow your heart and intuition - they somehow already know what you truly want to become.

—Steve Jobs

Creativity and expression, manifested through forms and images, serve as the primary languages of our psyche. Before we even venture into the realm of conceptual thought, it is through these artistic expressions that we connect most deeply with our inner selves. This connection to creativity is a vital part of steering our lives toward greater fulfillment and self-actualization.

By actively listening to and following our inner voice, we embark on a journey that not only enriches us but also has the potential to lead us to a life that is both rewarding and in alignment with our true selves. This concept echoes the belief that, often, those who stand out from the norm—the outcasts—are the ones who lead and bring unique contributions to the world. Their perspectives, formed on the fringes, offer fresh insights and leadership.

In the world of creativity, recognition often comes from external validation within one's professional community. Yet, the stories of some of history's most celebrated figures, such as van Gogh and Mendel, challenge this idea. Their lack of recognition during their lifetimes forces us to question the traditional metrics of creative success. These examples highlight the need for a deeper understanding and appreciation of creativity, one that transcends immediate acknowledgment and peers' recognition.

The idea of being an outcast often intersects with a deeper connection to our Source, a trait common among leaders and creative individuals. Reflecting on my own childhood, I often faced strict discipline for my inattentiveness and daydreaming during class. At the age of four, a severe illness led to hearing loss in one ear. This impairment made it challenging for me to hear or understand others unless they were speaking directly to me. Coupled with the frequent pain from my illness, my world was quite isolated. Yet, in this solitude, I found that I could hear and see things beyond the ordinary, perceiving what others could not. This unique sensory experience shaped my understanding of being different, or an "outcast," in the context of a deeper connection to something beyond the tangible.

The phenomenon where loss of one sense leads to heightened abilities in other senses is known as sensory compensation. Scientific studies have shown that when a sense like hearing or sight is diminished, the brain undergoes neurological changes to adjust. This can result in enhanced tactile, auditory, or visual acuity in the remaining senses. For instance, people who are blind often experience heightened auditory and tactile sensitivities. These adaptations are a testament to the brain's remarkable plasticity and its ability to rewire itself in response to sensory loss.

OUTLIERS

I remember weeping puddles on the desk one day, as I knew, in my heart, that it was a vital turning point in my educational experience as a child. I loved learning. I truly did; I did not enjoy going to school at all after that day.

It was a book report day. Riding with my father in his car on our way to school that day, I remember rehearsing my report with him and being thrilled to share what I had been learning with the class. When it was my turn, the teacher went from guarded to furious; she peered disapprovingly over her glasses and wrung her hands together. When I excitedly attempted to explain to the class that Jesus spent time meditating in the Great Pyramid and Atlantis was a landmass that had sunk to the bottom of the ocean, the teacher threatened me with a paddle (yes, that was still allowed several decades ago). She grimly reminded me of my "place" and admonished that certain things were not Christian, nor would they be tolerated in a Christian school. She called my father in for a parent-teacher meeting and further attempted to scold him for filling my head full of heathen stories. He assured her I was reading, comprehending, and conveying the stories of my own accord. I was in third grade at the time. Yes, that year again; the same year that my then-boyfriend, Scotty, and I were planning the escape to my grandmother's home. It was a remarkably busy year for me.

The same Christian schoolteacher recommended extensive academic testing. When I tested fully ten grade levels ahead in various subjects, it mortified the teacher. How could I be learning when I wasn't "present" and was not willing to interact with the other children other than one or two select others? All I wanted to do, according to the teacher, was "play." She suggested placing me in another classroom. She had already tried putting me into time-outs, moving me to other parts of the classroom, and sending me to the principal's office, all to no avail.

That negative experience was one of those proverbial blessings in disguise that did undoubtedly result in a greater good. To me, learning was supposed to be a form of play, and learning was meant to be fun. Today, I use forms of play to teach adults how to do things they may insist that they are not able to learn or cannot do. My classes, independent of Nidra and some clinic-based therapeutic yoga classes, are filled with hilarity and with joy. We have fun, especially in the retreat setting. We play. We eat treats and give each other lots of hugs. If there are tears, they are never intentional tears of frustration or of not belonging, they are tears of empathy and compassion. One of the kindest compliments I routinely hear is "follow the laughter—that's where you'll find her classes." I love this so much.

Lev Semyonovich Vygotsky highlighted that children's play is more than mere imitation; it's a creative reworking of experiences, reshaped to suit their needs and desires. This raises questions about the magical, artistic expressions in children like me, who perceive the world uniquely—feeling colors, seeing tones, and naturally communing with animals, even without play being modeled or encouraged by elders. This suggests a deeper, inherent capacity in children for imaginative and creative interpretation of their world.

SPIRIT AT PLAY

All of us are creative; we're born that way, and it is innate. We get squashed as we gain our momentum and our years, though. Children, however, if given a modicum of encouragement, will use play to channel this creativity. The genuine artist explores their tools, inspiration, forms, colors, and even their mind. Through play, we journey to realms that exist before consciousness and judgment. Play serves as the source of delightful surprises, a clear indication of the presence of spirit in both play and work. Freud stated that Leonardo DaVinci remained like a child for the whole of his life in more than one way. As quoted: "All great men are bound to retain some infantile part. Even as an adult, he [daVinci] continued to play, and this was another reason why he often appeared uncanny and incomprehensible to his contemporaries." My clients and students often comment that I'm more like a happy-go-lucky kid than a somber professional. One woman insists I'm "goofy and irreverent." And why not?

The question arises: does a child purely imagine, or are they more attuned and less critical, thus more closely connected to a Source of inspiration? Lev Vygotsky suggests that what children see and hear forms the foundation for their imaginative creations. They gather experiences as materials for the complex task of constructing fantasies. The intriguing part is understanding where the inspiration for this complex reworking originates. How does a child intuitively navigate through this creative complexity?

In psychology, this creative process, rooted in the brain's ability to combine elements, is known as imagination or fantasy. However, these terms are often used differently in everyday language compared to their scientific definitions. As per *Oxford Dictionaries*, fantasy is the product of imagination, existing within the mind, while reality exists independently. This distinction highlights a child's unique ability to bridge their inner imaginative world with the external reality they perceive.

Psychology is often only referred to as the study of the mind, the way we consciously form concepts and the way we understand the world around us, and the "soul" is an ignored part of the studies. Spirituality, conversely, can be defined in many different ways, and yet it is often regarded as a practical tool to achieve self-growth as it provides a portal for transcendence. It helps us transcend the analytical functioning and cognitive processing of the mind and creates space for other experiences. Spirituality is the experience of "Self-Transcendence," wherein one allows the experience of one's Self to move beyond the personal Self into an experience where the attachment to that individual Self disappears. At that point, one becomes part of all that "is," and we are considered to be "at one" with everything.

Dean H. Hamer, a behavioral geneticist, asserts that spirituality and the feeling of transcendence are inherent parts of our nature. He suggests this inherent spirituality drives the popularity of nontraditional religions in the US and the diverse array of religions globally. Hamer believes that the human propensity for spirituality, the urge to reach beyond oneself, is a fundamental aspect of our being.

Moreover, imagination, as Vygotsky points out, is the foundation of all creative endeavors and is vital across all cultural spheres. It fuels artistic, scientific, and technical innovations. Essentially, without imagination, our cultural and personal worlds would be devoid of the richness they currently possess.

A CELEBRATION OF ABILITY

Megan McCormick, driven by her passion for educating young children, achieved remarkable academic success. She earned her degree in education, graduating at the top of her class from Bluegrass Community Technical College in Kentucky. Her achievement is a testament to her dedication and the supportive environment created by her family. Her mother's philosophy was simple yet powerful: raising Megan without limits and acknowledging her abilities. This approach enabled Megan to break barriers, becoming the first individual with Down syndrome in the United States to graduate with honors from a technical college.

This inspiring story highlights a significant shift from traditional views on Down syndrome. Children with this condition are often unfairly labeled as slow learners or difficult to teach. However, Megan's story and research show that many individuals with Down syndrome possess a strong social inclination, often displaying a level of social engagement that surpasses that of their peers, including those without disabilities. This challenges the stereotypes and emphasizes the importance of recognizing and nurturing the unique strengths and abilities of each individual.

Children with Down syndrome are also, some believe, gifts from God with a special connection to Source put here with lessons for us all to learn. In Megan's case, I feel she is both.

Do our schools encourage respect and celebration of children's abilities and thus foster a connection with Source? Children are taught to pass one-size-fits-all exams rather than to nurture original thoughts; imagination and play are likewise squelched. It seems, however, that while creativity is cultivated through autonomy, it is, instead, being stifled by the continuous pressure to conform that restricts children's lives today. Creativity is crucial to success in the real world, yet are we not subjecting children to an educational system that assumes there is only one correct way to do things?

Parents lament that their children are stupid or stubborn or bored with school. It is my position, in this case, that boredom is synonymous with stupidity and that children are not innately stupid. Instead, I feel that children become discouraged and seek other avenues of expression, which may include stubbornness. Many of us know children who are labeled as disruptive and inattentive in school when, in fact, they are brilliant and may have a more open communication with Source. "I had one student run off chasing butterflies one morning very recently," said a teacher from my local area. "When I questioned her as to why she failed to come into the classroom when I repeatedly called out to her, she informed me, quite frankly, that the butterflies were about to die and that she was quizzing them about their amazing journeys." I thought that was beautiful.

Thanks to a raging infection, I almost died as a very young child and was consequently blessed with the loss of hearing in one ear and a proclivity for sensing things in unusual ways. Yes, I did often "turn a deaf ear" to the cacophony of a chaotic and toxic childhood as the people and the noises were often overwhelming. The noises still can be, and I'm often perplexed when people insist they must always have sound in the form of television programs or the radio continually playing.

Why are they so intent on distractions?

As I child, I preferred to be alone or spend time with my animal friends, and meandering around the desert in search of treasures was my way of finding quiet time to have my talks with Creator, whom I referred to as "Mommy-Daddy." As moving meditations or prayers, these long, long walks were filled with two-way discussions about everything of this world and others. Later I learned that God's name in Aramaic is that of "Great Birther." To this day, one of my most fundamental of mantras is that of *"Solvitur Ambulando"*—a Latin phrase meaning "it is solved by walking."

THE WAY

For me, all things have been solved with faith. I walk daily in meditation for an hour. I've walked numerous trails stateside and abroad over hundreds and hundreds of kilometers and have many more trips I'm planning to take. My two most recent "Big Trips" were the El Camino de Santiago, The Way of Saint James. I walked the Camino Frances (well over seven hundred kilometers) in 2020 and walked the shorter Camino Portugues route in 2022. There are seven major routes; the Camino Frances is the most popular.

The five-hundred-mile pilgrimage across the Iberian Peninsula is said to be a walk of the soul. Those of us who make this journey are known as pilgrims or *peregrinos* (peregrinas, feminine), and undeniably, we are in many ways, even if we do have the latest and greatest backpack, hiking boots, or GPS app on our brand-new phone. None of those trappings will ever compensate for the irrefutable spiritual lessons borne of the solitude one experiences when traveling alone, on foot, in a place far from home. Some of us eschew having phone service or GPS and simply follow the yellow arrows pointing the way to Santiago. I did. Some have their bags transported from place to place and forego walking when the weather is less than pleasant or predictable. I did not. Even still, walking hour after hour, day after day can be an intimidating and demanding endeavor, as it requires not only physical endurance but also the mental resilience to confront one's inner demons and navigate the emotional challenges that arise along the way. Our self-sufficiency is tested and bolstered, our inner strength is discovered, and our emotional resilience is honed during this arduous journey. We find ourselves facing and fighting demons that have been buried deep within, confronting fears that have long been ignored, and seeking inner peace amidst the relentless rhythm of the Camino. And for some of us, these inner battles are nothing short of extraordinary.

Many places I've traversed on foot over many kilometers, such as the Inca Trail, are also thought to be frequented in spirit by those who have gone before us and have left the planet physically. "That was the coolest and the scariest shit, ever!" noted one of my trail mates in Peru. He continued, "The trail gave way and all of a sudden, my gramma was right there and grabbed my arm. Thanks to her, I didn't fall." The trails are not haunted, necessarily. "They who you feel on the trail are angels of protection, protecting both of you and *Pachamama* (Mother Earth)" is how it was described to me. The Camino de Santiago is also rich with stories and personal accounts of spiritual encounters and otherworldly experiences. Numerous pilgrims have shared tales of supportive spirits and unique, often mystical, frequencies encountered along the route. Additionally, locals who live along the Camino speak openly about the distinct energies present in the area, further enriching the narrative of this historic pilgrimage as a journey imbued with spiritual and transformative qualities.

The Way of Saint James or simply "The Way" as the Camino de Santiago is also known, is a network of routes leading to the shrine of the Apostle Saint James the Great in the Cathedral of Santiago de Compostela in Galicia, Spain. It is believed that the remains of the saint are buried there. The earliest records date from the ninth century, in the time of the Kingdom of Asturias and Galicia.

According to Christian legend, the Apostle James was responsible for the Iberian Peninsula when the Apostles divided the known world into missionary zones. The Apostle James is the patron saint of Spaniards and Portuguese, and as such, is often identified as Santiago or São Tiago.

Seventh and eighth-century documents suggest that James spent a number of years campaigning on the peninsula before returning to Jerusalem, where in the year 44 AD he was beheaded by Herod Agrippa I. It is said that James's followers carried his body to the coast and put it into a stone boat, which was guided by angels and carried by the wind beyond the Pillars of Hercules (the Strait of

Gibraltar). The boat landed near Finisterre, in northern Spain. The local Queen, Lupa, supplied the team of oxen used to draw the body from Padrón to the site of a marble tomb (which she had also provided). Saint James was believed to have been buried there with two of his disciples. The body was said to have lay undisturbed until the ninth century.

Early in the ninth century, a hermit by the name of Pelagius had a vision in which he saw a star or a field of stars that led him to what proved to be an ancient tomb containing three bodies. He immediately reported this to the local bishop, Theodomir, who declared the remains to be those of Saint James and two of his followers. This, in turn, was reported to the King of Asturias, Alphonso II, who declared Saint James to be the patron saint of Spain, or of what would eventually be Spain. A village named Campus de la Stella (Field of Stars) and a monastery were established on the site. News of the discovery spread, and a small number of pilgrims began to arrive. King Alfonso II would later commission a larger temple to attract pilgrims from all over the world, competing with other prominent religious centers of pilgrimage such as Jerusalem and Rome.

It was believed that the site was responsible for miracles, and the wonders encouraged pilgrimage. This was actively endorsed by the Archbishop Gelmirez of Galicia and by the cathedral authorities, who were enthusiastically promoting Santiago as a pilgrimage destination. The monks of the Abbey of Cluny in France were also anxious to support the Spanish Church in its struggle against the Moors on the Peninsula.

The earliest recorded pilgrims from beyond the Pyrenees visited the shrine in the middle of the eleventh century. The earliest records of pilgrims that arrived from England belong to the period between 1092 and 1105.

There is also an interesting pre-history of the Camino; it seems The Way might have attracted pilgrims even earlier than the eighth century, as a route that followed the Milky Way all the way to

Fisterra (Finis Terrae, now known as Finisterre). Finisterre was believed to be the end of the world, a magical place where the living could get closest to the land of the dead and to the "other world."

It is said that many of the people who make the pilgrimage to Santiago are at a turning point in their lives, as I was. The medieval pilgrim was seeking forgiveness for sins or for the saint's assistance in some matter, and the pilgrimage was that of atonement. I've also heard The Way referred to as "The Trail of Tears."

I feel, as do many of my friends who have made modern-day pilgrimages do, that we are each called to make arduous journeys such as this. It is a retreat, a period of separation from all that is familiar, a time of letting go of the dailies as we know them in our present day-to-day existence, and a time of realignment with Self and our Creator. We pray with our footsteps, and we meditate by drinking in the divinity of Nature. This is not a matter of punishment nor spiritual reparation; it is for seeking a greater and purer connection with Source.

Assuredly there will be those within our circle of influence who will undoubtedly discourage our promptings and proclaim our callings to be anything other than what, in our hearts, we know them to be. People we love and trust may balk, sometimes to the point of hindering or even thwarting our journeys with excuses thinly veiled as irrefutable reasons. Please remember that they are human too, and parents, lovers, spouses, children, and friends will all have their opinions and justifications of why you cannot do what you know your heart is telling you that you must. Is this not a first test of our resolve? Upon my first mention of what one friend refers to as my "little five-hundred-plus mile solo stroll," my musings and excitement were met with many variations of the same sentiment: "Are you crazy?" and "You can walk here; why do you have go halfway around the world?"

So here's my question: why does anyone seek to do anything other than waste this precious gift of life we've been given? So many people firmly plant their backside on a worn-out sofa in front of an electronic amusement box airing insipid sit-coms and complain that their lives are boring or that learning or traveling isn't worth the time and expense. "Life is just a hamster wheel," said an acquaintance recently. When I asked him what he was doing to engage with life, he snorted and said, "Who has the time to do what they want when there are bills to be paid, work to do, and an endless stream of things breaking?"

To me, this lends a new perspective to the term "killing time."

The exasperated teacher who finally demanded that I be admitted for testing when I was in third grade had conveyed to my parents and other teachers that I was prone to daydreaming and my "checking out" was thus disruptive. This malignant digression firmly established a thorny and complicated set of rifts between the school, me, and my father. Many years later I would cross paths with this teacher's son in Nazca, Peru, a place that is twelve hours from Lima and an obscure, otherworldly place of lines that one can only see from the air. He shared that his mother had never forgotten the incident or me. Why had we crossed paths thousands of miles from home dozens of years later?

He wanted to know if I studied the occult or if I had gone for medical testing to find out if my brain worked differently than others. He felt his brain did and couldn't understand his compulsion to visit places such as Nazca. I asked him why he hadn't gone to the same school his mother taught at as he and I would have been in the same grade and classroom. He explained his mother was too challenged by him and wanted him to have the public school experience early on.

He also explained she was often angry and frustrated with him because he had playmates from another dimension. I assured him that I, too, had learned to forget many things I "knew" during childhood and was working diligently in my adulthood to remember how to connect with this Knowing. He was there, he explained, in search of many things that had never made any sense to him as a child. I asked him what his mother thought about his travels; he shrugged and said it was his journey now, whether or not if she liked what he was doing.

ADHD

Did I fit the standardized diagnosis of Attention Deficit Hyperactivity Disorder—ADHD—as a child? Yes, perhaps, I did. Thanks to a father with a disdain for Big Pharma and an insatiable appetite for learning, a home without television, and understanding grandmothers who were raised before the Great Depression, I learned to read as a toddler and had access, although not with my parents' permission, to the tools to craft and shape a myriad of things. Accordingly, I was able to channel my creativity despite the constraints and requirements of attendance at a very dogmatic grade school and a less-than-supportive home environment. As a child, I was routinely shamed for making my creative messes and fashioning things that had no practical value other than the joy of crafting it brought for me or to others. I would often get up in the wee hours of the night to sew or draw or glue pieces of treasures together to make something new and extraordinary. I was driven to do this—and often still am as an adult. By what or whom? I filled my school notebooks with sketches of costume-type ballroom dresses from another era. Later I would design and make formals and wedding dresses; later still, I would handcraft five-jointed teddy bears. Where had I learned to draw or "form fabric?"

Always highly energetic, my spirit was often tormented by the storms from within the confines of the family. Constant criticism derails almost anyone. My father, though an artist himself, often displayed a hypocritical stance toward the creation of art. While he engaged in artistic endeavors, he paradoxically criticized me for creating art purely for its own sake. And, growing up, I was often reminded that "no one likes a know-it-all," yet there was a clear expectation for me to excel in grade school and have ready answers for my father's broad range of eclectic questions. These questions could be as diverse as understanding the chemical combinations for creating explosions to speculations about the constructors of the mythical Lemuria. My father, who was a Mensa genius, also had a volatile nature, characterized by episodes of blinding rage.

Growing up with my father undoubtedly shaped many aspects of who I am today. Navigating his complex moods and meeting his high intellectual expectations taught me to think critically and adapt rapidly to changing situations. While I learned early on how to people-please as a solution to remain safe in that environment, it also fostered in me a resilience and an ability to understand and react to intricate emotional dynamics. This unique upbringing, while challenging, also sparked my interest in human behavior and mental health, particularly conditions like ADHD and the influence of allowing creative play. This fascination led me to observe patterns in how creativity is nurtured or stifled. Over the years, I've noticed an intriguing trend: the interplay between mental health conditions and the expression of creativity, and how this dynamic inevitably shapes individual experiences in the artistic domain.

An interviewer on NPR radio captured this sentiment well, stating, "I believe in my older years [...] I think I have adult ADHD or something [...] I'm wondering how much ADHD or ADD has contributed to having a stifled creative process." This comment resonates with my belief that many creatives experience a sort of psychic discontent, a frustration stemming from unfulfilled potential and an inability to fully express their creativity. It seems this restless energy and sense of blockage is a common thread among those in the creative fields.

Delving into the interplay between ADHD and the creative process unveils a complex dynamic. ADHD, characterized by symptoms like inattention and impulsivity, might seem at odds with sustained creative work. These traits can create challenges in focusing or seeing lengthy projects through to completion, potentially stifling the flourishing of artistic abilities. Yet, paradoxically, the same ADHD characteristics often spark a wellspring of originality and innovative thinking. The key lies in recognizing and adapting to the distinct ways ADHD impacts an individual's path in creativity. In light of this, the evolving landscape of our educational system becomes a matter of concern. As public schools increasingly cut back on art and music programs, essential platforms that support varied learning styles, including those affected by ADHD, are diminishing. These shifts in our educational priorities call for a deeper reflection on how we foster creativity and meet the diverse needs of all students.

This trend, documented in various research and reports, signifies a shift in educational focus, often to the detriment of holistic learning approaches that cater to diverse student needs. Recognizing the value of these creative subjects in nurturing different learning styles, some parents, those with the necessary resources and understanding, opt to move their children to private schools. This decision underscores a commitment to supporting their children's unique educational needs, which are not just academic but also encompass artistic and creative growth. Such choices reflect a deeper awareness of the multifaceted nature of learning and the importance of fostering all aspects of a child's development.

Imagine a child who shows a keen interest and aptitude in visual arts from a young age. Their parents notice this and decide to support this interest despite the child struggling in a traditional school setting, possibly due to an unconventional learning style. They enroll the child in a school with a strong emphasis on arts education or provide supplementary art classes outside of school. In this nurturing environment, tailored to their unique learning style, the child thrives, developing not only their artistic skills but also gaining confidence and improved academic performance across other subjects. This support helps the child realize their potential in a way that might not have been possible in a conventional educational setting.

An incredible teenager who worked for me on the weekends is another example. Considered to be "gifted" by many who know her, she and her sister drove an hour each direction to attend a self-directed learning high school, a support system that cost their parents thousands of dollars in tuition each year. These teens are both beautiful, ambidextrous, curious, artistic, and able to solve complex math problems rapidly without writing them down. They also performed in the Sailor Circus division of the Ringling Circus performances and trained with the circus after school five days each week. They can, among other feats, ride a unicycle while on a high wire with the other sibling doing a headstand on top of their head.

HELD HOSTAGE

The classroom schedule changes in response to Common Core examinations made across the states is just one example of what several parents have explained to me:

> The governors of 45 states and the District of Columbia took up the Common Core standards. They began implementing them with the support of the Obama administration, which aimed at common standards and assessments as a means of comparing achievement in math, language arts, and literacy across schools in the states. In short order, teachers and students started orienting themselves toward the Common Core set of mandatory standardized tests. And because a mechanism in the Common Core discussion often ties teachers' pay and job status to the results of student performance on those tests, many schools have taken the block of time regularly carved out for recess and put it towards classroom time to teach the test [...] "Preparing America's students for success" is one of the slogans often trumpeted by the Common Core initiative. It is a terrific aspiration [...] But if you ask most parents, teachers, and students, they will tell you that, under current conditions, it is closer to imprisonment than education. (Igel)

How can children flourish in a creative way when their recesses are taken away? Too many children have said that they hate going to school and even my friend's daughter, a bright and beautiful young girl, who loves to read and knit, returns home after purposely missing the school bus. The child explains that she has been troubled at school. She's frightened by the violence, afraid of the abuse from the "have-it-all-girls," discouraged by the restrictions of the educational system, and further, she has tears in her eyes as she attempts to clarify how angry she is with the limitations of her environment. "It's hot and noisy, and everybody is always mad, mad, mad." I felt the same way as a child. She further explains, "I can't think anywhere—not at home when the family is there, not at school. How am I supposed to learn?" This bright and beautiful child is only twelve years old.

It is not the most affluent of neighborhoods, and I also witness children who, with the limited support resources they have available to them, are working against a social tide to rise above their circumstances. "He was never a bad kid 'til the shootings the other day," says one father. "He used to like goin' to school. Now, well, he's just done gave up. Doctor say he's got a complex 'bout going to school."

Children today are facing an array of stressors that can be deeply unsettling. The rise in bullying, the prevalence of extreme violence in media, and the fast-paced omnipresence of social media are significant contributors to their stress. Studies indicate a growing concern about the mental health of young people, with chronic stress affecting their psychological well-being, behavior, and academic performance.

The impact of these stressors extends to how children perceive and react to the world. As explained by Diane Zimberoff, children develop behaviors to defend against psychological and physical threats. These behaviors, or "shadows" in psychological terms, initially serve as protective mechanisms. Over time, as these patterns align with archetypal powers, they form complexes. These complexes, initially developed to guard against harm, eventually become entrenched, operating unconsciously as an automatic response system in the child. This development of a reflexive response is a critical aspect of how children adapt to their environments but also speaks to the need for supportive and nurturing surroundings to foster healthier coping mechanisms.

How can we, as adults, help support and foster healthier coping for our children?

Vygotsky believed that effective education is about nurturing and guiding what already exists within a child. The goal is to awaken the child's innate abilities and direct their development in a specific direction. Traditional education often emphasizes left-brain activities, focusing on logic and analytical thinking. This approach can leave many children feeling frustrated or misunderstood, particularly when their natural learning styles are overlooked or suppressed. The confinement of spending every day in a structured classroom environment may hinder rather than foster a child's soul growth and creative development. As a result, we're seeing a decline in children's creativity, calling for a reevaluation of our educational approaches to better cater to the diverse needs and talents of all children.

Kyung Hee Kim, an education professor at the College of William and Mary, conducted an analysis of the Torrance Tests of Creative Thinking (TTCT) scores. These scores were collected from normative samples of children in kindergarten through twelfth grade over several decades. Kim's findings revealed a significant decline in creativity scores starting between 1984 and 1990, a trend that has continued. The decrease in these scores is not only statistically significant but also deeply concerning. Kim noted that the data reflects a marked decrease in various aspects of children's creativity. Children, according to her observations, have become less emotionally expressive, less energetic, less talkative, less humorous, less imaginative, less unconventional, less passionate, less perceptive, less capable of making unusual connections, less synthesizing, and less inclined to see things from different perspectives.

But is it possible to let our children explore their creativity freely, without imposing our expectations on them? I believe this approach aligns with a philosophy of detached, loving kindness. The act of creation, and taking ownership of what we create, enables us to delve into the wealth of images within ourselves. This process fosters a connection to a deeper Knowing, one that stems from our link to a higher, God-like consciousness. Such an approach can be transformative, both for us and for our children, as we navigate our creative journeys.

CHAPTER 18
PARADIGMS

O Birther! Father-Mother of the Cosmos,
you create all that moves
in light.
O Thou! The Breathing Life of all,
Creator of the Shimmering Sound that
touches us.
Respiration of all worlds,
we hear you breathing—in and out—
in silence.
Source of Sound: in the roar and the whisper,
in the breeze and the whirlwind, we
hear your Name.
Radiant One: You shine within us,
outside us—even darkness shines—when
we remember.

This is the translation of the opening line of the Lord's Prayer, Our Father Who Art in Heaven, that I prefer. God isn't out there. God is right here in each and every one of us, in our world, right now. Why, then, do people continue to affirm their separation daily?

Translated from Aramaic, the language of Jesus's time, these texts comprehensibly indicate that we are not separate. We and our Source are one—The Radiant One shines within us when we remember.

The translations come from the Nag Hammadi Library or Scriptures.

The Nag Hammadi Library is a collection of thirteen ancient books (called "codices") containing over fifty texts that were discovered in Egypt in 1945. This incredible discovery includes a large number of primary "Gnostic Gospels" such as the Gospel of Thomas, the Gospel of Philip, and the Gospel of Truth that were among texts once thought to have been entirely destroyed during the early Christian struggle to define orthodoxy. The discovery and translation of the Nag Hammadi Library, initially completed in the 1970s, has provided the impetus to a major reevaluation of early Christian history and the nature of Gnosticism.

CONTEMPLATING CHRISTIANISM

Some forms of meditation practiced by Christians, particularly those performed in monasteries, are a purer form of meditation, while other Christian meditative-type practices are forms of "contemplation." Rather than meditative in nature, the person who is praying is directing thoughts, in my opinion, in a disciplined and definite manner to address a particular theological matter.

This process of contemplation is also routinely used in yogi "talks" and often concludes with an effort to apply the concepts contemplated to one's life.

Prayer, at least in the West, is a much more recognizable form of this type of contemplative practice.

While sincere prayer probably cannot take place without entering a somewhat altered state, dutiful repetitions of standardized prayers recited to fulfill religious obligations aren't necessarily the same as meditating.

The relationship between meditation and prayer is nuanced, with both sharing similarities. Typically, they are inward-focused and meditative, often practiced in solitude. In a church setting, various elements like music, candlelight, offerings, symbolism, and specific postures are used to foster a sense of reverence and connection with that which is holy. These practices in a religious context are aimed at enhancing the feeling of unity with a something greater than we are as mere mortals.

While prayer often involves a meditative state, it is typically more goal-oriented. In prayer, individuals seek to invoke and establish a relationship with a deity. This contrasts with the meditative approach of "nowhere to go, nothing to do," which is more about being in the moment. Dionysios Farasiotis, for instance, describes Christian prayer as asking for God's mercy, which is believed to lead to theosis, or union with God.

Yet, when considering other forms of prayer, the lines between prayer and meditation become less distinct. Edward Maupin, a psychiatrist, noted that contemplative prayer was once the West's primary socially accepted form of meditation. He observed that the decline of prayer in Western societies has led to a loss of quiet, introspective experiences vital for nurturing the human spirit. This shift highlights the evolving nature of spiritual practices and their impact on individuals and cultures.

FORMS AND FUNCTIONS

Prayer sometimes takes a form similar to meditation, altering states of consciousness. *Japa* meditation, involving the meditative repetition of a mantra, is practiced in Buddhism, Hinduism, Jainism, and Sikhism. This mantra may be spoken aloud or silently within the mind. "Om," pronounced "A-U-M," is a common mantra in Japa, representing the Universe's creative energy. Regarded as the original sound of the Universe or the essence of God, "Om" is central to the Mandukya Upanishad. This text, focusing solely on "Om," delves into four states of consciousness, underscoring its spiritual significance.

The Mandukya Upanishad elucidates four states of consciousness, each symbolized by a specific aspect of the sacred syllable "AUM":

1. The "waking state," where the senses are outwardly oriented, corresponds to the letter A. By understanding this state, one gains mastery over their senses, leading to the fulfillment of desires and the attainment of greatness.
2. The "dream state," characterized by inwardly directed senses, is represented by the letter U. Mastery of this state leads to control over dreams, wisdom, and an elevation of the entire family's spiritual evolution.
3. "Deep sleep," a state of peaceful consciousness devoid of external and internal perceptions, is denoted by the letter M. Understanding this state grants knowledge of all, and everything converges into the Self. Patanjali's Yoga Sutras and Psalms affirm the significance of "Mmmm" as the name of God and the source of truth during sleep.
4. The fourth state, known as Turiya or Transcendental Consciousness, represents the soundless aspect of AUM or the gap between thoughts. Turiya is symbolized by "AUM" and, although indivisible, consists of three sounds. It is the very Self, transcending birth and death, symbolizing eternal joy. Those who recognize it as such enter the Self through their own Self, becoming embodiments of truth.

Furthermore, as the initial vibration of OM emerges from the unmanifest, it transforms, giving rise to all the diverse vibrations that constitute the Universe, ultimately resulting in the world as we know it. OM embodies the essence of all mantras, sounds, and vibrations in the Universe, serving as a representation of Pure Consciousness, the origin of all existence. It is the collective resonance of the Universe, symbolizing the Primordial Sound.

Moreover, as we exhale the syllables A-U-M, the vibration forms a profound connection with the original source of creation. When performed correctly, this sound resonates from the pelvic floor upward, extending through the crown of the head, filling the entire body with a pulsating energy that both empowers and brings tranquility.

Rama Jyoti Vernon teaches proper sounding this way:

"To sound the first two syllables, open the mouth wide as if you want to take in the fullness of the Universe. Pursing lips together helps stretch out the next two syllables. It's like both sides of the brain come together to form an arrow that is sent out with a sharp focus [...] Place the tip of your tongue on the roof of your mouth to sound the last two syllables, m, and ng, which symbolize the close of the creation cycle. Let the silence drape over you before inhaling again."

Beyond phonetics, the most insightful teaching in this context is that "exhalation embodies an egoless state [...] It's not a matter of me doing the Om; the Om expresses itself through me."

In Western monastic traditions, the repetitive recitation of words in devotion to God has long been employed to evoke a specific state, with the purpose of guiding the practitioner into a heightened sense of unity with the Divine. An example of this practice is the "Prayer of the Heart," observed by Russian monks and devout individuals in pre-revolutionary Russia.

Intended to purify the intellect, a specific prayer was practiced by adopting a passive mindset and rhythmically repeating the phrase "Lord Jesus Christ, have mercy on me." This repetition was believed to invite the influence of the Holy Spirit, as expressed by Dionysios Farasiotis: "When we wholeheartedly say 'Lord Jesus Christ,' we come under the guidance of the Holy Spirit, for, as Saint Paul asserts, no one can acknowledge Jesus as Lord except through the Holy Spirit."

The core emphasis here is the act of praying with unwavering faith to invoke the presence of the Holy Spirit. In my perspective, this can be likened to a form of hypnosis.

While it's important to note that prayer and meditation cannot be entirely equated, they also cannot be completely separated. These two practices share historical roots and often serve similar purposes. In essence, both prayer and meditation can be linked to self-hypnosis.

As mentioned earlier, the ultimate objective of meditation is to achieve a sense of unity with the Divine. Along this path, meditation can yield valuable byproducts, including heightened creative thinking. These transformative experiences can deeply impact both the physical and mental well-being of individuals. It's crucial to recognize that the mind and body are intricately connected, with each influencing the other.

VIPASSANA AS A TEMPLATE

Sitting in meditation for ten days in Nepal under the tutelage of S.N. Goenka's teaching lineage was among the most challenging things I have voluntarily taken part in thus far.

Vipassana "sits" range in length from three days to more than twenty days. Goenka was born in 1924, grew up a conservative Hindu, and was a successful businessperson. In 1955 he started experiencing severe, debilitating migraines and was unable to find medical relief, and on the suggestion of a friend, he met with the Vipassana teacher Sayagyi U Ba Khin. Ba Khin took Goenka on as a student; Goenka subsequently trained under him for fourteen years.

In 1969, Goenka was authorized to teach by U Ba Khin, who died in 1971. He moved to India, left his business to his family, and began teaching Vipassana meditation. The first meditation center opened at Kusum Nagar in Hyderabad, and in 1976, he opened his first meditation center, Dhamma Giri, in Igatpuri near Nashik, Maharashtra. Goenka taught meditation on his own until 1982 and then started training assistant teachers. He established the Vipassana Research Institute at Dhamma Giri in 1985. By 1988, Goenka had instructed numerous people, including several thousand Westerners.

Vipassana courses, in the tradition of Sayagyi U Ba Khin, are currently held at 310 locations in 94 countries; approximately 176 are permanent Vipassana meditation centers.

When someone applies and is accepted to undertake a Vipassana course, we agree to abide by five precepts: no killing, no stealing, no lying, no sexual misconduct, and no intoxicants. Also, notebooks, talismans, pens, pencils, reading materials, and electronic devices are left with the staff. There is no note taking nor reading or writing allowed. The sexes are also segregated.

There is also no talking, no eye contact, no communication. This is known as Noble Silence, and we all observed the Silence.

Participants can speak with the teacher assigned to their group during the designated lunch break or as the teacher requests. I was called to meet with the teacher several times during my sit; there was much to "untangle from," she noted. She encouraged me to disassociate from the intense sciatic pain I was experiencing since I was not my body.

Vipassana differs from mindfulness meditation, which focuses on awareness, and from transcendental meditation, which uses a mantra. Instead, it dictates a comprehensive mandate of non-reaction. In the stillness of those ten days, we can learn how much our mind distorts the reality we perceive. Many of us learn that much of what complicates our lives comes from suppositions we formulate and our responses to them.

The days begin with the gongs at 4 a.m., and we sit for our first meditation of ninety minutes. There are short breaks and brief mealtimes during the day. Students are housed dorm-style with members of the same sex, even if we arrive with a partner of the opposite sex. We are confined to the property with virtually nowhere to expend any physical energy that may be surging for us. The days are sixteen hours in length.

The first three days are spent with the focus directed and redirected to the breath. On the fourth day, Vipassana is introduced, as are the hours of "strong determination," wherein we sit without movement. Long sequences of body scans in a specific order are taught, and throughout, we are instructed to be aware of the sensations we feel. We are not to move; we are not to react. Instead, we are taught to refocus attention on the objective sensations.

During the ten days, we train to stop reacting to the vicissitudes of life. Many of us recognize how much we have changed by the tenth day, and some of us come away with a tremendous surge of creativity that feels almost overpowering. I know I did. As painful as the first few days were, the pain was worth the change for me.

Change is an inherent and essential aspect of personal growth and development. It's important to acknowledge that many individuals harbor apprehensions about change and often perceive it in a negative light. The fear of the unknown, more than any other factor, tends to deter people from embracing transformative changes in their lives.

One extraordinarily creative idea can change a person's life. In the quantum field, anything and everything that any of us will ever know, want to know, or may have cause to discover in the future is already in existence in the human mind. This discovery, nonetheless, necessitates the evolution of the human mind and its connection with the Universal Mind. We tap into this "already in existence" place of Oneness and become creators.

In the realm of consciousness, philosopher and spiritual teacher Jeddah Mali refers to our existence as the "Sea of Awareness." She eloquently describes this unified consciousness as our default setting, the most fundamental state of being. Within this unified consciousness, Mali explains, we engage in the act of creation, experience the unfolding of life's events, and receive continuous feedback.

According to Mali, enlightenment is the ability to dwell in all these elements simultaneously. It means inhabiting the undifferentiated sea of awareness, allowing the creative aspect to emerge, and being both the creator and the observer of the feedback that guides us toward alignment with the sea of awareness.

Anthropologist and historian W. H. Stanner coined the term "the Everywhen" (or Every When) to describe this realm of existence. For

Australian indigenous people, it is known as the "All at Once Time." In this dimension, the past, present, and future coexist alongside our conventional linear understanding of time. Albert Einstein profoundly observed, "People like us, who believe in physics, understand that the distinction between the past, present, and future is only a stubbornly persistent illusion."

Children, with their innate wisdom, often easily grasp the true nature of this paradox.

The question of whether we are on the right path and truly connected to the Oneness, especially in the midst of suffering, is a deeply contemplative one. It leads us to seek guidance and direction from a Higher Source.

Meditation and similar practices provide a gateway to accessing this intuitive guidance. Through these practices, we develop a heightened awareness of the subtle cues and insights that flow from our Higher Source. This guidance can manifest as inner wisdom, intuition, or a deep sense of knowing.

However, the challenge lies in the application of this guidance to our lives. While many of us may receive intuitive insights, it's not always easy to translate them into tangible actions that lead to happiness, fulfillment, and creative authenticity. Life's complexities, external pressures, and our own inner doubts can create obstacles.

Living a happy, fulfilling, and creatively authentic life requires not only receiving intuitive guidance but also having the courage and conviction to follow it. It involves aligning our actions, choices, and aspirations with the inner wisdom we receive. This alignment often involves making changes, taking risks, and stepping outside of our comfort zones.

In essence, the journey toward a more authentic and fulfilled life is a continuous process of seeking guidance, listening to our inner wisdom, and taking purposeful steps toward our true calling. It's about learning to trust in the guidance of the Higher Source and having the faith to follow the path it reveals, even when faced with challenges and uncertainties.

CHAPTER 19
THE COURAGE OF CREATIVITY

Be a gift and a benediction.

—Ralph Waldo Emerson

Many of our biggest challenges come from our immediate environments. We entrain and resonate with the people, places, and things that we surround ourselves with, and we're often diminished, deflated, or depressed by these interactions.

In this complex dance of life, our brains, hardwired for survival, often tilt the scale toward perceiving negative stimuli more prominently. This ingrained tendency, known as negativity bias, subtly shapes our interactions and experiences.

Moreover, this bias influences our decision-making. When faced with choices, we might lean toward avoiding negative outcomes rather than pursuing positive ones, even if the latter promises greater benefits. This risk-averse approach can limit our growth and opportunities, reinforcing a cycle of caution and restraint.

Amidst this, our desire for approval and acceptance from those around us—our "Earthly pack"—becomes a powerful motivator. In our quest for approval from our "Earthly pack"—our sphere of influence, our peers, our families, and even strangers—we often set aside what our intuition tells us is appropriate. This need to belong and be accepted can lead us to conform, often at the expense of our true selves. We might ignore our inner voice, intuition, or even compromise our values to fit in or avoid conflict.

In this complex interplay of environmental influences and innate psychological tendencies, finding a balance between external validation and internal truth becomes a crucial aspect of personal growth and well-being.

The neighbor's son discussed earlier joined a gang and now peddles drugs; he fits well into his environment and knows no other way out. "This my family, my life. It buy me nice cars and shit and I hang with my niggahs. Ain't nothin' wrong with that. It be play for me. So why quit?" he says.

The perception that this teen has is an illusion, or a veil of Maya. In esoteric terms, Maya is often translated as "illusion" or "delusion," and refers to the powerful force that creates the cosmic illusion that the phenomenal world is real. This boy is not yet aware or awake enough to understand he has choices, and indeed, some of his choices around "play" may indeed be delusional.

BIGGER WORK

Still, there are those who do much greater good in the world by heeding a higher calling and calling it play. "My heart led me to Nepal to work with women and girls," says Missionary Glenda McVay. "Their creativity, the artwork that my family and friends now sell here in the States, is freeing these young women and girls who were and are still in bondage. God directed me, He called me, and I listened." For her, this is playful and fulfilling, positive work.

Do you find time to play anymore, or has the relentless tide of "Must-Dos" in your daily life left little room for play? It's a question that strikes at the heart of our well-being, and for some of us, it's a troubling conundrum.

In the midst of our busy lives, it's not uncommon to confuse self-destructive behaviors with what we perceive as "Must-Dos." The demands of our schedules, the responsibilities we shoulder, and the weight of expectations can often eclipse the essential element of self-care. In this whirlwind, self-care becomes nothing more than an acrimonious afterthought at the end of the day—if it is given any thought at all.

It's a delicate balance to strike. Yet, as we explore the intricate landscape of our lives, it's vital to remember that play isn't a frivolous luxury; it's a fundamental ingredient of our well-being. It's a reminder that our inner child still yearns for laughter, creativity, and the simple joy of being present in the present moment.

There are personality traits that characterize creative people, such as tenacity and persistence, and individuals who are creative also seem to find the time and sometimes even force themselves to work in order to make the time to create. When we, as creatives, have that blank canvas or page or a lump of clay in front of us and nothing is immediately manifesting, we may experience a bit of anxiety or panic or even momentary terror. But we take those first actions and keep on moving forward. We make mistakes, and often, a lot of them, on our journeys. "Stop feeding your fear. Embrace it—doing so is what allows us to leave our biggest impact on the world," states author Josh Linkner. Linkner further reminds us that the WD-40 name in itself stands for this encouragement of creative failure. The abbreviation stands for "water displacement 40th experiment." "What the team at WD-40 knows and what we all need to embrace is that mistakes aren't fatal—they're simply portals of discovery. And sometimes we just have to create what some would consider a mess first" (Linkner, 2013).

While creativity is often portrayed as a lightning bolt that strikes once, in a big way, out of the blue, and without warning, in reality, it isn't a sudden, one-time flash for most of us. Some of us get messages all the time. "My creativity is a faucet," says Intensive Care Nurse Ann "Delight" Cash. "I am the spigot, and I cannot turn it off. If I do, I will suffer. My studio is stuffed so full of things I doubt I'll be able to use it all in one lifetime." Nurse Cash also has a flourishing shabby chic design business with customers around the globe.

My little art studio often looks chaotic and disorderly to outsiders. The space under my desk where I stash my journals and markers often does too. Even so, I know precisely what is where and how much of this or that is still in what part of what bin or what bottle. Many people who work in creative fields seem to prefer this same kind of environment.

Pablo Picasso said, "An act of art begins as an act of destruction," which seems likewise to describe the phenomenon known as "creative chaos." Often this chaos or crisis heralds a breakdown before our breakthrough for many of us. As Jung is quoted, "In all chaos, there is a cosmos, in all disorder a secret order."

Thus, we creatives also push limits; we're curious about our world and produce what we must, even if society rejects our work. We're contrarian, and we'll fall back on our faith. We often create chaos, sometimes in a very big way, as well.

Yes, creativity takes courage. The great German philosopher Friedrich Nietzsche said this: "'One must still have chaos in oneself to be able to give birth to a dancing star.' It is the chaos in ourselves that is Divine."

ILLNESS AND THE CREATIVE FORCES

Is it any wonder that some of us find that we become physically ill when we suppress our creative urges and shush the inner voice that speaks to us in the calm, clear presence of Knowing? Beethoven was said to have had bouts of suicidal lows. Vincent van Gogh has been documented as having suffered from depression, episodic derangement, and epilepsy. Painter Georgia O'Keeffe suffered from anxiety and depression. Brilliant comedian Robin Williams and globetrotting, brazen Master Chef Anthony Bourdain both committed suicide, and both were reportedly struggling with depression. My nephew, a gifted, top-ranked artistic photographer, committed suicide just after his fortieth birthday.

A Swedish study conducted in 2012 which followed 1.2 million patients found "that certain mental illness—bipolar disorder, in particular—is more prevalent in the entire group of people with artistic or scientific professions, such as dancers, researchers, photographers, and authors. Authors, specifically, were more common among most of the other psychiatric diseases, including schizophrenia, depression, anxiety, and substance abuse, and were almost 50 percent more likely to commit suicide than the general population" (Sternudd).

Anthropological findings support that contrarians, druids, shamans, and medicine people from all cultures share specific characteristics. They're intuitive, extremely sensitive, and empathic and frequently suffer from depression and emotional overload. They may have visions or dreams and have an uncanny affinity for the esoteric and for animals. As children, they may be sickly, traumatized, accident-prone, and challenging for their families of origin to understand. Because these people project such elevated levels of emotional energy and possess an intuitive understanding of others, people often seek them out for healing.

Individuals with these unique qualities manifest themselves in virtually every known culture. It is understood, in the highlands of Peru, for example, that shamans who fail to accept their gift, or fail to begin functioning as the Spirit channels they are intended to be, will become sick and perhaps even die. Many creative people express that they are unwell and unable to craft their art.

Most, if not all of us, are also Empaths. This can be exceptionally challenging from a pragmatic standpoint. Learning to protect ourselves from the constant bombardment of the energies of others is of the utmost importance if we are to remain healthy. We are like sponges.

As "sponges," our empathetic nature allows us to absorb emotions, energies, and moods from our surroundings. This capacity, while enriching our ability to connect and empathize, can also lead to emotional overload. Scientific research supports this notion, particularly studies in the field of Mirror Neuron Systems (MNS). These neurons, found in the brain, respond both when we perform an action and when we observe the same action performed by another. This mirroring mechanism is believed to be fundamental in understanding others' emotions, leading to what is commonly known as "emotional contagion."

Furthermore, psychological studies have indicated that individuals with high levels of empathy tend to have increased activity in the anterior insula and the anterior cingulate cortex—areas of the brain associated with emotional processing. This heightened activity suggests a greater susceptibility to experiencing the emotions of others as if they were one's own.

However, being highly empathetic can sometimes translate to taking on too much from our environment, leading to emotional fatigue or even burnout. This is particularly true in environments laden with stress, conflict, or negative emotions. Therefore, learning to discern and manage these empathic absorptions becomes crucial. Techniques such as mindfulness, setting emotional boundaries, and engaging in self-care practices can be effective in mitigating the overwhelming impact of external energies.

Our empathetic nature, akin to being sponges, has its roots in our neurological wiring and emotional processes. While it enables incredible connections with others, it also necessitates the development of strategies to protect and sustain our emotional well-being in the face of the constant influx of external energies.

There will always be the haters, the dream destroyers, and those who unashamedly wish to see others suffer. They may even stalk us when we summon the courage to extricate ourselves. Some of us have found we were born into families that are full of these types of people, and my hope is that we heal enough to recognize the gifts within the lessons that these people present for us.

We also find that those around us may not understand our drive and question not only our motives but our mental health, especially if we are empathic. "Many in a culture do not want to hear about innovation and new directions that creativity unleashes," writes Matthew Fox. "This is indeed Spirit's work—to awaken all things. That is the artist's work also: to resurrect and awaken all that is and all we perceive" (p. 75). And as legendary music icon Johnny Cash said, "Creative people have to be fed from the Divine Source. I have to get fed. I had to get filled up in order to pour out."

Children are naturally highly creative and empathic. I believe that frustration with the regimentation of classroom teachings may be a significant factor in the epidemic diagnosis of depression, obesity, and attention deficit/hyperactivity disorder (ADHD). There are certainly neurological conditions or chemically based cases where a person's brain may not function properly, making the diagnosis valid. However, this raises a question: does this justify the more than 3 million cases of ADHD diagnosed each year?

Given the dynamics of one's socialization or demographics, an admittedly creative person may be cast into the role of a social pariah. In attempts of adaptation or to avoid being "cut from the herd," we may further drive our creativity down to an acutely neglected place and, worse yet, believe that we are bad or wrong or somehow less than because we are creative or in touch with Source. We avoid facing ourselves: we seek alternate ways of creating noise, and we go along with the masses. We find any number of ways to squelch that inner voice. Sadly, we will often allow the uncalled-for opinions of others to shame us into hiding our gifts.

ANOTHER ERA

Coupled with the proliferation, ease, and accessibility of digital electronics, smartphones, and televisions, is it any wonder that our children are less creative, sicker, heavier, and more challenged now than ever before? Obesity is out of control. "Sure, she's a little plump. So what? She's a kid. It's just easier to hand her the iPad and let her surf the web than to get her to do anything around the yard," said a young, very overweight mother recently when I queried her as to whether her clinically obese daughter might want to get moving and learn to propagate some of the plants I have in my garden.

She shook her head and indicated that she did not. "Besides, we hate being outdoors," she said.

Hate being outdoors?

Not only did this girl's mother believe her daughter was "plump," when, in fact, the girl was obviously and uncomfortably obese, this mother was defaulting to electronic babysitters rather than fostering natural curiosity and encouraging movement for this child. We are built to move!

In the US, the average American family's television is on for about six hours every day, accounting for approximately 40 percent of an individual's free time daily. Virtually everyone is connected via smartphones, tablets, laptops, and computers. "The younger generation is just watered down now," says my neighbor about her thirty-something-year-old son who, upon getting fired from "one more" job, has moved home once again with child number three in tow. "He just spends all his time on the iPhone. Seems he's getting more and more stupid by the day. He's looking for happiness in the 'great out there,' way out there in a make-believe world."

The challenge herein is that by attempting to silence our inner voice, our intuition, and our connection with Source, we limit our true potential and our ability to lead full and happy lives. As taught in Buddhist philosophy, true refuge lies not externally but within oneself.

In many of the programs I've been involved with, we frequently utilize meditation and meditative states as a means to tap into deeper levels of awareness, and interestingly, children tend to achieve these states with remarkable ease. As previously mentioned, meditation can be seen as a form of prayer or deep introspection.

It's common to observe children engaging in self-dialogue or connecting with a benevolent, unseen force greater than themselves, perhaps reflecting their natural inclination toward spiritual or introspective experiences. This ease with which children enter meditative states may be attributed to their having fewer filters, less mental noise, and a lower tendency to be influenced by ingrained patterns of thought and behavior.

Children's natural propensity to enter meditative states with fewer filters and biases highlights their open and uncluttered minds.

This openness may be key in understanding how prayer functions as a channel for consciousness. In my view, prayer is a channel through which we can allow something beyond us, a Higher Power or God, to work through us. Various spiritual teachings suggest that without the right mental attitude, a sort of psychic blockage can occur, hindering the connection between our conscious mind and the Higher God-Mind.

Children, with their unimpeded and expectant minds, often believe their questions will be answered, a belief that can be diminished or altered through adult influence. Their approach to meditation and prayer can offer insights into how unobstructed consciousness interacts with the otherworldly or higher realms of thought and existence.

Prayer is a gateway of one's consciousness, I believe, and one way that we may allow God to work through us. Various teachings emphasize that we will encounter a psychic blockage of sorts between the conscious and Higher God-Mind without the proper conscious mental attitude.

How many of us as adults have abandoned the expectation that we will get our questions answered?

Children often understand this expectation of answers far better than adults and will excel if encouraged. Says middle school teacher Meg Keller, who has more than two decades of teaching to her credit: "My kids are 'super learners' by society's definition. They are children. I insist that they find the answers by asking and looking and trying new ways of doing things. 'Who am I supposed to ask?' they will say. And I'll tell them that they already know, and they have the answers within them, and more importantly, that they just need to ask themselves. Yes, in my opinion, that asking is prayer or meditation or insight or God-granted knowing. In the school system, I'm not allowed to call it any of those things. I tell them to calm themselves down, tune themselves in, ignore what might be 'logical,' and get their answers. I insist that they grow and to explore and to exploit their gifts" (Keller).

Embracing our creativity honors the complexities and ambiguities of our Soul's growth during our incarnation. Creativity and spirituality beckon us to access our intuitive processes, and they ask us to set aside those processes of reason or logic. Logic isn't a necessity for children; some things just "are." In the creation of our artwork, we enter that altered state of intuitive awareness wherein time often collapses. The Creative Self flows through us, often taking us to places we cannot ordinarily access in our normal waking state. We follow our bliss, and hours may evaporate.

Personally, when I am in my studio, my special place of magic and wonder, it seems that time warps. There were days I'd work ten to twelve hours nonstop at my usual profession so I can make a space of an hour or two to spend time with my art. And there are times when I stand back in detached awe and watch as astonishing things emerge from the clay or the glass with the help of my hands. How does that happen? Where did I ever learn to create the myriad and prolific number of mosaics from the Earth's treasures and magical sculptures from the soft earth? Certainly not in this lifetime. Fascinated by molten glass, I taught myself—or remembered how—to kiln form. Clay work magically found me—another long and magically "coincidental" story—when I was giving up on my creativity.

As a child, I was never encouraged to draw or sculpt, nor was I ever formally educated in art. The sad reality is the exact opposite was true. Early attempts at sharing my work were met with a rueful cluck of the tongue or an admonishment of "What is the purpose of this?" from many of the adults in my life. Later, a spiteful sibling who was considered to be "the artist in the family" (and spent tens of thousands of dollars on an art degree only to change his major three times) maliciously critiqued one of my first publicly displayed works and declared, "Who would ever buy that thing?"

That thing was an audacious mosaic that had been accepted by a prominent gallery.

A heartfelt treasure crafted of recycled glass and reclaimed lumber; the work depicted the vibrant magenta plumerias propagated from a cutting gifted to me from Hawaii. The piece now hangs in a residence in Ohio. "It brings me such incredible joy every time I look at the piece. It is hanging over my fireplace, in the very heart of my home, and I absolutely love the piece," the buyer later wrote in a note of appreciation. I love that she loved it.

My home and gardens are also filled with cheerful clay dragons—one of which was on display at a famous art center for some time. Another message from the Divine, I ended up in a clay hand-building class one summer afternoon when I was headed for the wheels to learn to throw pottery. I had no prior training in clay art hand-building, and when the instructor said, "Let your heart guide you," a dragon manifested. Later, when I researched the meaning of the totem, I learned that the Dragon is said to be the master of the four elements of fire, water, air, and earth. According to some sources, the Dragon is also the symbol of primordial power.

To me, creating my art and sharing this God-given gift with others is a way of honoring Spirit. And today, without the benefit of a formal art education, I teach others—from young children to those who are in their nineties—how to use art and movement as forms of therapy and very healing play. It was only when I decided that I could, as part of honoring my truth, create art for art's sake and heed Creator's calling that I was able to access this altered and safe space of my bliss. Bringing the joy of art to others' lives is part of this bliss and part of my truth.

In the realm of expressive arts, the true magic lies not in the meticulousness of technique or the grandeur of the final piece. It's about the raw power and process of using art in all its forms for the deep work of healing and integration. It's this journey, the act of creation, that throws open the doors to anyone willing to walk this path. The art then transforms into a living, breathing entity, its evolution and practice becoming a crucible for self-discovery, healing, and growth.

Echoing this sentiment, the spiritual life—mirroring the ethos of expressive arts—is a testament to valuing the process over the product. In spirituality, yoga, healing arts, and many kindred paths, the cornerstone is the practice itself. This is reminiscent of the pilgrimage, a concept I often reflect upon, and the myriad and magical lessons from the Camino de Santiago. It's a movement, an ongoing odyssey, not just a destination. This idea resonates deeply with the continuous evolution of childhood, where each moment is ripe with potential for growth, learning, and boundless discovery, regardless of the stage of life we find ourselves in.

Spirituality is also largely about growth, awareness, and assimilation, with our spiritual path leading us to a place of Unity or Oneness. Perhaps creativity is as well.

When the objective is practice over product, the process of accessing one's creativity can create a safe space for discovery. We all need safe spaces and sanctuary so that we may flourish. This process also creates a meditative space of being objectively present in the present moment. Creative pursuits provide us with insights into our lives and, for many of us, access points to Spirit, which are not readily available through cognitive ways of identifying with our physical world. We can embrace our intuition and suspend our judgments and rely on a real and responsive Universe that is acting and reacting to our requests and interests.

The fascinating world of neuroscientific research echoes the concept that the arts serve as a portal to a realm of "non-cognitive" understanding, distinct from traditional cognitive processes.

Neuroaesthetics is a field of study at the intersection of neuroscience and aesthetics. It explores how the brain perceives, processes, and responds to art and beauty. This field examines how artistic experiences, like viewing artwork or listening to music, can trigger emotional and cognitive responses, and how these responses are represented in the brain. Neuroaesthetics seeks to understand the neural basis of aesthetic experiences, including the psychological and physiological effects of art on the human brain.

When we immerse ourselves in creative endeavors like painting, music, or writing, neuroscientific studies highlight a significant increase in activity within the right hemisphere of the brain, a region associated with creativity, emotion, and non-linear thinking.

Functional magnetic resonance imaging (fMRI) studies have further revealed that engaging in the arts activates the brain's default mode network, which is intricately linked to imaginative thought, empathy, and deep reflection. This activation points to a cognitive process in the realm of art that is fundamentally different from the logical, analytical pathways dominated by the brain's left hemisphere.

In the field of neuroaesthetics, research uncovers how art can evoke a tapestry of emotional and cognitive responses, far beyond simple analytical thought. Art, it seems, can ignite emotions and thoughts through a complex interplay, engaging both our emotional responses and sensory experiences in ways that traditional cognitive processes do not.

These insights from neuroscience substantiate the idea that the arts open up a unique channel to knowledge and understanding, one that engages the brain's intuitive and emotionally rich capacities, aligning with the essence of non-cognitive means.

This "non-cognitive" approach of creating art taps into the intuitive, emotional, and sensory aspects of our being. It encompasses the subtle nuances of feeling, the abstract language of symbols, and the transformative power of aesthetic experience. Through art, we can connect with aspects of our consciousness and the world around us that are often left unexplored by more conventional methods of comprehension.

The beauty of this concept lies in its recognition of the diverse ways in which we can understand and interact with our surroundings. It acknowledges the richness of human experience and the multitude of ways we can interpret and make sense of our existence. The arts, in this context, become more than just a form of entertainment or aesthetic enjoyment; they are a vital means of accessing deeper layers of meaning, emotion, and understanding, bridging gaps that logic and language alone cannot span.

In embracing the non-cognitive means offered by the arts, we open ourselves to a world of imaginative possibilities and transformative experiences, enriching our lives and broadening our perspectives in wonderful and often unexpected ways.

In the act of creating art, we embrace a powerful form of freedom. It's here, in this creative space, that we can fully reclaim our emotions, giving life and voice to our deepest dreams. This process becomes a journey of identifying and expressing the core values that define our individual truths. It's a sacred space where our inner narratives find their form and expression.

Extending this freedom of artistic expression to our children is crucial. We need to nurture and encourage it. Allowing children to explore art in their own way becomes a vital pathway for them to discover and articulate their feelings, dreams, and understandings. It's through this artistic exploration that they learn to communicate their unique perspectives and cultivate a deeper connection with their inner selves. This, in essence, is not just about creating art; it's about shaping a space for growth, self-discovery, and the articulation of one's personal truths.

KEY PHASES

Graham Wallas, a distinguished social psychologist from the late nineteenth and early twentieth centuries and the author of *The Art of Thought*, outlined four key phases in the creative process: preparation, incubation, illumination, and verification. This framework mirrors the journey many of us undergo in our own personal awakening. Wallas describes these phases as the initial preparation for the creative work, followed by a period of stepping back to allow insights to emerge, then experiencing moments of inspiration or illumination, and finally, the actual process of creation itself.

Just as our spiritual practices demand, the practice of artmaking calls for spaciousness and time for incubation. In the midst of our bustling lives, this process provides a much-needed opportunity to slow down. There's a natural rhythm in creativity that oscillates between receptivity and activity, essential to the ebb and flow of the creative process. This "creativity construct," as previously mentioned, mirrors the journey of spiritual awakening for many individuals. These stages of creative rhythm also reflect the cycles of growth and development we see during childhood and adolescence, underscoring a universal pattern of evolution and self-discovery.

Embracing our creativity is a vital way to connect more deeply with our Source and to remain fully present in each moment. I hold a firm belief that it is in alignment with the Creator's will for us to nurture and express our creativity, irrespective of our age. This conviction is rooted in the understanding that creativity is not just an activity; it's a state of being that transcends age and time.

When we engage in creative endeavors, our body and mind enter a state of relaxation, allowing the often-dominant neocortex—the part of our brain responsible for functions considered uniquely advanced in humans, such as abstract reasoning, aesthetic appreciation, judgment, and language—to ease its constant activity. In this state, the relentless narrative of the "thinking brain" begins to quiet down, moving to the background of our consciousness.

As we immerse ourselves in creativity, we find that the incessant chatter of thoughts starts to dissipate. This shift is not just a mental phenomenon but a holistic experience that affects our emotional and spiritual well-being. In these moments of creative engagement, we often experience a sense of timelessness and a deep connection with something greater than ourselves—a connection that is not hindered or diminished by our physical age.

A notable example of an artist who gained fame later in life is Grandma Moses, whose real name was Anna Mary Robertson Moses. She began her painting career in her late seventies, initially as a hobby to keep busy after arthritis made it difficult for her to continue with her embroidery work.

Grandma Moses didn't receive significant recognition until she was seventy-eight, when an art collector saw her work displayed in a drugstore window and decided to include some of her paintings in an exhibition of unknown painters. Her work quickly gained popularity for its charm, simplicity, and depiction of rural American life. She became known for her vibrant and naive style, depicting scenes of farm life and the changing seasons.

Her late-blooming success is a heartening example of how age is not a barrier to creativity or recognition. Grandma Moses continued to paint until her death at the age of 101, leaving behind a legacy that continues to inspire and remind us of the value of pursuing our passions at any stage of life.

Grandma Moses' journey beautifully underscores that engaging in creative activities at any age carries immense benefits. These endeavors keep our minds active, playing a crucial role in maintaining cognitive functions. They endow us with a sense of purpose and can be an abundant source of joy and fulfillment. Importantly, creative expression provides us with a language that goes beyond words, offering a channel for emotions and thoughts that might otherwise remain unvoiced.

In my view, creativity is a Divine gift, an endless well of potential meant to be explored and enjoyed throughout our life's journey. It stands as a powerful instrument for personal growth, deepening our spiritual connections, and bolstering mental well-being. This highlights the importance of continually nurturing our creative skills, embracing them as an integral part of our existence, no matter our age or the stage of life we find ourselves in.

When we engage in creative activities, our thought processes shift from the linear to the expansive, tapping into deeper, more primitive brain functions. This shift often leads to a stream-of-consciousness that unfolds archetypes, heightened awareness, and deep-seated feelings. In this creative flow, even somatic memories can surface, revealing themselves in our art as unexpected shapes or innovative ideas.

This phenomenon is echoed in the structure and function of our brain, particularly in the neocortex, which presents a unique case of functional asymmetry despite its anatomical symmetry. Unlike other symmetrical body structures like the adrenals, kidneys, and ovaries, which perform identical functions, the two hemispheres of the brain have distinct roles. The left hemisphere primarily handles speech and linear thinking—the kind we step away from in creative work—while the right hemisphere governs spatial and temporal processing, areas we engage more deeply when we create. This specialized functioning of the brain underscores the transformative power of artistic expression, as it involves different brain areas, encouraging us to think and perceive beyond our usual patterns.

There is a theory that posits creativity predominantly resides in the right hemisphere of the brain. Despite the right and left hemispheres being extensively connected via the corpus callosum, the right hemisphere is often associated with distinct qualities. According to experts, it is the center for curiosity, synergy, experimentation, metaphorical thinking, playfulness, solution-finding, artistry, flexibility, synthesizing, and generally, risk-taking behaviors. This suggests that while the two hemispheres are interconnected and work in tandem, they each contribute unique functions and characteristics that play a crucial role in our cognitive processes.

The right hemisphere, for example, will take an intuitive idea and further experiment with, visualize, and integrate that idea with other ideas and ultimately develop a possible outcome, project, or solution.

Doing something with that result or solution, however, requires different methods, and research has shown that these particular processes are more likely located in the left hemisphere.

The possibility, and indeed probability, is high that a creative individual oscillates between the specialized modes of the brain's hemispheres to devise practical solutions to real-world problems.

This fluid back-and-forth movement is a hallmark of creative thinking. Children, in their uninhibited approach to the world, exemplify this seamlessly. They often ask, "Why not?" reflecting their innate ability to tap into diverse cognitive resources without constraint.

If the right hemisphere were isolated from the left, functioning solely within its unique modes of thinking, it might be limited to generating only abstract, fantastical ideas or unconventional concepts that could be challenging to implement in reality. The left hemisphere plays a crucial role in guiding and grounding the imaginative tendencies of the right hemisphere.

When considering the creative process through a left brain / right brain lens, it unfolds in a balanced sequence: interest engages both hemispheres, preparation is led by the left, incubation by the right, illumination again by the right, and verification by the left, with application involving both. This represents an equal involvement of "left" and "right" brain processes, ensuring a harmonious blend of imaginative and practical thinking.

Our physical brain serves as a conduit for our true minds, which exist as a field of energy. Techniques such as meditation, prayer, contemplation, and other practices including art and yoga, can help in quieting an overactive brain. This, in turn, enables us to tap into this energy field, enhancing our presence in the moment.

Being fully present means that all aspects of your awareness—focus, attention, thoughts, and feelings—are concentrated on what you are currently doing or whom you are with. Whether you are conversing with someone, paying full attention to their words and presence, or immersed in a task, your entire being is centered on that moment and activity.

Children are experts at this.

In the altered state of creative flow, we engage the practices of quietude, of contemplation, and of connection, which for some is also a form of prayer.

Prayer can be seen as a form of cooperation with the Divine. In embracing our creativity, we often learn to surrender to a process that is beyond our individual control, letting go of the urge to steer the outcomes purely from a cognitive standpoint. Allowing our creative endeavors and artistic expressions to unfold as a part of our spiritual practice is akin to making time for and nurturing our relationship with the spiritual realm. This approach opens us up to the full potential of our innate creativity, a precious gift that we have been endowed with.

There's a certain efficiency in the way the Divine or the Universe operates, often surprising us with how seamlessly and unexpectedly it can bring about positive outcomes and opportunities. This can be particularly evident in moments of creative inspiration and expression, where we may find ourselves in awe of the seemingly effortless way in which creative ideas and solutions—gifts—present themselves.

Some of us see these gifts from the Universe as answered prayers.

We can likewise learn to cultivate a sense of spontaneity and playfulness that opens our imaginations to new possibilities. Making new things for the joy of doing so encourages inquisitiveness and, for many of us, an extraordinary sense of wonder and anticipation. We're awakened, and we're thriving. We've transcended our limiting self-thoughts and the automatic responses of the body-mind. We have learned something new by creating and allowing our joy to work through us as Creator has intended.

Theologian Jeremy Begbie has noted that the drive to create and appreciate art appears to be a universal human trait. This impulse encompasses activities like etching images on stone walls, delighting in the harmony of musical notes, and crafting words into meaningful patterns. These artistic endeavors go beyond simple self-expression or earthly amusement. They serve as pathways to reveal and unfold the world around us in unique ways, acting as vehicles for discovery and understanding.

In the world of a child, every day is filled with discovery and a sense of wonder. They thrive on exploring and learning, constantly following and feeding their innate curiosity. It seems that children are naturally endowed with the right mindset for this—an attitude of continuous expectancy and openness, which flows intuitively from a Higher Source. As adults and guardians, it's our responsibility to nurture, encourage, and remind children of this intrinsic connection to creativity and discovery. Moreover, it's equally important for us to remind ourselves of this truth, to reconnect with our own sense of wonder and openness to the world.

GENETIC TENDENCIES

We cannot effectuate change when we have trained ourselves—our body and mind—to constantly and consistently be living in a predictable future based on the known experiences of our past. Familiar emotions will naturally create a corresponding future; how can it be otherwise? The moment of change is now, and we can condition ourselves to live in the now and To Be Here Now. We can stay present and create new neural pathways, sever those connections with past programming, and experience the elevated feelings and emotions of a more positive future.

We likewise cannot rid ourselves of certain genetic tendencies, yet we can indeed alter them.

Today, less than 5 percent of all diseases stem from single-gene disorders. Ninety-five percent of all illnesses, however, are borne of chronic stress, environmental factors, and lifestyle choices. Lifestyle choices can lead to toxic overload, yet how can two people be exposed to the same toxins at the same time react so differently?

It may have a lot to do with expectations.

The concept of expectation bias plays a significant role in the health of healthcare professionals, for example, who are regularly exposed to various pathogens. This psychological aspect, coupled with their adherence to strict infection control measures and robust immune systems, contributes to their overall health. Healthcare practitioners, armed with extensive knowledge of disease prevention and a routine of thorough protective measures, may develop a mindset where they expect not to fall ill. This expectation can foster a form of mental resilience, reinforcing their physical health. The expectation bias theory posits that by anticipating good health and rigorously following preventive strategies, healthcare workers might indeed be less prone to sickness. Their mental outlook, therefore, in conjunction with practical health measures, forms a comprehensive shield against the high-risk environment they navigate daily. This is what they do, live and expect and highlights the powerful interplay between psychological resilience and physical health practices in maintaining wellbeing, even in the face of constant exposure to potential health threats.

Building on the idea of expectation bias in healthcare professionals, this concept dovetails elegantly with the realm of epigenetics. Epigenetics explores how our behaviors and environment can cause changes that affect the way our genes work. Interestingly, while our genetic code provides a blueprint, epigenetics suggests that our perceptions, beliefs, and actions can influence gene expression. In the context of healthcare professionals, their resilient mindset and rigorous health practices, influenced by expectation bias, might not just psychologically shield them but could also be impacting their genetic expression. This aligns with the epigenetic view that our environment and behaviors, including our mental state and lifestyle choices, can alter gene expression in ways that bolster our health. Thus, the mental resilience and anticipatory health behaviors of healthcare workers could potentially have an epigenetic effect, contributing to their overall well-being and possibly influencing their biological response to pathogens. This fascinating intersection of psychology and genetics underscores the significant interconnectedness of our beliefs, behaviors, and biological processes and how they collectively shape our health.

Epigenetics is one of the most active areas of research today. The conventional model stated that DNA controls all of life and that all gene expression takes place inside the cell. In short, this left us saddled with our genetic inheritance.

Genes, though, are activated by chemical signals and can express in specific ways. Stressful emotions cause dysregulation of the cells and thus creates a perfect environment for disease to flourish. By changing our thoughts, emotional reactions, and making better and more positive choices, we send our cells new signals.

While the DNA code we are born with may stay the same, once a cell is activated in a new way with new information, the cell is free to create thousands of variations of the same gene.

We really can change our outcomes.

Remaining entrenched in negative emotional states can trap us in a cycle where the same neural pathways are continuously activated, potentially leading to the onset of certain diseases. This cycle underscores the importance of managing our internal state, even when we cannot control external circumstances.

This concept of internal management connects with how individuals relate to their spirituality. While people's specific religious beliefs may shift over time, the underlying inclination towards spirituality often endures. This innate spiritual pull can be harnessed and deepened through practices like meditation, prayer, and creative arts such as music and painting. These practices offer a means to positively influence our internal state, providing a counterbalance to negative emotions. They serve not just as tools for spiritual exploration but also as pathways to cultivate a healthier mind and emotional well-being, bridging our inner experiences with our overall health.

I hold the belief that the qualities of creativity and spirituality are deeply embedded within us, and they will inevitably find ways to express themselves. This expression is akin to how our art sometimes mysteriously emerges and evolves when we are on the path of growth that our Creator intends for us. Just as a seed naturally grows toward the light, our innate creativity and spirituality seek to manifest in our lives, guiding us toward our true potential and purpose.

CONSTRUCTS AND FUNCTIONS

While a person may not be an actual extension of the world they are part of, or the work they do for a living, he or she may surely die because of that situation, circumstance, or the karma-luggage. The energies get misdirected and become problematic, toxic, or even life-threatening in efforts to find release. Our prana short-circuits. Vital parts of us wither and die.

We freely spend billions of dollars on health care every year, and self-help peripherals are a multi-billion industry. Traditional wisdom recognizes that the person heals the person; we forget, however, that the pills so many of us so quickly ingest "fail to cure whatever disease we may have without our cooperation."

We ultimately choose.

I understand the depth of feeling angry with the Creator, a sentiment you might be experiencing too. Please don't let that kill you. In my darkest times, a gentle yet annoying voice within me urged me to listen, to question and test my faith, and to keep going even when I felt close to permanently checking out. If you're in a similar place, I encourage you to pay attention to that quiet inner voice, to give it your trust and faith.

While nurturing this faith may seem challenging in such moments, it's not just about spiritual solace; it also plays a huge role in our overall well-being. Research, including insights from Newberg and Waldman, shows that practices like meditation aren't merely spiritual exercises; they have tangible effects on our neurological health. Similarly, as White notes, yoga offers a space to experience both the physical and the spiritual, bridging the gap between our tangible reality and deeper energies. These practices help heal our spiritual rifts and foster a more cohesive balance between our mind, body, and the unseen forces of our existence.

In the realm of holistic well-being, meditation has been shown to have significant effects on our mental and spiritual health. Andrew Newberg, MD, a renowned researcher on the neurological basis of religion, has noted that for individuals who may not prioritize religious beliefs, focusing on concepts like hope, optimism, and a positive future can produce effects in the brain that are similar to those observed during religious meditation. Dr. Newberg emphasizes that meditation can be a powerful tool for alleviating doubts and anxieties and reinforcing faith in oneself, others, and potentially in something greater and beyond our human existence. This connection between meditation, faith, and our inner world forms an integral part of our holistic journey toward well-being.

Further research indicates that the act of contemplating a concept like "God" can initiate changes in neural functioning. This process involves the activation of different brain circuits, the formation of new dendrites, and the creation of new synaptic connections, making the brain more receptive. These changes suggest that focused thought on such subjects can indeed transform the brain's structure and function.

Understanding the impact of meditation and similar practices on the brain is crucial. These practices can lead to significant neurological changes, which are vital due to their transformative effects on the brain's architecture and functions. Such alterations not only enhance our receptivity but also deeply influence the way we interpret and interact with our surroundings, marking a substantial shift in our cognitive and emotional processing.

Please understand that this heightened receptivity affects not just our cognitive abilities but also profoundly influences our emotional and spiritual realms. It enhances both our objective understanding and subjective experiences, refining our capacity to perceive, process, and react to the world with greater depth and subtlety. This more nuanced approach allows for a richer engagement with our surroundings on multiple levels. We become better attuned to our own thoughts and feelings, as well as the thoughts and emotions of others. This heightened sensitivity can lead to increased empathy, improved emotional regulation, and a deeper connection to ourselves and to others.

Furthermore, these neurological changes can foster a greater sense of clarity and purpose in life. When our brain is more receptive, we are better equipped to explore complex concepts like hope, optimism, and a positive future. This exploration can, in turn, lead to a renewed sense of meaning and fulfillment in our daily existence.

In essence, valuing the changes that occur in the brain through practices like meditation is about embracing the opportunity for personal growth, emotional well-being, and a deeper connection to the world around us. It's like unlocking new doors to possibilities that extend well beyond our individual minds, enriching our human experience.

Managing our mental state is crucial for both healing and personal growth, demanding a commitment to personal responsibility for our mental health. This encompasses actively making conscious, positive, and healthy choices about our thoughts, attitudes, the company we keep, and the environments we engage with. By intentionally fostering these choices, we can significantly boost our overall well-being and cognitive functions. Adopting this proactive approach not only enhances our mental and emotional resilience but also cultivates a more optimistic and constructive perspective on life. Managing our mental state is crucial for both healing and personal growth, demanding a commitment to personal responsibility for our mental health. This encompasses actively making conscious, positive, and healthy choices about our thoughts, attitudes, the company we keep, and the environments we engage with. By intentionally fostering these choices, we can significantly boost our overall well-being and cognitive functions. Adopting this proactive approach not only enhances our mental and emotional resilience but also cultivates a more optimistic and constructive perspective on life. Remember, what we focus on expands.

I turned to yoga training seeking a way to heal without surgery, and what I discovered was resilience, a reconnection to my life, a healthier group of people to play with, and a renewed connection to my faith. This journey into yoga marked the beginning of the greater work I am meant to do in the world—helping others heal holistically. Weiss and Weiss once said, "Helping others to heal, to understand, and to progress along their spiritual paths is the soul's noblest duty." Reflecting on this, I realize the significance of finding myself in that yoga studio on that particular day. Was I initially defiant? Yes.

Engaging in the process of healing and personal transformation is undeniably challenging, especially when it involves shifting away from long-held paradigms and outdated patterns. The hardest part of this journey often lies in taking those initial steps, as they require us to confront and challenge our deep-seated ways of being. This can be a daunting task, as it involves not just a reevaluation of our beliefs and behaviors, but also the courage to face the unknown and embrace change.

In this process, we are called to critically examine the beliefs and habits that have defined us, questioning their relevance and helpfulness in our current lives. It's about recognizing that what once served us may no longer be beneficial, and that growth often necessitates leaving behind familiar yet limiting patterns. As we embark on this journey, we might encounter resistance, both from within ourselves and from those around us who are accustomed to our old ways.

Moreover, this transformative work requires a sustained and concerted effort. It's not just about making a single choice to change, but rather about consistently choosing growth, even when it's uncomfortable or challenging. It involves developing new habits, nurturing healthier relationships, and building a supportive environment that aligns with our evolving selves.

Ultimately, the work of healing and changing our paradigms is an ongoing process of self-discovery and growth. It's about learning a new language and gradually building a new way of being that is more authentic and aligned with our true selves. While the path may be difficult, the rewards of such deep personal transformation can be extraordinary and can create precessional ripples of far-reaching changes.

I firmly believe that when the Spirit guides us with a "Go," it intuitively leads us to bring our ideas into physical reality. My journey has been one of intuitive guidance, and it continues to shape my path, in whatever form it may take now. Does it sometimes feel intimidating and disruptively awkward? Absolutely. Do those around me always offer support and understanding? Unfortunately, no. But these challenges are part of the journey, shaping and strengthening my resolve as I continue my work.

Self-care is essential, and the responsibility for authentic and necessary self-care rests solely with you. No amount of effort spent on others can fulfill the deep-seated longing or fill the void when something vital is missing in your own life. It's important to recognize the clear distinction between self-care and self-destruction. In toxic environments, it's not uncommon for individuals to engage in self-destructive behaviors as a means of self-protection. However, it's crucial to remember that your well-being is your responsibility. Others are not accountable for your self-care; you are the one who must take charge of your own health and happiness.

When life began to feel nearly unmanageable for me a few years ago, I felt a deep calling to embark on the Camino de Santiago, a journey that I eventually extended to include Finisterre and Muxia—places the Romans considered the edge of the world. My trek began in Pamplona, Spain, and I walked the entire route solo, carrying only an eleven-pound backpack. Many fellow pilgrims believe that the true Camino journey begins the moment one decides to take on the pilgrimage. For me, reaching this decision was a turning point, a *descanso*, where I felt I had no other choice but to follow this calling.

Following my Camino journey, I've experienced significant physical and emotional healing. I've regained the full functionality of my arm and shoulder without the need for medication or surgery. There's a greater sense of peace in my heart now, and my perspective on life has grown much more compassionate. My work, though sometimes incredibly demanding, is deeply fulfilling and offers endless opportunities to serve others. The people I meet in my office bring me great joy, and I make it a point to express my gratitude and affection to and for them.

Living in a continuous state of healing, I'm well acquainted with the presence of samsaras. People often wonder how I maintain my cheerfulness, especially when my work involves interacting with numerous individuals, some of whom present considerable challenges, on a weekly basis. To those who may be curious, I explain that I maintain an open and active communication with the Greater Creator and that I am still perfecting the art of intentional breathing. I am committed to a shared journey of personal healing and growth, steadfast in my role as a lifelong learner, constantly evolving and acquiring new insights throughout my time on Earth.

As stated in the Bible, Ecclesiastes, 3:1, "To every thing, there is a season and a time to every purpose under the heaven." I, like so many others, had lost all hope and retreated to heal or die. Instead, a samsara occurred, and with it, the death of the life I knew before. Maya Angelou said, "I did then what I knew how to do. Now that I know better, I do better." Let us all strive to do better.

Embracing yoga and therein contemplating God, even in my bleakest hours, did irrefutably change the trajectory of my life. I encourage you to contemplate God, your God, whatever your Great Birther, Higher Power, or Source, may be to you.

CHAPTER 20
JOY AS A DAILY EPITOME

Joy is the infallible sign of the presence of God.
—Pierre Teilhard de Chardin

Life, for me, will be lived as a blessed and daily celebration. Call it what you will; for me, it's a personal imperative and love-centric, even though, at times, it can still be incredibly challenging. The Creator gave me hard, hard schoolings; I collided with the lower energies, got back up, and embraced the lessons of the Higher places. I survived. Are the difficult initiations over? No, most assuredly, they are not. Am I okay with that? Absolutely. The perspectives have shifted, and I recognize there is always a gift within the paradigms of difficulties we may face in life. My wish for you is to embrace the possibilities of a Higher place as well. And, likewise, for you to be able to rise each day before the sun to embrace the sunrise as the gift of another day in this physical beingness.

Ultimately, our most courageous and important creative act is the positive, purposeful, and productive living of our daily lives—and that of bringing joy to others' lives in celebration. Real creativity, for me, is about honoring our lives and the world around us as our Greater Creator intended and in celebrating the life we have been blessed with by sharing our love, our joy, and our creative gifts with the world.

I think all of us are meant to live this way and help each other reach higher places of compassion, love, and understanding.

It takes courage to make changes, though. For many of us, it requires colossal daring to experience new ways of living in the places where life-numbing fear used to dictate our outcomes. By choosing to embrace change, we become the playwrights of our own experiences.

There was a prayer my father used to have us recite on the way to school each day when I was quite young that was as difficult for me to understand as it was austere in context. Here's why: my father struggled his entire incarnation with simple happiness.

Maybe he was terrified of life every damn day. I believe he was.

The prayer went like this: "Say happy things, think happy thoughts, and put joy into people's lives."

He finally made his way full circle to self-effacement in the last ten years he was on the planet, and he used to get so angry with me when I questioned the hypocrisy of the prayer before that time. The last ten years, though, when we met via telephone for our "ten o'clock telephone Tuesday" date, we both said the prayer together and ended with "I love you." And we meant all of the words from our hearts.

The phone in my office would ring at 10 a.m. on Tuesdays for a long while after my father left the planet. Here I am so many years later, and I still start to dial his number for a chat.

JOY IN TANGIBLE FORMS

This act of "putting joy into others" lives, is, indeed, a part of the art of living a happy life, is it not?

Those of us who must create art do so for the joy it brings. For some of us, art is joy in tangible form. The art may be that of crayons or oil paints, or clay, or it may be movement in the form of dance or hugging. For me, happiness smells like a forest or a long stretch of pathways on the Camino in the early morning hours. Sunshine and warm rain both feel like a whole-body hug. Soft, warm beach sand and a carpet of pine needles are dessert. Artwork is joy as matter-form to me.

Please remember to be gentle with yourself. To quote Cohen, "There is a crack in everything, that's how the light gets in." Perfect people are not real; real people are not perfect. We are all a little broken.

So shine your joy in whatever form of artwork it takes and lovingly share your gifts with the world. You will effectuate energetic ripples beyond what you will know. A woman whom I have met only briefly a couple of times over the years sent me a note recently that served as a special reminder. She shared that I gave her a broken part of herself back simply by holding space for her to do her inner work. She further wrote: "You gave me meditation and a space to heal; maybe I felt seen by you, maybe you saw the little me inside that I had no connection to." I had no idea. She had been exquisitely challenged and embarrassed by someone she held dear when she had disclosed something particularly important to her. I took the time to just be with her, to listen to her, and to hug her. I understand being embarrassed by people I thought cared for—and about—me. Embarrassed, belittled, and crushed, as a child artist, for example, I hid my artwork. Always. I would stealthily creep out at night, risking certain punishment if I were caught. The best times for creating my "nonsense" were those "vacations" to the beach when I was a child. Mom was drinking, always drinking, to suppress the feelings she felt; Faud was always away fishing in his own form of seeking peace.

During those beach days, the younger siblings were somehow corralled, and I was finally free. My creativity was my lover, my best friend in the world, my solace, my confidant. I was talking to God, and God was answering through my hands. The "adults" would chastise: "What is this? Why are you wasting time?" and later, certain "experts" would finger their carefully groomed goatees as they spewed vicious opinions.

They were just that, however: vicious, asinine, judgment-riddled opinions.

A journal from seven years ago recently surfaced: "My creativity is my Life's Breath, and I am dying. Breathe, and breathe now," was scribbled within the unruliness of the free-written pages. My creativity led the way through the darkness and into the light then. Where did I go as the shards of broken trash glass, pieces of dunnage lumber, and sand stirred into leftover bits of construction glue turned themselves into murals? I had no idea. Time would morph and disappear. It was a liminal time; it was the Void of nothingness and All-ness. The vastness of the unknown and higher place of being. Love being made manifest.

I had no idea then that these murals would later be sold in galleries thousands of miles away. I was talking to something greater. My artwork was the reflection of my time at that time: shattered, outcast, irreverent. My Source-driven, God-approved, big ol' "F-U" to all the "WTF are you wasting time like this for?" Those mosaics made of recycled materials brought in thousands of dollars—from world-class art galleries—when I needed it most. I could not have consciously known how or why or when. So many people questioned why I was "wasting precious time" making those mosaics. It was therapy. It was prayer. It was meditation. That "It" pulled me forward to the Life I have now. The *It* kept me on the planet and, in doing so, has helped me help others cross some of the deepest, most terrifying chasms—from attempted suicide to the loss of a child.

You can survive and thrive. I wasn't certain I would stay here on the Big Green Footstool called Earth, and at this moment, you may not be certain of your resolve to stay either. The pivotal fact is that you've been with me this far and somewhere, somehow, please know that we are connected energetically and that you can and will survive. You have the ability within you to find your "direct connect" to the Source beyond your present set of circumstances. All that past that you have created is creating your present and your soon-to-be future. You can change that right here, right now, and embrace a new future that is bigger, bolder, so much more alive, and infinitely more radiant. As C.S. Lewis wrote, "There are far, far better things ahead than any we leave behind."

In retrospect, my creativity has always saved my life, and as the Divine is my witness, I believe in my heart that the gift of creativity that we are each given is our God-given direct connection to our own Divinity. And you are welcome to call Divinity whatever suits you. The point I'm making here is that Divinity is the Higher Power, the parts beyond the *you* that inhabit your physical Self as you are now.

You are creative and you have inherent gifts. The challenge is that we move so fast in our worlds with busyness and must-dos and minutiae that we forget that we must stop, slow down, and get quiet enough to hear what we are being told by the Divine within us. We must learn to turn down the volume on the outside world and shield ourselves from the energies that are so damn negative and pervasive, and it just isn't always that easy. I believe that people seek to squash the very creative essence out of others because they are absolutely terrified. Don't let them squash you too.

And please, find those precious heartfelt moments to return to your Self and play for the simple joy of timelessness in the moment. When we play, we're grateful for so much without being in that place of time and matter. If a moment is all you can begin with, then begin with that. As I always tell my clients, you have the courage to begin, and in that beginning, you do indeed have the courage to succeed.

I'm often asked why I work with some of the very difficult cases I work with. I do so because I see a spark, and if a person is honestly willing to do their work, I will hold space for them. Those of us who work with broken people to help bring about healing do so to bear witness to the healing and the joy that it brings forth in them, in ourselves, and in the world at large. I believe that we can find our value and our purpose—our exponential and precessional gift—at the intersection of what brings us joy and where we have labeled something in our life as a success.

What is your exponential gift? You know in your heart what it is and how it can be shared. I implore you to find the sweet space of silence to go within and find the answers, not in a withdrawal from life, but in a transcendence of the external haze. The Law of

Awareness states that whatever we are willing to be with, we go beyond. We each have innate intelligence and can find the intrinsic lucidity within a personal quietude. Together we can all achieve more, entrain at a higher frequency, and bring about healing where there has been disease before. Together we can channel the magic that is a vital component of who and what we are made of. What you may call a miracle, I know, now, in my heart, as Truth. I wish the same for you.

A beguiling child showed up at the studio where I train a few days ago, adorned for the children's yoga class in a neon pink, multi-layer diaphanous tutu, replete with hundreds (if not thousands) of sequins. Upon complimenting her on her attire and spinning several quick pirouettes with her at the front desk, I asked this bright spark of unbridled joy whom I had just met what we were celebrating. Her reply was, "*Every* day!" She was beaming. "I say that too!" I told her, "I celebrate life *every* day too!" She hugged me tight around my legs. "I already *know* that, and we are the best!" she stated.

"Do you like my dress?" she asked. I nodded. "I love it, I really do!" "Mom hates this pretty thing, but I love, love, love it," she said, and next came the statement that really got my attention:

"Mom doesn't see what *we* see."

I cast a glance at the babysitter, a teenager in faux fur and the latest Lululemon-lookalike yoga pants. She winked back at me and mouthed, "I made the dress for her; she's amazing," and patted the child on her head.

"I love it too!" I stated, and gave the little one a hug. "You are the pretty thing, and you look just like a chrysanthemum when you spin!" I told her. ("The magical Fibonacci Sequence at play again," I thought). She then sized me up and gingerly fingered the sweater I was wearing. "Purple. The other very best color!"

The little one then stepped back, held both of my hands, looked me in the eyes, and declared, "I AM a chrysanthemum, and I love you, and you are covered with purple mountain flowers, and *we* are made of magic! That's why we celebrate *every* day! And you are a mountain, and the mountains are calling you home! Now let's go play!"

I had crocheted the sweater during a stint at Kripalu, the enchanting yoga and wellness retreat that I love so much located in the Berkshires of Massachusetts. Taking my yarns with me is something I always do when I travel, and I allow my creativity to flow through my hands unabated. How had this tiny sprite intuited mountain flowers and my love of the mountains when we lived in a state that is a semi-tropical sandbar? I asked her if she'd ever been to see the snow. "Nope. Born here," was her reply as she kissed my cheek. With that, she skipped off to class, blowing kisses to those she made eye contact with along the way.

Ah yes, magic and joy and play and, most importantly, celebration. We are all. I agree that we are made of magic, and I believe we are meant to exist in loving, perpetual, and, yes, in a proud and uncompromising Spiritual and creative response to what the Higher Power has in mind for each of us. We all are each and *every* day.

Is this creative response one of play and celebration? I have faith that it is.

ABOUT THE AUTHOR

Laura Weber Garrison, PhD, is an artist, educator, international retreat facilitator, holistic health counselor, and psychotherapist who specializes in trauma resolution.

With a PhD in Holistic Health and over two decades of experience, Dr. Garrison has developed extensive expertise in working with challenged and at-risk populations. She specializes in holistic, integrative, yoga-based therapeutics, with a particular emphasis on neuroplasticity and restorative modalities. She remains committed to lifelong learning and development, consistently pursuing further studies as a dedicated practitioner, instructor, and perpetual student.

Dr. Garrison holds certifications in Advanced Clinical Hypnotherapy and Yoga Therapy, including the designation of Yoga Therapist from the International Association of Yoga Therapists (IAYT). She is also recognized as an E-RYT Continuing Education Provider and certified as a Yoga Alliance Certified Educational Professional (YACEP) by Yoga Alliance. Additionally, she serves as an approved Professional Development Program Leader (ADP) through the IAYT and is an Instructor in iRest Integrative Yoga Nidra

Within her private practice, Dr. Garrison has supported clients facing various challenges, including severe trauma, stress and anxiety management, PTSD and C-PTSD, mind-body disease, life transitions, abuse, eating disorders, grief, mood disorders, and addictions. She also facilitates transformative groups, workshops, and international retreats, offering signature programs such as Empowered Transitions™: The Courage to Begin Again; Empowered Transitions™ Retreat to Recalibrate: Accelerated Healing and Learning; and the Ten Big, Bold Weeks Program™.

Outside of her professional endeavors, Dr. Garrison has embarked on profound journeys of pilgrimage and study, exploring countries such as Peru, China, Korea, Italy, Mexico, Nepal, and Egypt.

She has completed the Camino Frances de Santiago and the Camino Portuguese, obtaining a Compostela on both occasions. Additionally, she has plans to walk the Camino Frances from Pamplona to Muxia in 2024. These experiences have significantly expanded her cultural understanding and deepened her connection to diverse spiritual practices.

WORKS CITED

Alpert, Y. (2015, February 11). Mastering the Om: A Guide for Beginners. Retrieved January 2023, from YogaJournal.com

Ancient Jewish History: The Ark of the Covenant. (n.d.). Retrieved from Jewish Virtual Library: https://www.jewishvirtuallibrary.org/the-ark-of-the-convenant

Anderson, M. N. (2019). Growing through Grief: The Group Process. (L. Garrison, Interviewer)

Andreasen, M. N. (2006, December 15). Creativity, Learned or Innate? (I. Flatow, Interviewer)

Avgerinos, J. (n.d.). The Essence of Yoga: Why Asana Is Only a Small Part of the Equation. Retrieved November 2016, from Chopra.com.

Baer, R. A. (2003). Mindfulness Training as a Clinical Intervention. Clinical Psychology Science and Practice, 125-143.

Ballen, W. (1997). Freud's views and the contemporary application of hypnosis: Enhancing therapy within a psychoanalytic framework. Journal of Contemporary Psychotherapy, 201-214.

Beck, M. (2008). Steering by Starlight. New York: Rodale.

Blakeborough, K. (2016, August). Mom Broke My Brain. (L. Garrison, Interviewer)

Braden, G. (2007). The Divine Matrix. Carlsbad: Hay House, Inc.

Braden, G. (2016, August). Resilience from the Heart. Retrieved December 2016, from GreggBraden.com.

Breuer, J., & Freud, S. (2010). Studies on Hysteria. In Freud- Complete Works (p. 10). Ivan Smith.

Broadway, B. (2004, November 13). Is the Capacity for Spirituality Determined by Brain Chemistry? Retrieved December 2016, from Washington Post.

Burkan, T. (n.d.). Firewalking Theory. Retrieved September 2023, from TollyBurkan.com.

Burns, D. (1967, 1981) 1994). Buddhist Meditation and Depth Psychology. Sri Lanka: Wheel Publications, Buddhist Publication Society.

Camarata, P. S. (2016, December 17). Lessons from Down Syndrome: Learning from Herbie. Retrieved December 2023, from Psychology Today.

Cameron, J. (1992). The Artist's Way: A Spiritual Path to Higher Creativity. New York: Jeremy P. Tarcher/Putnam.

Capacchione, P. L. (n.d.). Divine Creativity. Retrieved December 2023, from www.soulfulliving.com.

Carrington, P. P. (n.d.). How Does Meditation Differ from Prayer? Retrieved November 2023, from PatCarrington.com.

Cash, D. A. (2016, October). Let's Make Pretty. (L. Garrison, Interviewer)

Cooper, B. B. (2013, November 4). How Our Brains Work When We Are Creative: The Science of Great Ideas. Retrieved December 2016, from blog.bufferapp.com.

Cope, S. (1999). Yoga and the Quest for the True Self. New York: Bantam Books.

Davis Ph.D., B. (2013). There Are 50,000 Thoughts Standing Between You and Your Partner Every Day. Huffpost.com.

Davis, M. (2013, May). BCTC graduate is a role model for us all. Retrieved December 2023, from Kentucky.com.

De Koven, B. (2016, December 19). Doing Pointless Things for Fun. Retrieved December 2023, from Psychology Today.

Donald, K. (1984). Self-Hypnosis to Self-Improvement. Indiana: Accelerated Development, Inc.

Doran, W. (n.d.). The Eight Limb, The Core of Yoga. Retrieved January 2017, from ExpressionsofSpirit.com.

Doss, C. (1979). I Shall Mingle. Friday Harbor: Long House Printcrafters and Publishers.

Dyer, W. (2003). Getting into the Gap. Carlsbad: Hay House.

Ellison, K. (2006, September 1). Mastering Your Own Mind. Retrieved November 2016, from PsychologyToday.com.

Equanimous, M. (2015, February). The Meaning of the Word Guru "Weighty" or "Dispeller of Darkness"? Retrieved January 2017, from linkedin.com.

Farasiotis, D. (2008). The Jesus Prayer and the Hindu Mantra. Retrieved November 2023, from orthodoxprayer.org.

Forbes, B. (2007, August 28). Stuck in a Rut? Retrieved November 2023, from YogaJournal.com.

Fox, D. (1995, September). Integration of the cognitive and the psychodynamic unconscious. American Psychologist, pp. 798-799.

Fox, M. (2002). Creativity. New York: Jeremy P. Tarcher/Putnam.

Fromm, E., Lombard, L., Skinner, S., & Kahn, S. (1988). The modes of the ego in self-hypnosis. Imagination, Cognition and Personality, 335-349.

Gabriel, R. (. (n.d.). Appreciating OM: The Sound of the Universe. Retrieved November 2023, from Chopra.com.

Goldin, P., & Gross, J. (2010, February). Effects of Mindfulness-Based Stress Reduction (MBSR) on Emotion Regulation in Social Anxiety Disorder. Retrieved December 2016, from ncbi.nlm.nih.gov.

Gray, P. P. (2012, September 17). As Children's Freedom Has Declined, So Has Their Creativity. Retrieved December 2016, from Psychology Today.

Gross, D. G. (2014, December 30). The Individuation Process: Finding Your True Authentic Self. Retrieved December 18, 2017, from www.TheHuffingtonPost.com.

Gruzelier, H. B. (1984). Psychophysiological evidence for a state theory of hypnosis and susceptibility. International Journal of Psychophysiology, 131-139.

Hahn, T. N. (2016, December). Listening Deeply for Peace. Retrieved December 2016, from Lionsroar.

Harris, B. (2003). Thresholds of the Mind. Beaverton: Centerpointe Research Institute.

Harris, B. (n.d). The Holosync Solution. Beaverton: Centerpointe Research Institute.

Harris, B. (n.d.). The Science Behind Holosync® and Other Neurotechnologies. Retrieved November 2016, from Centerpointe.com.

Harris, B. (n.d.). Understanding Holosync - Workshop Synopsis. On Holosync Solutions.

Hartman, D. (2015, September 1). How Complexes Create Archetypal Reality in Childhood [Jung]. Retrieved November 2016, from wellness-institute.org.

HeartMath. (n.d.). Science of the Heart. Retrieved January 2023, from Heartmath.org.

HeartMath. (n.d.). The Heart-Brain Connection. Retrieved January 2017, from HeartMath.org.

Herrmann, N. (2016). Is it true that creativity resides in the right hemisphere of the brain? Retrieved December 19, 2016, from Scientific American.

Igel, L. (2015, January 1). The Common Core Is Taking Away Kids' Recess—And That Makes No Sense. Retrieved December 19, 2016, from Forbes.

James, C. (2015, August 11). NYU Study Examines Top High School Students' Stress and Coping Mechanisms. Retrieved December 2016, from NYU.edu.

Johnsen, L. (2014, July 8). The Koshas: 5 Layers of Being. Retrieved December 2016, from YogaInternational.com.

Johnson, W. (1982). Riding the Ox Home. A History of Meditation from Shamanism to Science. Boston: Beacon Press.

Keller, H. (1905). The Story of My Life. New York: Doubleday & Co.

Keller, M. (2016, July). Why My Kids Aren't Behaving. (L. Garrison, Interviewer)

King, S. (1985). Mastering Your Hidden Self: A Guide to the Huna Way. Illinois: Theosophical Publishing House.

Kubler-Ross, E. (2007). On Grief and Grieving: Finding the Meaning of Grief Through the Five Stages of Loss. Scribner; Reprint edition (June 5, 2007).

Leichtman MD, R. R. (1982). Active Meditation: The Western Tradition. Ohio: Arial Press.

Linkner, J. (2013, March 3). Embracing Creative Failure. Retrieved December 20, 2016, from Forbes.

MacIsaac, T. (2014, March). What Are Orbs in Photos? Spirits? Dust? Retrieved February 2017, from theepochtimes.com.

Mali, J. (2008). Seeds of Enlightenment Changing the Paradigm Series. Minnetonka: Learning Strategies Corporation.

Masters, P. L. (1973). Meditation Dynamics. Burbank: Burbank Publishing.

Masters, P. L. (2012). Masters Degree Curriculum. Burbank Printing.

Masters, P. L. (2012). Ministers/Bachelors Degree Curriculum. Burbank, CA: Burbank Publishing.

May, R. (1979). The Courage to Create. New York: W.W. Norton & Co.

McCraty Ph.D., R. (2015). Science of the Heart: Exploring the Role of the Heart in Human Performance. Boulder Creek: Heartmath Institute.

McCraty, P. R. (2004). The Energetic Heart: Bioelectromagnetic Communication Within and Between People (pgs. 541-562). Retrieved February 2023, from www.heartmath.org.

McCraty, P. R., & Zyas, P. M. (2014). Cardiac Coherence, Self-Regulation, Autonomic Stability, and Psychosocial Well-Being. Frontiers in Psychology, 1-13.

McDowell, S. (2018, January). Does the Bible say women are inferior to men? Retrieved 2019, from https://fervr.net/.

McFadden, K. (2017, October). The Circus. (L. Garrison, Interviewer)

McVay, G. (2016, December). What Took You from Raymond James to Nepal? (L. Garrison, Interviewer)

McVay, J. (2016, October). Straight Talk from a God's Man. (L. Garrison, Interviewer)

Meek, P. W. (2012, October). Real Stages of Grief. Retrieved 2019, from Psychology Today.

Morrow, R. A. (2019). How to Recognize When Your Loved One Is Dying.

Murphy, J. (1973). Telephysics: The Magic Power of Perfect Living. New York: Parker Publishing Company, Inc.

n.a. (2012, August 7). Heart Intelligence. Retrieved November 2016, from Heartmath.org.

n.a. (2016, January 11). Jon Kabat-Zinn: Defining Mindfulness. Retrieved December 2016, from Mindful.org.

n.a. (2016, August). Pranayama. Retrieved January 2023, from Wikipedia.

n.a. (2016). Sigmund Freud Quotes. Retrieved December 2020, from AZquotes.

n.a. (n.d.). Cognitive-behavioral therapy. Retrieved December 2023, from minddisorders.com.

n.a. (n.d.). en.wikipedia.org/wiki/Japa. Retrieved February 2021

n.a. (n.d.). en.wikipedia.org/wiki/Namaste. Retrieved February 2023

n.a. (n.d.). en.wikipedia.org/wiki/Suggestion. Retrieved February 2022

n.a. (n.d.). Jung's Archetypes. Retrieved December 2022, from http://changingminds.org.

n.a. (n.d.). Namaste. Retrieved January 2017, from India-Infofacts.com.

n.a. (n.d.). Neocortical Functions - Neural Bases Of Behavior. Retrieved December 2016, from Psychology.jrank.org/.

n.a. (n.d.). Neuroanatomy. Retrieved January 2017, from psychology.wikia.com.

n.a. (n.d.). Primordial Sound Meditation . Retrieved December 2023, from Do-Meditation.com.

n.a. (n.d.). Reference.com. Retrieved December 2016

n.a. (n.d.). Samsara (Buddhism). Retrieved November 2023, from Wikipedia.org.

n.a. (n.d.). Sankalpa—The Power of Intention. Retrieved December 2023, from LivingSukha.com.
n.a. (n.d.). Science of the Heart. Retrieved January 2023, from HeartMath.org.
n.a. (n.d.). Scientific Research Validates Holosync's Benefits. Retrieved December 2016, from Centerpointe.com.
n.a. (n.d.). The 4 Paths of Yoga. Retrieved December 2023, from Chopra.com.
n.a. (n.d.). The Nag Hammadi Library. Retrieved December 2023, from http://gnosis.org.
n.a. (n.d.). The Super-Easy Way To Get All The Benefits of Meditation—In a Fraction of the Time. Retrieved January 2017, from Centerpointe.com.
n.a. (n.d.). What is Mindfulness-Based Stress Reduction (MBSR)? Retrieved November 2021, from umassmed.edu.
n.a. (n.d.). What is Transcendental Meditation? Retrieved December 2023, from TM.org.
n.a. (n.d.). Yoga and the Law of Detachment. Retrieved December 2023, from Chopra.com.
n.a. (n.d.). Yoga Nidra. Retrieved February 2023, from Wikipedia.org.
Nefertari. (n.d.). Retrieved 2023, from https://en.wikipedia.org/wiki/.
Networks, A. (2009). Nikola Tesla. Retrieved December 2023, from History.com.
Newberg, M. A., & Waldman, M. R. (2010). How God Changes Your Brain: Breakthrough Findings from a Leading Neuroscientist. Ballantine Books.
Nilsson, R. (n.d.). The Relaxed State and Science. Retrieved December 2023, from yogameditation.com.
Ogden, C., MD, C., BK, K., & KM, F. (2014). Prevalence of childhood and adult obesity in the United States, 2011-2012. Journal of the American Medical Association, 806-814. Retrieved from Center for Disease Control.
Olson, J. (2013). The Slight Edge. Greenleaf Book Group Press.

Painter, P. C. (2007, January, Vol 3, Issue 2). The Relationship Between Spirituality and Artistic Expression: Cultivating the Capacity for Imagining. Newsletter. Spirituality in Higher Education - UCLA.

Pilgrims.Org, A. (n.d.). https://americanpilgrims.org/history-of-the-camino/. Retrieved 2022

Rinpoche, C. T. (2017, January). The Bodhisattva. Retrieved January 2017, from LionsRoar.com.

Santorelli, E. M., & Kabat-Zinn, P. J. (2014). Mindfulness Based Stress Reduction: Standards of Practice 2014. University of Massachusetts Medical School.

Schwarz, J. (1978). Voluntary Controls. New York: EP Dutton.

Shevrin, H. (1973). Brain wave correlates of subliminal stimulation, unconscious attention, primary and secondary-process thinking and repressiveness. Psychological Issues, pp. 56-87.

Sternudd, K. (2012, October 16). Link between creativity and mental illness confirmed. Retrieved December 2016, from ki.se Karolinska Institutet.

TBO. (2015, December 17). Police seek community's help after another teen killed in St. Pete. Retrieved December 2016, from TBO.

The Wellness Institute. (2014). Heart-Centered Hypnotherapy Training. What is Hypnosis? Issaquah: The Wellness Institute.

Van Praet, D. (2017). Why Negative Thoughts Are Normal. https://www.psychologytoday.com.

Vygotsky, L. S. (2004). Imagination and Creativity in Childhood. Journal of Russian and East European Psychology, vol. 42, no. 1, 7-97.

Walton, A. G. (2010, August 2). Meditation: Hype or Help? Retrieved December 2016, from The Doctor Will See You Now.

Walton, A. G. (2011, June 22). Penetrating Postures, Part II: The Psychology of Yoga. Retrieved December 2016, from Forbes.com.

Ways, C. (2019). The History of the Camino de Santiago. https://caminoways.com/the-history-of-the-camino-de-santiago.

Weiss, M. B., & Weiss, A. E. (2012). Miracles Happen: The Transformational Healing Power of Past-Life Memories. HarperCollins.

What is the Ark of the Covenant? (n.d.). Retrieved from JW.Org: https://www.jw.org/en/bible-teachings/questions/ark-of-the-covenant/.

White, G. (2007). Yoga Beyond Belief: Insights to Awaken and Deepen Your Practice. Berkeley: North Atlantic Books.

Wilkens, J. (2022, December). Off to the Doctor and Out of the School. (L. Garrison, Interviewer)

Wisehart, D. J. (2011). Encyclopedia of the Great Plains: Sweat Lodge. University of Nebraska-Lincoln.

Zimberoff, D. (2014). What is Hypnotherapy? The Wellness Institute Heart-Centered Therapies.

Zimberoff, D. (n.d.). A Jungian Approach to Evaluating the Development of Complexes in Childhood. Retrieved November 2016, from Wellness Institute.

Index

acute mountain sickness. *See* AMS
addiction, 149, 224
ADHD, 245, 246, 269
adrenal glands, 26, 27, 28
affect, 18, 19, 20, 24, 25, 35, 67, 79, 111, 198, 228, 283
Affect dysregulation, 18, 20
affect regulation, 19
agape, 82
Āgyā, 82
Al-Anon, 72, 149, 167
alpha, 52, 117, 118, 197, 216
alpha-blocking, 216
AMS, 101, *See* acute mountain sickness
amygdala, 26
Anāhata Nāda, 81
Anna Quindlen, 7
ANS, 16, 17, 18, 19, 20, 21, 23, 26, 28
Apostle James, 241
Aramaic, 239, 253
Ark of the Covenant, 95, 96, 301, 308
Asana, 200, 301
AUM, 256

autonomic nervous system, 16, 26, 27, 28, 115, 117, 158, *See* ANS
autopilot, 54, 139, 153, 157, 164, 208, 223
Bessel van der Kolk, MD, 9, 124
Bhagavad Gita, 55, 106
Bible, 191, 230, 231, 290, 305
Bill Harris, 34, 56, 66, 106, 116, 117
boundaries, v, 42, 45, 59, 74, 125, 126, 128, 129, 144, 155, 158, 168, 170, 181, 268
brain, 20, 25, 26, 27, 30, 34, 52, 55, 71, 72, 83, 111, 112, 113, 114, 115, 116, 117, 118, 129, 130, 141, 195, 197, 199, 202, 203, 210, 212, 216, 234, 237, 244, 250, 257, 267, 268, 269, 274, 275, 277, 278, 279, 280, 285, 286, 304
brain wave patterns, 117, 197, 216
Buddhism, vii, 217, 218, 219, 255, 306
Camino, ii, 14, 180, 182, 183, 240, 241, 242, 273, 289, 292, 300, 308

CBT. *See* cognitive behavioral therapy
Chakra, 78, 80, 81, 82, 83, 84, 85
Christian, 49, 82, 84, 218, 235, 241, 254, 255
cognitive behavior therapy. *See* CBT
C-PTSD, 41, 151, 299
creation mandala, 90
creative flow, 278, 280
David Hartman, ii, 52, *See* Wellness Institute
Deepak Chopra, 214
delta, 118, 197, *See* brainwave patterns
Descanso, 165, 289
Dharana, 200
dharma, 41, 42, 116
Dhyana, 200
Diane Zimberoff, ii, 198, 249
Dirgha pranayama, 29
Dissanayake, 5
DNA, 283
dopamine, 27
Down Syndrome, 238, 302
dukkha, x
Dysautonomia, 17
dysregulation, 17, 18, 20, 23, 115, 283
Earth School, 9, 10, 46, 53, 147, 207, 219
Eckankar, 49, 50
EEG, 216

Ego activity, 140
ego passivity, 140
Ego receptivity, 140
Egypt, 77, 88, 89, 91, 92, 93, 94, 95, 96, 97, 230, 254, 299
electrocardiogram, 111
electroencephalographic. *See* EEG
emotionally dysregulated, 20, 21
Empath. *See* empathic
empathic, 108, 109, 131, 180, 181, 267, 268, 269
Empaths, 108, 109, 181, 267
Energy Field, 84
entrain, 67, 72, 111, 263, 295
Entrainment, 67
epigenetics, 283
equilibrium, 17, 18, 19, 20, 25, 73, 181, 202
Ezer, 232
fawning, 23
firewalking, ix, 104, 105
flower or life. *See* Sacred geometry
fMRI, 274
freeze, 16, 20, 23
Freud, 8, 187, 209, 214, 236, 301, 306
functional asymmetry, 278
Geljun. *See* Geljun Sherpa
Geljun Sherpa, 101
genetics, 283
Giza Plateau, 91, *See* Egypt

Gnostic Gospels, 254
Goenka, 36, 258
Great Pyramid, 91, 92, 93, 94, 96, 97, 231, 235
guru, 209, 229
Hakim, 91, 92, 93, 96
Hatha yoga, 35, 205
HeartMath Institute. See HMI
High Heart Chakra, 85
Himalayas. See Nepal
Hindu, 78, 83, 200, 217, 258, 303
human state, 224
hyperactivation, 25
Hyper-arousal, 21
hyper-vigilant, 56, 157
hypo-aroused, 25
hypothalamus, 26
implicit, 55, 144, 209, 210
Inca Trail, 241
insulin, 27
intuition, 109, 110, 233, 261, 263, 270, 274
Japa meditation, 255
Jeddah Mali. See Mali
Jesus, 96, 116, 231, 235, 253, 257, 303
Joy Anderson, 14
Julia Cameron, 4
Jung, 6, 9, 107, 230, 266, 304, 306, See Carl Jung
Kabat-Zinn, 203, 204, 306, 308
Kathmandu, 36, 103, 104

King's Chamber, 94
Korea, 143, 144, 145, 146, 299
Kripalu, 140, 296
left hemisphere. See brain
limbic system, 26
liminal, 127, 162, 168, 192, 294
locus ceruleus, 26
Machu Picchu, 74, 77
Mali, 260, 305
Mandukya Upanishad, 255, 256
Manipūra, 81
Matt Kahn, 169
Maya, 264, 290
Megan McCormick, 238
metaphysical, 41, 49, 123, 218
Miki Bryant, 121, 133
Mirror Neuron Systems, 267
mirror neurons, 109, 110
Moses, 96, 231, 277, 278
Mūlādhāra, 80
munay, 82
Nadi Shodana, 30, 199
nadis, 30, 32, 33
Nag Hammadi Library, 253, 254, 307
Namaste, 218, 306
Neely Bryan, 175
Neely's Ark, 175
Nefertari, 87, 307
Nepal, 36, 100, 103, 258, 264, 299, 305
Neuroaesthetics, 274
Neuroanatomy, 227, 306

neuroplasticity, 129, 299
neurotransmitters, 27, 114
Nidra. *See* Yoga Nidra
Nietzsche, 266
Niyama, 200
Noble Silence, 37, 259
non-cognitive, 274, 275
orbs, 97, 98
oxytocin, 112, 113
Pachamama, 152, 241
pancha kosha, 227
paranoia, 109, 110
parasympathetic, 16, 17, 19, 20, 21, 26, 27, 28, 29
Patanjali, 78, 200, 256
pathogenesis, 22
Paul Masters, 3
people-pleasing, 23
Pinnacles, 146
PNS. *See* parasympathetic nervous system
pranamayakosha, 33, 227
pranayama, 16, 29, 30, 32, 201
Pratyahara, 200
psychic utero, 47
PTSD, 18, 187, 211, 299
Pyramid of Khufu. *See* Great Pyramid
quantum field, 205
quantum law, 223
Quechua, 84
Raja Yoga, 200, 201

resilience, xv, 6, 18, 22, 24, 26, 56, 65, 130, 168, 180, 240, 246, 282, 283, 287
Richard Miller, Ph.D, vi
right hemisphere. *See* brain
Rumi, 154
Sakshi, 24
salutogenic, 22
Samadhi, 200
samsara, vii, x, xiii, 7
Samsara, 306
samsaras, xiii, 104, 129, *See* samsara
Sankalpa, 228, 306
Sanskrit, 16, 24, 33, 78, 79, 116, 218, 228, 229
self-realization, 4, 50, 200, 224
Serge King, 51
serotonin, 27, 28, 113
shamans, 78, 230, 267
Shlokas, 201
Siva, 205
SNS. *See* sympathetic nervous system
Solvitur ambulando', 167
somatic, 10, 24, 55, 66, 67, 156, 211, 222, 278
Stephen Cope, 32, 33, 42, 47, 221
subtle body, 79
suicide, viii, 70, 127, 153, 157, 266, 267, 294
Svādhishthāna, 80

sweat lodge, 75, 76, 78
Sweat Lodge. *See* inipi
sympathetic, 16, 17, 19, 20, 21, 26, 27, 28, 202
thalamus, 210
The Way, 240, 241, 242, 243
theta, 52, 55, 117, 118, 197, 199, *See* brainwave patterns
tolerance, 7, 15, 18, 21, 24, 25, 71, 180, 231
Tolly Burkan, ix, 99, 104, 301
trance, 51, 52, 55, 88, 118, 119, 121, 198, 216
trance state, 51, 52, 88, 121
trancework. *See* trance
Transcendental Meditation, 215, 307

Uijayi pranayama, 30
Vikalpa, 204
Vipassana, 36, 38, 204, 227, 228, 258, 259
Vishuddhi, 82
Vygotsky, 236, 238, 250, 308
Wayne Dyer, 139, 198, 205
WD-40, 265
Wellness Institute, 52, 133, 199, 308, 309
Wisdom Keepers, 88, 89, 91, 93, 95
Yama, 200
Yoga Nidra, vi, 116, 118, 119, 202, 228, 299, 307, *See* nidra
Yoga Sutras, 78, 200, 256
Yoga Sutras of Patanjali, 78

www.ingramcontent.com/pod-product-compliance
Lightning Source LLC
Chambersburg PA
CBHW020334010526
44119CB00002B/60